English for Business

J Chilver
B.Sc.Econ.Hons., D.B.A., A.C.I.B. (and Trustee Dip.), Grad. I.P.M., M.B.I.M.

Dr Joseph Chilver was formerly Senior Lecturer, Dorset Institute of Higher Education

THOMSON

Australia • Canada • Mexico • Singapore • Spain • United Kingdom • United States

English for Business

Copyright © J. Chilver 1992

The Thomson logo is a registered trademark used herein under licence.

For more information, contact Thomson Learning, High Holborn House, 50-51 Bedford Row, London WC1R 4LR or visit us on the World Wide Web at:
http://www.thomsonlearning.co.uk

All rights reserved by Thomson Learning 2004. The text of this publication, or any part thereof, may not be reproduced or transmitted in any form or by any means, electronic or mechanical, including photocopying, recording, storage in an information retrieval system, or otherwise, without prior permission of the publisher.

While the publisher has taken all reasonable care in the preparation of this book the publisher makes no representation, express or implied, with regard to the accuracy of the information contained in this book and cannot accept any legal responsibility or liability for any errors or omissions from the book or the consequences thereof.

Products and services that are referred to in this book may be either trademarks and/or registered trademarks of their respective owners. The publisher and author/s make no claim to these trademarks.

British Library Cataloguing-in-Publication Data
A catalogue record for this book is available from the British Library

ISBN 1-84480-102-0

First published 1988 by DPP
Second edition published 1992 by DPP
Reprinted 2001 by Continuum
Reprinted 2003 by Thomson Learning

Typeset by Judy Hobden and Cath Chadwick

Printed in the UK by TJ International, Padstow, Cornwall

Preface

Aims

This book has three main aims:
1. To provide a programme of study for students whose second language is English, to improve their command of English and so enhance their career prospects. Students are familiarised with the various business settings in which they will be expected to use English, and taught the basic skills to enable them to operate effectively in these situations, i.e.:
   a) comprehension and interpretation of written reports and other business documents;
   b) simple analysis of graphically and numerically displayed information;
   c) summarising and precis writing
   d) production of expanded passages from brief notes;
   e) composition of letters, memoranda, reports and faxes etc.
2. To give students the opportunity to test these skills during the programme of study. This book will prepare them for the new monthly examinations for the Institute of Commercial Management's Certificate and Diploma in Business English (for which this book is the recommended text), and all three levels of the English for Business Examinations for the London Chamber of Commerce and Industry.
3. To aid students on various RSA, BTEC and secretarial courses who wish to improve their English while at the same time increasing their knowledge of business.

Approach

In teaching the various skills called for in business, the author has, at all times, recognised the need for the student to be acquainted with the various situations in which they will be used. The book is therefore divided into four parts:

Part One contains a general outline of the skills mentioned in the Aims, and a review of the basics of grammar and punctuation.

Part Two illustrates applications of the skills to the various aspects of business. In this second edition the graded exercises have been substantially expanded. Following the original pattern of the book, they provide even more practice which will prove of value both in a formal examination setting and in the workplace.

Part Three provides further practice for all levels of both the ICM and LCCI examinations; questions are to be completed within the time constraints imposed in the examination room. Answers are provided.

Part Four offers a glossary of the most common business colloquialisms, followed by a business dictionary with brief explanations of terms, as an aid to vocabulary development. Finally, there is a section to which students can refer to check their answers for those exercises which are asterisked.

Notes on the Second Edition

The book has been substantially updated and expanded.

There are new chapters on Information Technology, and Stocks, Shares and Take-overs. All the chapters in Parts One and Two have been expanded, with the addition of more short exercises to consolidate vocabulary and longer tasks such as writing an essay on a discussion topic. There are also more exercises based on correspondence and meetings.

Part Three has two new chapters providing sample practice papers for the Institute of Commercial Management's Certificate and Diploma in Business English.

Contents

Preface

Part One: **The ground rules** 1
    1. Understanding business data 3
    2. Modifying business information 11
    3. The written word in business 18
    4. Grammar and punctuation 42

Part Two: **The functions** 53
    5. Factory production 55
    6. International marketing 68
    7. Advertising... 84
    8. Transport and distribution 96
    9. The office 107
    10. Business meetings 121
    11. Personnel management 132
    12. Finance and accounting 143
    13. The board of directors 153
    14. Business decisions 162
    15. Information technology 171
    16. Stocks, shares and take-overs................................. 179
    17. Money and banking.. 191
    18. Insurance 203
    19. Exporting 217
    20. Government and business....................................... 235

Part Three: **Examination practice**
    21. ICM Certificate in Business English......................... 244
    22. ICM Diploma in Business English 250
    23. LCCI Level One... 256
    24. LCCI Level Two... 265
    25. LCCI Level Three.. 273

Part Four: **Dictionary and answers**
    Common business coloquialisms 280
    Business dictionary... 289
    Answers 298

Part One

The ground rules

In business the English language is used as a vehicle for the exchange of information and instructions, and you need to develop certain basic skills to participate successfully in this exchange. This part of the book identifies and examines these skills, and looks at some of the situations in which they are used in business.

Chapter One covers skills relating to the comprehension of information. In business we are required to understand and interpret a great variety of data. We look first at two techniques to help us understand written material. After applying the techniques to some sample passages the focus is switched to the comprehension of visual presentations. After a look at some of the ways in which statistical data can be presented you are given an opportunity to interpret some simple examples.

Chapter Two deals with skills relating to the modification of information. As information passes from person to person or from department to department, it may need to be abbreviated, and here a technique is introduced which helps you to summarise or take notes effectively. At other times a brief message may need to be expanded and the technique required for this is also examined. Practical exercises are included.

In Chapter Three the focus is on skills related to written communication. The cardinal rules regarding letter-writing are explained and the student has an opportunity to apply the theory to practical situations. Other forms of communication with the public such as circulars and advertisements are also considered, followed by written material such as memoranda and reports which are designed for the transfer of information within the business.

In Chapter Four we examine basic rules of grammar and punctuation. We look at the parts of speech and identify some of the common pitfalls which can mar work. Again practical exercises are included. For many of you this chapter will be no more than a short revision course, but it is a vital part of the preparation for the exercises which follow in Part Two.

1: Understanding business data

Comprehension of written material

A dictionary definition of 'comprehension' is the act of understanding. Very often in business we find ourselves reading documents and letters which need some effort before they can be understood. However, we face similar problems long before we start earning a living. For example, James' parents bought him a computer game for his birthday. Now, before he can play the game, he has to read and understand the instructions. Meanwhile his elder sister, Fiona, has been reading her history books trying to discover why the Industrial Revolution started in Britain rather than anywhere else in the world, and his younger sister, Marsha, has taken up knitting and is having difficulty making sense of the instructions in the pattern her mother has given her.

Of course there is another side to these activities which should be mentioned here. The instructions for the computer game and the knitting pattern, as well as the history text books, are produced by commercial organisations for their customers. James, Fiona and Marsha may well be working for such organisations when they start work, in which case they will learn that the need in business is not simply to understand (or comprehend), but to do so with speed and accuracy. Time is expensive in terms of pay for workers, rent for buildings and interest on bank loans, while inaccuracy leads to mistakes, miscalculations and losses. Businesses need to make profits and compete against other firms effectively if they are to survive.

It is therefore essential for students looking for employment in business to develop skills in comprehension if they wish to succeed in their careers, and examiners in English for Business often set tasks for candidates to test their understanding of material such as they would encounter in the real world. Obviously the material will vary, but no matter how difficult a passage is to understand, the task will be made easier by following a set routine.

It is suggested you should:

Stage 1

Read the passage at normal speed to gather a general impression of the contents.

Stage 2

Read the passage more carefully a second time, taking care over any more difficult sections. Refer to the dictionary if any new words are encountered or where you are unsure of the meaning of a word.

Stage 3

Underline key words and phrases. This is a particularly useful practice when the narrative is lengthy or complex.

Stage 4

Read the passage once more at normal speed. By this stage you should be getting a clear idea of the message.

1: Understanding business data

An example

You might apply this technique to the following passage taken from a local newspaper. The figures in the right hand margin indicate the line numbers and are there to make reference easier:

> Concern has come from the county planning committee about a building to house waste materials at the site of the new nuclear power station. The application for a treated waste store comes from the UK Atomic Energy Authority. The committee heard that the building would have a significant effect on the environment.
>
> The councillors were concerned about the colour of the building and its height, and thought it should be turned at a different angle to be less obtrusive from the main road. The committee decided to object to the building on the grounds of its obtrusiveness.
>
> Two years ago a similar power station in Scotland won permission for the medium-level waste generated by the power station reactor. In that case the waste was to be enclosed in concrete and steel drums and retained in a specially fireproofed building identical to the one proposed here.
>
> A UK Atomic Energy spokesman declared after hearing the committee's verdict, 'A waste storage unit is essential if we are to provide power for local industries. In designing the building, safety has been our prime concern, but we will certainly do all we can to placate the environmentalists.

(Line markers: 1, 5, 10, 15)

From a first reading *(Stage 1)* you might gather that a local power station has applied to the local authority for permission to store nuclear waste.

In the second reading *(Stage 2)* some students might refer to their dictionaries to check the meaning of 'significant' (line 5), 'obtrusive' (line 8), 'generated' (line 11), 'placate' (line 19) or 'environmentalists' (line 19). They would discover the following definitions:

significant	= having a considerable influence or effect;
obtrusive	= obvious;
generated	= produced;
placate	= soothe or pacify, remove the fears;
environmentalists	= those who are concerned to preserve nature.

Stage 3 calls for an underlining of key words. These might be:
  i)   the county planning committee (line l)
  ii) the new nuclear power station (line 2)
  iii) the UK Atomic Energy Authority (line 3)
  iv) obtrusive (line 8)
  v)   a waste storage unit (line 15)
  vi) safety ... prime concern (line 16)
  vii) environmentalists (line 17)

Now we can go on to the fourth reading, after which we can hopefully answer some of the questions which might be posed. For example:
  a) Who is making the application? The United Kingdom Atomic Energy Authority.
  b) Who is considering the application? The county planning committee.
  c) What is required? Permission to build a waste storage unit.

d) Why has the application been turned down? The building would spoil the look of the surrounding countryside.
e) What will have to be done before the application is approved? The building will have to be made less obtrusive.
f) What is the danger if this happens? In the present design safety has been considered more important than the environment.

Exercise 1

By now you should have a good understanding of the newspaper report, and you might use the same method in connection with an item from Singapore Bulletin, Volume 15 Number 6. Suggested key phrases have been highlighted to make your task easier.

Infringement of copyrights is a global phenomenon, its rapid growth being closely linked with the fast pace of technological advancement.

New technologies like photocopying machines, satellite transmissions and cassette, computer and videotaping **have generated new problems** which have tested existing legislation and enforcement capabilities in individual countries.

Singapore was no exception.

Legal proceedings taken against the producers and vendors of pirated cassette tapes **failed to bring about convictions** in court either because of inadequate laws or the many loopholes that existed in the law, or a combination of both.

Undeterred, Singapore pirates used high-speed cassette tape **dubbing equipment to produce millions of copies** of music cassettes each year. Many were readily sold to local music lovers and tourists, while the bulk made their way to the Middle East and Africa – at the expense of the US and British copyright holders. Not contented with this, the pirates spread their activities to other areas of intellectual property such as videotapes, photo-copying of books and computer software, thus compounding the problem.

The tough **new Copyright Act aims to eradicate Singapore's image as a 'pirate's haven'** by wiping out this lucrative, multimillion-dollar illegal business. The new act provides for stiff penalties, including jail terms of up to five years and/or fines of up to $10,000 per illegal copy, or $100,000 whichever is the lower.

With the new copyright law, Singapore will enhance its image in the eyes of the business world. Businesses will he attracted to set up operations in Singapore because of the protection that the new copyright law accords. **With the pirates out of the way, businesses and individuals will rightfully be ensured protection of their intellectual property.**

Now answer the following questions. In the first question short and clear-cut answers are called for. In the second question the answers will be slightly longer and call for a broad understanding of the material.

1. a) Why is infringement of copyrights a growing problem? (line 2)
   b) Why had legal proceedings been ineffective in Singapore? (lines 10/11)
   c) What had happened to the bulk of the Singapore pirated copies of music cassettes? (lines 14/15)

1: Understanding business data

    d) What items other than music cassettes were involved in the trade? (lines 17/18)

    e) What was the purpose of the new Singapore Copyright Act? (lines 20/21)

    f) What benefit did the Singapore government expect as a result of the legislation? (lines 24/26)

    g) What would happen to people who broke the law? (lines 21/23)

2. a) Why is it difficult to eradicate the pirating of copyright globally?

    b) Why do you think Singapore became a haven for the pirates?

    c) To what extent do consumers suffer (or benefit) from this sort of piracy?

    d) Why do you think the article discussed the illegal activities in terms of 'piracy'?

    e) How do you think a problem like this should be tackled?

    f) What is meant by the term 'intellectual property' in the last sentence of the article?

    g) What title would you give to the article we have been studying?

After completing this exercise you will realise that answering the questions has helped you toward a much better understanding of the topic covered by the article, and this has given you another technique for understanding business narratives.

The questioning approach

This may be used as an alternative to the first method, but can also be used in addition. It involves asking yourself a series of basic questions about the material being studied, in much the same way as has been done in the first two examples. As you answer the questions your understanding of the narrative will improve.

Exercise 2

Read the following passage and this time use the questioning approach completing the list with four more questions of your own. Then write your answers to all the questions.

Fire Insurance Brigades

Following the Great Fire of London in 1666 it was realised that a more efficient fire service was required. Up to that time fire-fighting was supplied by the various parishes throughout Britain, but at best they were untrained and poorly equipped. During the last quarter of the seventeenth century the newly formed fire insurance offices assumed responsibility for fighting in the capital and eventually in most major towns and cities throughout Great Britain. They had a substantial vested interest in taking on the task as they were the ones to lose most by an inefficient or non-existent fire service.

The early part time fire insurance company firemen in London were mostly watermen who plied their trade on the Thames providing a water-taxi service. These men were eminently suitable for this task as they were self-employed and therefore could be called upon at a moment's notice, and were generally fit and strong which helped when they were called upon to operate the hand pumped fire engines of the period.

In the early part of the eighteenth century, these watermen probably did not have anything in the way of a formal uniform, with the exception of a badge worn on the left arm which served as a distinguishing mark and was numbered to show that they had a licence to operate boats on the river.

By the middle of the eighteenth century a number of these watermen/firemen were almost fully employed by the fire insurance companies of the day and wore a colourful distinguishing uniform. Sometime after 1820 two types of uniform were provided for each man. The first was an expensive and elaborate uniform for 'dress' or ceremonial occasions and was worn when the men took part in such ceremonies as the Lord Mayor's Day Parade or when the firemen marched, often with a band, to help publicise their insurance company.   20

25

From 'Fire Insurance Company Buttons' by Fergus Bain & Brian Wright published by the Fire Mark Circle 1985

Questions

1. When did the insurance offices assume responsibility for fire-fighting? (line 4)
2. Why could the watermen be called upon at a moment's notice? (line 10)
3. What was the purpose of the number on the badges worn by the watermen? (lines 16/17)
4. Why did the firemen take part in the Lord Mayor's Day Parade? (line 24/25)
5. ....
6. ....
7. ....
8. ....

Comprehension of visual presentations

It is sometimes possible to present data visually in the form of graphs or diagrams – so as to make their meaning clear at a glance. Here we will consider four different kinds of diagram: pie charts, bar charts, Gantt charts and graphs.

Consider the case of Delta Food Products. The sales of the different product lines over the past year are broken down in the following table:

	Sales in £ million last year
Iced Diamond Cakes	12
Crumble Cookie Range	24
Chocolux Confections	6
Miscellaneous	6
Total	**48**

Pie charts

This data can be visualised in the form of a pie chart. It should be obvious from the figures that one half of Delta's sales arise from the Crumble Cookie Range. That is easily their most popular line. The Iced Diamond Cakes account for a quarter of the sales. The final quarter is equally split between the Chocolux Confections and the remaining product lines.

1: Understanding business data

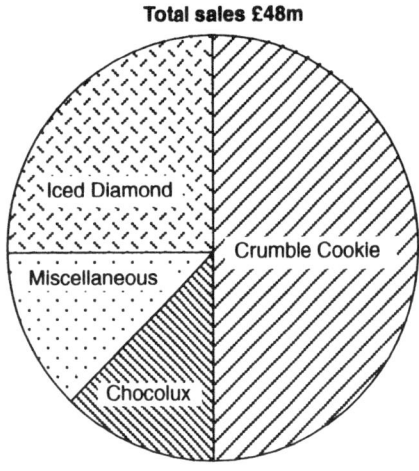

There are 360° (degrees) in a full circle, and we can work out how many degrees in the circle to allocate to each of the product lines by dividing the sales of the product by the total sales and multiplying the result by 360:

$$\text{Iced Diamond Cakes} = \frac{12}{48} \times 360 = 90$$

Using a protractor we then allocate 90° of the 360° of the pie to the Iced Diamond Cakes. We then repeat the calculation for the other products until the whole of the pie is used up. The distinctions can be heightened by shading or colouring the different segments of the pie.

Bar charts

Another way of expressing data visually is by means of bar charts. If we elaborate the sales data to include sales for the year before last, the table now looks like this:

	Sales in £ million	
	Previous year	*Last year*
Iced Diamond Cakes	10	12
Crumbly Cookie Range	16	24
Chocolux Confections	12	6
Miscellaneous	6	6
Totals	**44**	**48**

To show the data in the form of bar charts, the bar charts are drawn to scale and measured from the base line which may be horizontal or perpendicular.

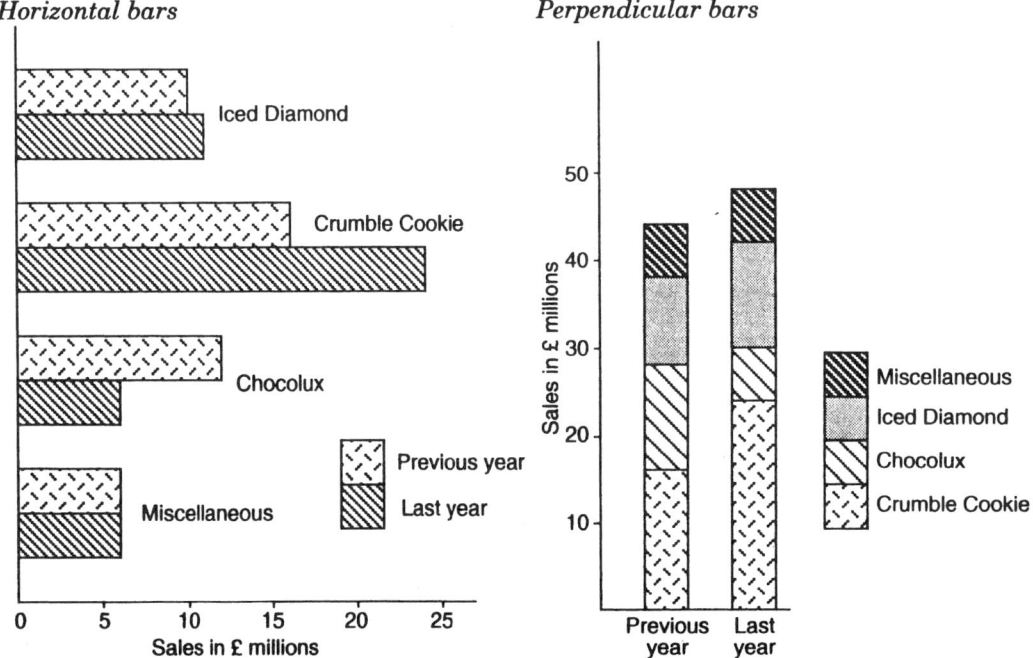

1: Understanding business data

The perpendicular bar chart is also a 'composite' bar chart because it includes a breakdown of the individual products in each bar.

Gantt charts

A variation of the bar chart is the Gantt chart, used in connection with the process of control in a business. It gives an instant visual comparison between expected and actual performance. The example below shows the production levels (target) and the output achieved (actual) on Delta's Chocolux production line. The performance would be recorded at the end of each day and the chart would provide information for the line managers who could see at a glance whether the targets were being met.

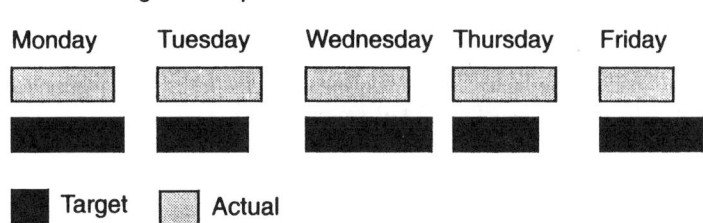

On which days did the Chocolux production line exceed its target?

Graphs

The most common form of visual presentation is the graph. Graphs are two-dimensional. The x-axis records one dimension, usually the time dimension. The y-axis records another range of data which changes in relation to the time (or other) series. The unbroken line in the graph below shows Delta's sales over the past six years. The broken line shows the sales of one of Delta's major competitors.

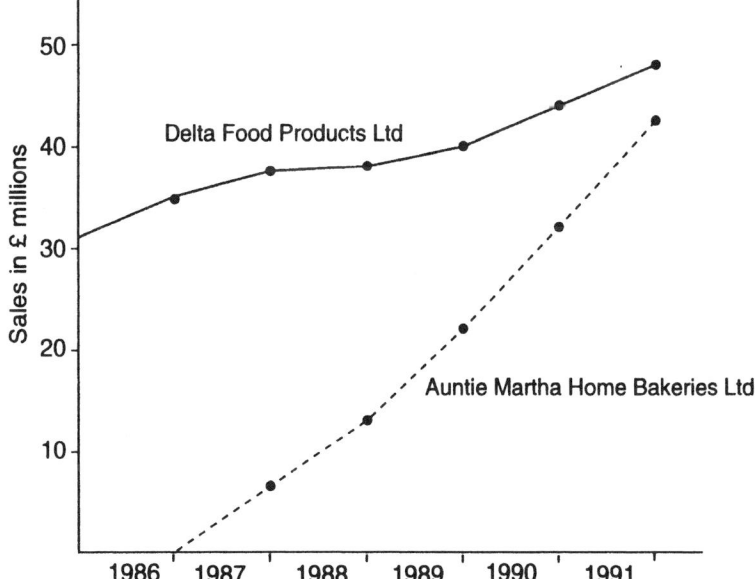

The benefit of all these diagrammatic representations is that they present the data in an easily assimilable form. This is no doubt one reason why they appear so often in company's Annual Reports to their shareholders. Shareholders do not want to go through the tedium of analysing the statistics in detail, but they do want to know what is happening generally.

1: Understanding business data

Those who are more directly involved in the business need to be able to interpret data presented to them in whatever form. They also need to be able to express the ideas that emerge from the analysis.

Exercise 3*

Concentrate your attention on the diagrams. On this evidence:

1. Which Delta product was most popular with the customers last year?
2. Which product increased its sales most over the last year?
3. Sales of which product fell most last year?
4. Are Delta's sales generally rising or falling?
5. How is Delta performing in comparison with its main competitor?
6. What sales would you expect from Delta next year?

2: Modifying business information

Summarising

As information passes from person to person, from department to department, or from level to level within an organisation, it may need to be reproduced in an abbreviated or summarised form. Only the refined material will go forward and this implies that people in business are often required to distinguish between important and trivial elements in communications. This is the essence of the task in business, but we are all familiar with the art of summarising in one form or another in the course of our daily lives. Consider, for example the following situation.

Gillian is watching a late night film on television. It is featuring the famous female pop group, the She Devils. After about twenty minutes of the film the door opens quietly and Gillian's elder brother, Jonathan, joins her to see the rest of the film. Fortunately, at that moment there is a commercial break so the disruption is less than it might have been. First he wants to know which film she is watching. What is it called? Who is in it? And then he asks, 'What's happened so far?' Gillian wants to get the explanations over as soon as possible so she can enjoy the film when it continues. A lot of things have happened in the first twenty minutes of the story. Should she tell Jonathan that the opening scenes were of the She Devils performing at a live concert, and that they had started with the number 'Fire Worship' which had taken the group to the number one spot in November last year? Should she tell him that Mariana, the lead singer, had had an argument with their manager and had thrown her high-heeled shoe at him and cut his forehead? The commercials will only last for a few minutes and so Gillian has little time before the film resumes. She decides to tell her brother just the *essence* of the story so far.

'The She Devils have gone on tour to America,' she says. 'Mariana has fallen in love with a Puerto Rican guitar player and he's trying to persuade her to leave the group and stay with him in Los Angeles. She's just gone round to his hotel and found him beaten up ... And that's where you came in.'

Most of us will have been through a similar routine at some time or other. Gillian's task in *summarising* the She Devil story for Jonathan requires the same sort of skill as when she is asked to summarise a passage in an English examination.

'Summarise the following passage in 150 words,' instructs the examiner. Gillian looks at the 500 word narrative and has to decide which strands are vital to an understanding of the story, and which parts can be left out, or glossed over, without seriously reducing the impact. Obviously, the shorter the summary, the greater the loss of detail. Sometimes a passage will be easy to shorten because information falls into clear-cut compartments of *vital* and *irrelevant*. Consider another situation, this time in a business setting:

Peter Baker has set up an advertising agency and employs John Waters as his Office Manager. This conversation occurred last Friday evening.

JOHN:	Did you sign those letters Mr Baker?	
BAKER:	I put them in the out-tray. I made a slight change to the Caldwell letter.	
JOHN:	Oh yes, I see ... Mr Baker I wonder if you could spare me a few minutes on a personal matter?	
BAKER:	OK John. As long as you don't keep me too long. My train goes at six.	
JOHN:	Alright, Mr Baker. It's about my salary. As I'm sure you know, my last pay increase was eighteen months ago, and I've had more responsibilities	

2: Modifying business information

	since Miss Oldroyd left. As you know I've bought a house and the mortgage repayments are over £300 a month.
BAKER:	If you saw my bank overdraft you'd realise you're not the only one with problems. but I know you've got to live too. And I'm very pleased with the effort you've made since Miss Oldroyd left. What sort of figure have you got in mind'?
JOHN:	Well, I was hoping for another £1,000 a year.
BAKER:	£1,000? I can't go that far, but I tell you what. Let's make it an extra £10 a week for now and we'll have another chat in six months' time. If we get the Caldwell contract, I might be able to be a bit more generous. Does that seem fair?
JOHN:	Yes Mr Baker, that seems very fair.
BAKER:	We'll start with the new amount next month OK? Have a good weekend.
JOHN:	Good night Mr Baker and thank you very much.

Suppose you were asked to recount that conversation as briefly as possible. Most of what has passed between them is incidental (of little importance). Our task in summarising the conversation is to pick out the key phrases. If we had to reduce what John was saying to a single short sentence, what would that sentence be?

'Can I have an increase of £1,000 a year in my pay?'

If we also reduce Peter Baker's response to its bare essentials, what does that become?

'You can have £520 a year.'

So, if we are looking for the briefest possible description of what has happened it becomes:

Peter Baker agreed to pay John Waters another £520 a year.

Exercise 1

The passage below is for you to summarise. First, pick out and underline what you regard as the key phrases, then explain what has happened in your own words. Be as brief as possible, without omitting any vital details.

David is the Area Sales Manager for a famous cosmetics firm. He is interviewing one of the most recent recruits to his sales team.

DAVID:	Did you have a good journey down from Newcastle?
JANE:	Not too bad. The traffic was very heavy around Birmingham, but it was alright once I reached the motorway.
DAVID:	Well, I've been having a look at your sales figures for the last quarter. I see we set you a target of £60,000 sales for last month, but you only reached £50,000. That's disappointing, but I know you haven't been with us very long, so we have to be patient. That's why we've given you the same target of £60,000 for this month, but it still means you've got to increase your sales by 20 per cent. Tell me Jane, what difficulties are you finding?
JANE:	There aren't any particular problems. I must admit I spend a lot of time with the buyers for the department stores, but I often find it difficult to close a deal with them. I spent a couple of hours with the Chief Buyer at Bonnies in Sunderland last Friday. I got her interested in the new range

2: Modifying business information

	of blushers. She ordered £5,000 worth. I thought I'd made a real killing, and then she cut down the rest of her order by £5,000 and I was no better off.
DAVID:	I've run into that problem too. The only thing I can suggest is that you keep trying and don't get down-hearted. Every person in the team has got to work like a beaver. We've got to increase our sales this year, or we're in trouble. The Managing Director's told us he's thinking about closing down the Pimlico plant. If that happens we're all in danger of losing our jobs. Perhaps you ought to spend more time visiting drug stores.
JANE:	Yes, I've thought about that myself.
DAVID:	I'll make a note in my report that you're going to give more attention to the smaller retailers, and we'll see whether that produces better results.

Having successfully completed the above exercise, you should now be ready to tackle a more difficult passage. In order to help you in this task the four stage method suggested for comprehension is now further developed. A methodical approach is obviously called for and it is proposed that whenever students are faced with the task of summarising they base their plan on the words TRACK DICE. This is a mnemonic, a device for aiding the memory.

T =   Task
Make sure you understand the terms of reference, the task you have been set.

R =   Read
Read through the passage once to perceive the general drift. Then read it again more carefully.

A =   Ask
Ask questions such as 'What is this about?', 'What title could it be given?'

C =   Clarify
Look at any difficult words or passages. Try to work out their meaning from the surrounding text.

K =   Key words and phrases
Which are the vital parts of the narrative? Where possible underline them. Use broken lines to show the secondary phrases, those you consider to be fairly important but not vital.

D =   Draft
Make a rough draft of your summary, using your own words to link up the elements.

I =   Improve
Refer back to the instructions. Read the passage once more and make any necessary amendments.

C =   Count
Is there a limit to the number of words you are allowed to use in your summary? How many words have you used? Add or subtract according to the degree of importance.

E =   Edit
Read through the draft once more before editing and producing the summary in its final form.

2: Modifying business information

Summarising would be a much simpler task if there were no time constraints, but both in the business world and the examination room time is of the essence. That is why a methodical approach is imperative, as is written practice.

Exercise 2

Give a title to the following passage and reduce it to about one third of its present length, using the technique explained above. In this exercise certain key phrases have been highlighted to help you.

> **Some people think of a career in business as boring.** They probably visualise the clerk in the office wading through piles of routine correspondence, filling in forms and endlessly placing documents in filing cabinets. Of course the jobs of managers are more interesting, but even they are only making decisions such as how many plastic containers to make this month and what price to charge for them.
>
> It is true that **much of business is routine**. We live in a mass production society. People are often no more than appendages to their machines. Automation and robotisation were offered as ultimate solutions to the problems of boredom in the work place, but workers actually engaged on robotic production lines would no doubt argue the case.
>
> Yet there is another side to the coin. Far from being boring, the world of **business could be likened to a jungle**. It is no place for the naive or the uninitiated. You create a new product or service, and within days **competitors** have used your ideas to make even better products. You lower your **prices** to the point where you can barely make enough profit to survive and someone comes along and lowers their prices even further. Should you be fortunate enough to make a profit, the government will gobble it up in **taxes** before you can do anything with it.
>
> Hardly a world where you can afford to sit vacantly under the shade of the factory or office block with glazed eyes. **If you wish to survive** in the modern business world **you need to understand what is happening**. The jungle can be a rewarding place, but only for the mentally alert and fleet of foot.

Note-taking

Closely allied to summarising is note-taking. The same principles apply. Students will already have practised this art to some extent. They will have made notes as they read their text books, probably using key words and phrases to remind them of important points. Many will have made notes during the course of a lecture, sometimes the lecturer helps by giving hand-outs or dictating notes. The hope is that these key thoughts will strike a chord in the memory when they are re-read at a later stage, particularly when examination time comes around. The student in the examination room will try to recall the vital words and phrases expanding them into a worthwhile answer to the question on the examination paper.

The same skills are called for in business, particularly in recording what has happened at a meeting. When a group of people come together to exchange ideas and reach conclusions, there is generally a great deal of talk. When the group come together at a later stage to continue the discussions, memories might be a little hazy. For this reason it is general for a record to be made of what has been said. These formal records are described as *minutes*.

While normal proceedings in a meeting may or may not be noted, it is obligatory to record any *decisions* which have been made, because these will normally be binding on the group.

You are now invited to 'listen in' to two different business meetings:

2: Modifying business information

1. Alpha Engineering Company Limited – a meeting of the Safety Committee

The company makes switchgear equipment for the motor industry. There are some 650 employees – mainly male. Tim Brandon is the Chief Shop Steward and is also the Transport and General Workers Union representative on the committee. He is reporting to the committee with regard to an accident which happened recently to one of the workers. Our task is to make a note of his speech to the committee in a form which would be acceptable as a formal minute, using no more than 30 words.

'Gentlemen, I have to bring to your notice a very unfortunate incident which occurred in the Welding Section last Monday. Some of you already know the details, but I am bringing it to the attention of the committee generally. Julia Styles joined us last August as a trainee welder. The first female welder we've had at Alpha, but she's been getting first-class reports from her supervisor. It was a bit of a novelty to start with, but the lads got used to having her around, and she was settling in nicely.

'On Monday it seems Julia was changing a gas canister when there was an explosion and she was badly burned around the face. Even her hair caught fire, but fortunately, some of the lads were quickly on the scene and smothered the flames. Julia's still in hospital. It looks as if she's going to be there for some time, and they reckon she'll need plastic surgery.

'Now, gentlemen, it seems obvious that Julia has a right to compensation, but when I took this up with the Works Manager this was disputed on the grounds that Julia hadn't been carrying out the proper safety procedures. I've reported the case to union headquarters, and they're now involved.

'The lads in the Welding Section sent her flowers and a couple of them have visited her in hospital. I'm sure the members of this committee will join me in wishing Julia a speedy recovery. I suggest we also send her some flowers.'

There was unanimous approval.

Here is an example of how you might write the minutes for this meeting, using the TRACKDICE rules given earlier:

Task	Record what has been said in no more than 30 words.
Read and re-read	Once to get the general outline and then more closely for the details of what happened.
Ask	What is this about? Answer: a serious accident to one of the welders.
Clarify	One of the trade union representatives is reporting to the Safety Committee. Names of people involved will have to be mentioned though these reduce the number of words available for the description.
Key words and phrases	trainee welder ... changing a gas canister ... explosion ... in hospital .... plastic surgery ... compensation disputed ... union now involved ... send flowers. *(18 basic words)*
Draft	Tim Brandon (TGWU) referred to the explosion which happened when Julia Styles, a trainee welder, was changing a gas cylinder. She is still in hospital and will need plastic surgery. The union are looking into the question of compensation. The committee agreed to send her flowers.
Improve	Tim Brandon said his union were looking into the issue of compensation following the accident to Julia Styles, a trainee welder, when a gas cylinder exploded. The committee is sending flowers to the hospital.

2: Modifying business information

Count   33 words

Edit   '… were looking into the question of …' wastes words.

The final draft of the minute might read:

> Tim Brandon said his union were considering compensation for Julia Styles, trainee welder, in hospital following a gas explosion last Monday. The committee is sending her flowers.
>
> *(30 words)*

No two people will use precisely the same words to note Tim Brandon's contribution to the meeting, but we can look at our edited version critically.

a) Does it omit any vital facts?
b) Are any further reductions possible?
c) Are there any inaccuracies in the recorded note?

If the answers to those three questions are 'no', we can accept the minute as satisfactory.

It could be argued that it is wrong to give up one-fifth of the note (six words) to the comparatively trivial business of the flowers, but the defence of this treatment is that it was a decision by the committee and therefore requires to be recorded.

2. The Brompton Electronics meeting

James Davies, the Chairman of Brompton Electronics, is addressing the company shareholders at their Annual General Meeting. He is telling them how the company has fared during the past twelve months. Some of his news is good, some bad.

'We've introduced a new range of computer games for teenagers this year. We've marketed them under the brand name of Scotland Yard. I'm sure you've seen the advertisements we've been putting over on television. The games are based on a very simple principle. The players are given a series of clues and from these they've got to work out who committed the crime. Our most popular game so far has been the Great Train Robbery, but our newest, Counter Espionage, looks like overtaking it before long. Both have sold close on 50,000 copies to date.

'All this success has been achieved at a price. The development costs have been substantial. I hardly need to tell you the cost of sustaining a national television advertising campaign. However, if we want to make profits we've got to invest and, with this in mind, the company's directors felt that Scotland Yard was a worthwhile project.

'So far, so good, but two problems have arisen within the last few months. The first is that counterfeit copies of Scotland Yard have started appearing in the home market. Of course they are affecting our sales. They're often selling at nearly half the price of our own products. Our legal advisers say there is nothing we can do.

'The second problem is just as serious for us as shareholders. The Scotland Yard project has eaten up a lot of our working capital, and we are now facing a rather serious cash flow problem. In short, ladies and gentlemen, I am recommending that this year's ordinary dividend should be halved to five per cent.'

The shareholders agreed to the proposal for a reduction in the dividend.

Exercise 3

Make a brief note of the Chairperson's speech (30–40 words) in a form which would make it suitable as a formal minute.

Expanding

While expanding can be seen as the opposite of summarising, the use of key words and phrases remains as the recommended technique. Imagine that you are asked by the local Chamber of Commerce to give a talk about your part of the world, be it village, county or town. How difficult it would be for most people to stand up in front of strangers, or comparative strangers and give a talk like that! Yet it would be much less of a burden if you took along a series of prompting cards. How much easier it would be to give the talk if you had in front of you a series of cards with key words or phrases written on them:

my family's connections – schools and colleges – churches – sports clubs – industries – commerce – shopping centres – rivers – roads – people – interesting personalities – beauty spots – public houses – doctors – hospitals

The list does not need to end there but, if you shuffle the cards into the order you prefer, you will no doubt find your speech will dramatically improve with these combined memory aids and prompters. It is interesting to note how the mind reacts to the intrusion of a single word. Psychologists and psychiatrists sometimes use word association tests in their procedures.

The question might be, 'What comes into your mind when I say the word 'pop'?'

One person might answer 'disc jockey', another might respond with 'lemonade'. Whatever the response, the word 'pop' has acted as a catalyst. One word leads to another. One word leads to a train of thought. Check this chain-type reaction on yourself.

Your task

What do the following words conjure up in your mind? Think about each word for a few minutes and make a note of the thoughts they evoke.

princess   nuclear   Olympics   fashion   play

For example, the word 'princess' might make you think of the words 'royal' or 'fairytale'. You might associate the word nuclear with Chernobyl, someone else might think of fuel.

3: The written word in business

Letters

In spite of the great advances made in the field of communication the letter remains one of the most effective ways of conveying information from one person to another. Bearing in mind the important role played by the letter in the world of business students need to distinguish between good and bad practices in letter writing. The acceptable forms and styles need to be understood.

The critical importance of the letter is its impact on the receiver. We are dealing with customers or members of the public (potential customers) without whose support the business would fail and our jobs disappear. Of course this is true of all our contacts with the public but the letter is difficult to retract or to deny, and these features mean that we need to be particularly careful and precise when we compose letters.

General guidelines

The most important quality to cultivate for writing letters is empathy. Empathy requires you to 'stand in the shoes of' the recipient. How would you react to this letter if it was addressed to you? It is a quality closely allied to tact and diplomacy. However there are other guidelines which you will need to bear in mind.

1. Deal with **all the points** raised in an **incoming** letter. There is always a danger in a complex letter that some of the questions raised will be unanswered.

2. Reply to letters as **promptly** as possible. Time is sometimes of the essence. Consider for example a letter which asks. 'In order to save myself enormous losses, should I sell my government stocks before the impending budget?' The recipient is too busy to answer before the Chancellor of the Exchequer's pronouncements so when he gets round to replying he has to write 'Yes you should have done!' Hardly the way to nurture clients!

3. Keep the language **as simple as possible** particularly when you are writing to a non-expert. At the same time do not go too far in that direction so that the recipient feels he or she is being treated as an idiot.

4. Avoid **irrelevancy and triviality.**

5. **Check** the letter carefully before it is signed and leaves the office. The letter is an advertisement for the efficiency of your business. Advertisements are supposed to make people want to be associated with your organisation but some letters have the opposite effect.

6. **Avoid making promises you cannot keep**, and if, for example, you agree to provide certain information by a certain date make a diary note so you are reminded to act.

7. **Avoid attacking other people or firms** particularly by name. Your letter might be produced in court when you are charged with damaging a person's reputation (called 'publishing a libel' in legal language).

8. **Be careful you are not committing your organisation to an unwanted course of action.** An agreement between two parties may be enforceable at law. A contract does not usually need to be evidenced in writing but the production of a letter could support a claim to the court that a contractual obligation exists. Andrew, a car dealer, writes to a customer 'I agree to buy your Ford motor car for £3,000'. He may then be

committed to the purchase in spite of the fact that he meant to quote a price of £2,000. The larger sum was a typing error.

Here is an example of a letter and reply:

Letter

Anthony P Briggs
Chartered Accountant
55 North Road, Harrow, Middlesex HA1 2PR
Telephone: 081 111 0000

```
Mrs Thelma Grant
46 Grange Road
Harrow
Middlesex HA4 1WE

5th January 199-

Dear Mrs Grant,
```

I have now drafted the accounts for Grant's Garden Shop. Will you kindly check them before they are typed. The Directors' Report seems to have varied from the statutory format last year and I have included a separate sheet showing the normal headings which I hope you will be able to follow. Your review of the business last year was more detailed than the average presentation, so it would be possible for you to reduce its length this year, but of course it is entirely up to you.

Please let me have the accounts back with any queries so I can have them completed as soon as possible.

With best wishes,

Yours sincerely,

Anthony Briggs

Anthony Briggs

Points to note

1. It is common practice to leave out commas and full stops in addresses when typewriters and word processors are used.

2. When the letter is sent from a large office a reference is often quoted at the heading of the letter (e.g. GPN/GH). When a reply is sent the reference should he quoted in order to ensure that it gets to the person dealing with the subject matter as soon as possible.

3. The postcode should always be quoted as this speeds up the processing of the letter in the sorting office.

4. For record purposes the date is an important part of any letter.

3: The written word in business

Reply

Mrs Grant's reply to her accountant might take the following form:

46, Grange Road,
Harrow HA4 1WE
Tel. 081 945 6789

12th January 199-

Anthony P. Briggs Esq.,
Chartered Accountant,
55, North Road,
Harrow HA1 2PR

Dear Mr Briggs,

Thank you for your letter of the 5th January enclosing the draft accounts. They seem quite satisfactory and I return them for your further attention.

Please let me know if anything else is required.

Yours sincerely,

Thelma Grant

Thelma Grant

In this letter commas and full stops have been included in the addresses which shows where they would appear if used. You will note that Mrs Grant has addressed her accountant as Esquire (abbreviated to Esq). Professional men are often addressed in this way. It is also usual to quote qualifications after a person's name when these are known. If a person quotes these qualifications when writing to you it is courteous to quote them when replying, for example:

> Ms Jean Hardcastle BA Dip Ed

In the letter from the accountant 'Dear Mrs Grant' is the salutation. 'Yours sincerely' is the complimentary close. Certain salutations and complimentary closes are conventionally linked with each other. Thus:

salutation	*complimentary close*
Dear Sir	
Dear Madam	Yours faithfully
Dear Sirs/Mesdames	

The above forms are used when the writer does not know the name of the recipient.

When the writer does know the name of the recipient, any of the following forms can be used, as appropriate:

Dear Jeremy/Jennifer*(informal)*	
Dear Mr/Mrs/Ms*/Miss Smith	
Dear Dr Smith	Yours sincerely
Dear Sir/Lady John/Jennifer	
Dear Lord/Lady Abercrombie	

* Used when it is not known whether the addressee is married or single, or when she indicates that this is how she wishes to be addressed.

Exercise 1

You are the Office Manager in a plastics manufacturing company. You have to reply to the following letter received from a potential customer. Your diary shows you are free on 7th April.

Follow the format of the letters on pages 19 and 20.

R. Corbett & Son Ltd.
14–16 West Way, Ipswich, Suffolk IP5 3PJ
Telephone 0220 434343

Our Ref NOV/QRT

The Office Manager
Allardyce Plastics Ltd
33 Gordon Square
London NW1 7HM

16th January 199-

Dear Sir or Madam,

Thank you for sending me your catalogue of plastic components; a number of items are of interest to me. However, before I place an order with you I will need to discuss terms and discounts. I shall be in London on Monday, 7th April, and wonder whether it would be convenient for me to call on you, say between 2 and 3pm on that day.

Yours faithfully,

Robert Corbett

Robert Corbett
Managing Director

3: The written word in business

Exercise 2*

Find 15 errors in this letter.

```
                                              Miss Mabél Tang Bin
                                                     Apartment 617
                                                  The Red Dawn Hotel
                                                           Hunghom
                                                           Kowloon
                                                         hong Kong
Mr Andrew Corrigan
Principal
English Language School
Wordsworth Lodge
Purbrook
Shropshire SY3 DX

Dear Mr Corigan,

I hope you had an enjoyable and successful trip to Bombay and Karachi and
that the move into the new school building is going according to plan.
The advertising campain in Hong Kong has rather run out of steam I fear,
mainly because I am not hearing from the UK printers. They have still not
sent the stock of amended brochures and I need these before I place any
advertisements in the two Chinese langauge newspapers. I an growing con-
cerned that if the advertisements are not placed soon, then the period for
vetting applications for scholarships and a place on the new courses in
September will of necessity be very rushed.

If you still wish me to place the advertisements would you please let me
know as soon as possible. I will then have a stock of the broachures (as
discussed in my previous letter to you printed here in Hong Kong and have
these ready to forward to respondents to the newspaper advertisements,
which I will place as soon as I have the go-ahead from you. This will
releive you of the necessity to send a stock out to me.

I have recently sent copies of the Schools brochures to the commercial
studies departments ofthe various Technical Institutes here in Hong Kong.
It will be interesting to hear whether this results in more enquiries
about the courses.

Yours faithfully,
```

Letters of Enquiry

Most business transactions develop out of an initial enquiry from a potential customer. They have received your company's catalogue, read your advertisement in a newspaper or magazine, or you have been recommended to them by another (satisfied) customer.

Letters of enquiry should be handled with great care because each of them could be the starting-point for a long and mutually beneficial trading relationship. Mishandled, they represent a lost opportunity which may never return, and will most likely end up benefiting your competitors.

Fresh Food Distributors Ltd are a new firm which caters for a number of large office blocks in the City of London. They prepare food for office workers along the same lines that airlines provide snacks for their passengers, and these food packs come in an assortment of shapes and sizes. Because of the traffic congestion in London they are taken from the kitchens to the offices by a fleet of motor cyclists, whose machines have specially large panniers attached. The ideas was the brainchild of a young Japanese lady, Takiko Sato, who noticed when she was posted to London by her company, that the English office workers were badly served in comparison to their Japanese counterparts. In Tokyo, many office workers find restaurants overcrowded at lunch times, and prefer to each lunch in their own offices. Having set up the business, she is now finding that the plastic containers available on the market do not keep the food hot (or cold) enough, and she is now looking for a suitable supplier of containers. This is vital to the business which has the slogan, 'Hot food delivered to your desk'.

The letters which follow indicate a typical pattern of enquiry and reply between business firms, in this case leading to a successful outcome.

Enquiry

Fresh Food Distributors
Unit 15, Vesta Industrial Estate, Southwark Close, London SE1 0AA   Tel: 071 515 1515

Date:

Ms Alyson Hall
Marketing Manager
Elmo Plastic Containers Ltd
Grange Works
Lymington
Hampshire SO41 9AP

Dear Ms Hall

Thank you for sending your catalogue of plastic containers for food products, together with quotations for quantity purchase. You were kind enough to offer to send samples of any products which interest us, and we would appreciate samples of your Pristine 95 range, particularly the watertight 1.5, 2.0 and 3.0 litre sizes.

Your catalogue refers to the possibility of various divisions being built into the containers, and we would certainly need these. More importantly we need to include a device which will help us to keep the food in the container hot for a period of 1 to 2 hours. With the winter coming this will shortly be a critical factor. In Japan we keep the food hot by introducing a vacuum surround for the containers, but I have failed to find any firm in England which can provide this. Another Japanese technique is to provide an outer shell for every 50 containers, which also has the effect of retaining heat.

We could obtain all these containers from Japan, but it is essential that we have a constant and reliable supply daily, and that is why we are looking for an English supplier if possible.

We look forward to receiving your samples and then perhaps we can see what options there are.

Yours sincerely,

Takiko Sato

Ms Takiko Sato
Managing Director

3: The written word in business

First reply

Elmo Plastic Containers Ltd

Grange Works, Lymington, Hampshire, SO41 9AP   Telephone 0590 9955 Fax 0590 1155

Date

Ms Takiko Sato
Managing Director
Fresh Food Distributors Ltd
Unit 15, Vesta Industrial Estate
Southwark Close
London SE1 0AA

Dear Ms Sato,

Subject: Pristine 95 Range Containers

Thank you for your letter of [date], and I am sending the samples you have asked for by Express which means you should have received them by the time this letter arrives. Ms Hall is on a business trip to the Netherlands and Germany for the remainder of this week, but I have referred the contents of your letter to her. She would welcome the chance to meet you and, as she will be in London on Tuesday and Wednesday of next week, wonders whether a meeting on either of those days would be possible. Any time after midday would be acceptable fro m her point of view.

Incidentally, I have enclosed with the samples some of the divisions which are currently being produced, but please remember shapes and sizes can be designed to suit your special needs, and they can either be fixed or detachable.

Please let me know if I can be of further assistance.

Yours sincerely,

Paul Greenaway

Paul Greenaway
Deputy Marketing Manager

Second reply

Elmo Plastic Containers Ltd

Grange Works, Lymington, Hampshire, SO41 9AP   Telephone 0590 9955 Fax 0590 1155

Date: Page One

Ms Takiko Sato
Managing Director
Fresh Food Distributors Ltd
Unit 15, Vesta Industrial Estate
Southwark Close
London SE1 0AA

Dear Takiko,

First let me thank you again for your kind hospitality yesterday. The food and the presentation were excellent and I can understand why your business is flourishing. I hope that Elmo can help you to be even more successful in the future!

I felt our discussions were very useful and since I came back to my office I have discussed your problems with our production department. They have no doubt they can design and produce the containers you require in the quantities you require. I promised to give you some quotations and here they are. You will see they are very close to the prices I predicted.

> Page Two
>
> **Insulated containers with self-seal lids and divisions as agreed:**
>
> | | Order amounts | Per unit (£s) |
> |---|---|---|
> | **1.5 litres** | Up to 1000 | 1.50 |
> | | 1001 to 3000 | 1.05 |
> | | 3001 to 6000 | 0.75 |
> | | above 6000 | 0.55 |
> | **2.0 litres** | Up to 1000 | 1.85 |
> | | 1001 to 3000 | 1.30 |
> | | 3001 to 6000 | 1.00 |
> | | above 6000 | 0.80 |
> | **3.0 litres** | Up to 1000 | 2.50 |
> | | 1001 to 3000 | 2.05 |
> | | 3001 to 6000 | 1.65 |
> | | above 6000 | 1.15 |
> | **Insulated outer shell containers** | | 22.50 |
>
> I confirm that all containers will carry the FFB logo in red and blue together with your company's address and telephone number. Whether or not the individual containers are returned to you, I am sure this will be good publicity for your business.
>
> Our production department have agreed to accept a target date of three weeks from today. As promised, I will get your first order of 1000 of each size to you immediately they are available. We can deal with the need for any modifications as they arise.
>
> Please let me know if I can be of further help in the meantime.
>
> Thank you again for your hospitality - and your confidence.
>
> Yours sincerely,
>
> *Alyson Hall*
>
> Ms Alyson Hall

Note: The letter from Alyson Hall may sound surprisingly informal, but she has obviously had a meal with Takiko, and during that meal they would have used first names. Having reached that point in their relationship it would be rather unfriendly to revert to a more formal style.

Sensibly, Alyson is showing interest and enthusiasm for her customer's business.

Collection Letters

Most transactions between business firms are for credit. In the previous example Takiko will not be expected to pay cash for the plastic containers when they are delivered. She will be given a 'breathing space' of about one month before Elmo expect her to settle the account. This is normal business practice. In general it gives the purchasers time to sell the goods before they have to pay for them.

Of course some businesses are slow paying their accounts and they have to be 'chased'. The larger the amount involved, the more vital it is for us to take appropriate action.

Customers may be slow to pay for a number of reasons. For example:

a) They may have genuinely forgotten that payment was due.

b) They may need a few more days or weeks before they are in a position to pay. In these circumstances we sometimes say they are having cash flow problems.

3: The written word in business

c) They may deliberately delay payment on the grounds that they prefer to have the use of the money for as long as possible.

d) Some large companies, realising the importance of their custom to small businesses, are adept at making their suppliers wait for payment. This improves their own cash flow considerably.

e) They may be in serious financial difficulties, in which case we may need to take legal action without delay.

When writing letters reminding customers of outstanding debts, it is always wise to remind ourselves that without customers we have no business. It may take months or even years to find customers. It could take just one thoughtless, careless word to lose them. However, we do expect to be paid. Our job is to walk a tight-rope between being too tough and too soft.

In the letters which follow you will see how Anglo-Chinese Importing Consortium start off politely, but begin to apply more pressure on their customer with the passing of time.

Stage 1:

Anglo-Chinese Importing Consortium
66-70 Longford Place, London N1 1ZZ Telephone 071 111 1000

Barton's Carpet Emporium
55-57 Lower Clapham Road
London N16 2YY

15th March 199-

Dear Sirs,

Reference: Invoice 139541/X February 11th

According to our records the above invoice for £13,335.00 has not yet been settled and we would appreciate an early payment. If payment is already on the way to us please ignore this letter.

Yours faithfully,

Thomas Johnson

Thomas Johnson
Credit Control Department

Stage 2:

Anglo-Chinese Importing Consortium
66-70 Longford Place, London N1 1ZZ Telephone 071 111 1000

Barton's Carpet Emporium
55-57 Lower Clapham Road
London N16 2YY

5th April 199-

Dear Sirs,

Reference: Invoice 139541/X February 11th

Our records show that the sum of £13,335.00 on your account has still not been paid. It is now two months since the goods were delivered to you and we would ask you to clear your account within the next seven days. If you are experiencing any difficulties regarding payment please contact me personally.

Yours faithfully,

John Lee

John Lee
Credit Control Manager

Stage 3:

Anglo-Chinese Importing Consortium
66-70 Longford Place, London N1 1ZZ Telephone 071 111 1000

Barton's Carpet Emporium
55-57 Lower Clapham Road
London N16 2YY

23rd April 199-

Dear Mr Barton,

Outstanding Account: £13,350.00

It is now ten weeks since we delivered to you a consignment of high-quality Chinese rugs. We have waited patiently to hear from you, but have heard nothing. No explanation has been offered for the delay. No payment has been made.

The amount outstanding is substantial and in the circumstances we have no choice but to hand the matter to our solicitors from whom you will no doubt be hearing in the course of the next few days.

It is a considerable disappointment to us because we have always enjoyed doing business with you.

Yours sincerely,

John Lee

John Lee
Credit Control Manager

Points to note

1. The first letter was signed by a clerk, the second by the Credit Control Manager, and the third is addressed to the proprietor of the carpet store personally. What starts off as a routine matter becomes more serious and finally very serious.

2. There are no fixed periods between the stages. Nor is there a limitation to the number of stages. Much will depend on:

    a) The amount outstanding.

    b) The previous history and credit worthiness of the customer.

    c) The financial reputation of the customer. One would obviously be less concerned if the customer was a well-known and reputable company. A stage three letter would probably never be written in that case. Instead, there would be a succession of reminders.

    d) How long Barton's Carpet Emporium have been customers.

    e) Any additional evidence which is available. For example, John Lee might visit Barton's and discover they are doing a brisk business – in which case he might be re-assured. Conversely, he might see sales notices across the windows – 'Everything at half-price' – or even more alarming 'Closing down sale – everything must go'. Or there could be rumours 'in the trade' that Barton's are in serious financial difficulties, which would speed up the whole process. In any case he might use the opportunity of a visit to talk to the proprietor.

Letters of Complaint

General trade correspondence deals with information about products and services offered. Correspondence involving enquiries orders and estimates can be regarded as routine but letters expressing dissatisfaction need to be considered in a separate category. The problem may be a faulty product or inadequate service though the complaint may also be con-

3: The written word in business

nected with an unpaid account. Special thought and care is required when you are replying to a customer's complaint about the goods or services your firm has provided. People tend to be very sensitive and should be dealt with accordingly but it is not enough to simply placate or reassure the customer. Action is often more important than words.

Here is an example of a letter of complaint; it is to a local supermarket.

---

                                                           116 Esplanade Road
                                                                                    Poole
                                                                          Dorset BH6 2QQ

22nd September 199-

The Manager
SupaSave Stores PLC
High Street
Poole
Dorset BH3 9BB

Dear Sir,

Last week I visited your store as usual to pick up my groceries for the week. One of the things I bought was a tin of baked beans. When I got home to unload my shopping the beans were missing. I checked the receipt the girl had given me at the check-out and the 67p for the beans was shown on the list. I telephoned the store on Monday to tell them about it and the girl on the telephone was quite rude to me. She said it had got nothing to do with the store and I should have been more careful.

I am 75 years old and find it difficult enough to get to the store. When your girl was rude to me it was very upsetting.

Yours faithfully,

Thomas Carter

Thomas Carter

How does the manager of SupaSave Stores deal with this letter? To some extent he will be bound by company policy, but let us assume he has some discretion in the matter. His reply might be along the following lines.

SupaSave Stores plc
High Street, Poole, Dorset BH3 9BB   Tel: 0151 887744

24th September 199-

Mr Thomas Carter
116 Esplanade Road
Poole
Dorset BH6 2QQ

Dear Mr Carter,

I am sorry to hear about the lost can of beans and your unhappiness with regard to the subsequent telephone conversation. I have spoken to the young lady who took your call and she tells me she had no wish to sound discourteous. Please make a point of asking for me when you visit the store next time. I can assure you we do value the goodwill of customers like yourself.

Yours sincerely,

Kenneth Curtis

Kenneth Curtis
Manager

3: The written word in business

Points to note

1. Mr Curtis has avoided admitting that the telephonist was rude. He has also avoided the temptation to give Thomas a replacement can of beans. He will have the opportunity to talk to Thomas face-to-face before deciding how to deal with the complaint. He will no doubt consider producing a replacement can of beans if on talking to Thomas he feels that this will safeguard Thomas's custom for the store.

2. Regardless of the merits of the case, the girl who took the telephone call from Thomas was wrong if she was in any way rude to him. Courtesy is a vital requirement in business.

The following is an example of a letter dealing in detail with a complaint from a customer of another supermarket. The story will unfold as you read the letter.

Bestbuy Supermarkets plc
Head Office: 35 New Road, Clerkenwell, London EC2 1AA   Telephone: 071 767 6767

Our reference CD/2439

Mrs H Brady
368 Jordan Street
Linton
Surrey GD1 1WW

Date:

Dear Mrs Brady,

We were very concerned to learn from the Manager of our Linton branch, Mr Peterson, that you believed your purchase of Belgarda Tuna may have been responsible for your daughter being unwell. This product is obtained from a very reputable supplier whose standards are generally of the highest order. We are therefore extremely disturbed at this possibility.

Regrettably, as the sample you kindly returned had been opened for some time, conclusive microbiological tests could not be carried out to establish its condition at point of sale. Neither were we able to obtain a sample of the same canning code batch for examination, as these had all been sold.

We can assure you that tuna fish for Bestbuy Supermarkets is carefully selected and is processed under conditions of stringent hygiene to our own high specifications. It is subjected to rigorous quality control at source and our own food chemists make regular checks on deliveries.

Our Canned Goods Buyer has explained that in cold weather the oil in the can may tend to thicken, but this does not detract from the product in any way and should not cause a stomach upset. Our Chief Chemist added that sickness can result from numerous causes. Therefore, to establish its origins conclusively, it would be necessary to test samples of everything eaten and drunk by the sufferer for at least 48 hours prior to an attack.

We very much regret, therefore, that we are unable to present you with definite conclusions in this unfortunate matter. We are extremely sorry for the inconvenience and discomfort your daughter suffered but, in the light of the above, we think it possible that something other than the tuna caused her to be unwell. However, as you were dissatisfied with your purchase, and your local manager Mr. Peterson clearly values your custom, we would like to offer you the enclosed credit note for £25 as a gesture of goodwill and without prejudice*. It can be spent at any BestBuy store.

Yours sincerely,

Patricia Shaw

Ms Patricia Shaw
Personal Assistant to Sales Director

*The phrase 'without prejudice' has legal implications. It is used to avoid a situation where Mrs Brady takes the company to Court and claims (through her lawyers) that the payment of £25 made by the company was an admittance that the goods sold were faulty.

Circulars

The distinction between a letter and a circular is that the former is normally addressed to an individual while the latter is sent in the same form to large numbers of potential customers. The distinction is sometimes blurred because circulars these days are often cleverly contrived to look like personalised letters. They are almost invariably a form of advertising and as such need to be persuasive. They also need to be checked very carefully because any mistake that is made will be repeated as many times as the number of circulars distributed.

One of the aims of a circular is to let the public know about a product or service on offer to them. In other words it is a form of advertising. Regrettably and expensively for those footing the bill the majority of circulars addressed to the public end up in the waste bin. This explains why many advertisers include a free gift element in the circular. At least then more people might be interested in the accompanying literature.

The ground rules for circulars

1. The presentation should be eye-catching.
2. The message should be persuasive.
3. The message should be simple and straightforward.
4. It should be easy for the recipient to respond (a prepaid envelope might be enclosed).

An example of a circular is shown here. The merit of this example is that there are no postal costs. The costs are limited to the printing of the circular.

3: The written word in business

---

greetings cards   *sweets & tobacco*

Prince's News
65 Prince's Road, Ruddington RN4 5GP
Telephone 033 131313

Dear Customer,

We have become agents for the Ruddington Rugby Club Cashline Daily Draw and we are taking the liberty of enclosing this leaflet for your interest and consideration, in the hope that you will participate. The cost is only 50p per week for each 10 chance daily entries, which gives you ten chances to win £100 each day Monday to Friday, every week, plus £5 consolation prizes.

All you have to do is complete the attached form and return it to us at the shop, after which there are no further forms to fill in - no postal orders - no postage - no collectors at your door.

On receipt of the form we will make you a member of the draw and issue you with a membership card containing your ten numbers for each 50p invested.

Winning numbers will be printed in the Ruddington Evening Mail daily.

Always at your service.

Maurice & Michelle Morton

Maurice and Michelle Morton
Your newsagents

✂ ---

Please complete and return this form to us at:

    Prince's News, 65 Prince's Road, Ruddington RN4 5GP

Please register me as a member of the Ruddington Rugby Club   YES/NO

Name _____

Address _____

_____

_____

Date _____

Please tick the number of chances you would like:

    10 chances to win @ 50p weekly   ❑

    20 chances to win @ £1 weekly   ❑

    40 chances to win @ £2 weekly   ❑

Exercise 3

Bearing in mind the guidelines given on page 30 how would you improve the circular produced by Prince's News?

Advertisements

Advertising will be dealt with as a business topic in Chapter Seven but here the advertisement will be looked at as another example of communication taking place in the business world. When we look at the basics of an advertisement the public (or a section of the public) are being made aware of the availability of a product or service. The advertiser is trying to 'paint a picture' in the mind of the recipient. The aim is to persuade the audience (or as many of them as possible) to part with their money. The aim is achieved by means of a mixture of words and images. In developing material for advertising certain basic questions need to be answered:

1. To which audience is the advertisement addressed?
2. Is the advertising material appropriate for that audience?
3. How effective is the advertisement likely to be?

These questions are equally applicable whether we are dealing with advertising on television or in newspapers and magazines.

Advertisers are as bound by the law as any other members of society. In general terms, they may make their offerings sound attractive but not overtly mislead the public. The state can be expected to use the law to protect its citizens.

The importance of empathy has already been mentioned and a knowledge of psychology will help the advertisers to be persuasive. Psychology also helps us to understand that every human being has an ego and is seeking respect from others. If we fail to show respect to those we interact with in business, we must expect to incur their wrath.

The sample advertisement shown here gives us a number of clues as to how the mind of the advertiser works.

The products being sold are apple pies. There is nothing novel about apple pies, but the modern fad is for natural, unadulterated foods. This is the message being put across in the advertisement.

Advertising has been given a special place in the Ground Rules section to emphasise that every outward going communication is a form of advertisement for the organisation. It is positive if it makes the recipients better disposed towards the organisation. It is negative if it does harm to the organisation's reputation. And the success of the organisation is vitally important to those who look to it for wages and pensions, promotions and holidays with pay.

Exercise 4

Auntie Martha Home Bakeries Ltd have received the following letter from a potential customer. You are asked to prepare a reply for the Marketing Manager who wants you to tell Ms Green:

a) There has been a great demand for the pies and there is a shortage in supplies at the present time.

b) The Area Sales Manager has been informed of Ms Green's interest and will arrange for a representative to call very shortly. Although the sales are being made through the large supermarket chains initially, it is proposed to use the smaller retail outlets in the very near future.

3: The written word in business

S.G. Green
Your friendly corner shop
5 Adelaide Terrace, Northampstead, Yorkshire Y05 9K Telephone 4546 0041

15th September 199-

The Marketing Manager
Auntie Martha Home Bakeries Ltd
The Granary
Westhampstead
Yorkshire Y03 7QW

Dear Sir,

I read with interest your advertisement in the local papers for the apple pies. I found it most amusing. I did purchase a sample for myself to find out whether the product was as good as you made it out to be. I must admit I was impressed. Which brings me to the point of this letter.

While I cannot pretend to operate a supermarket (in the normal sense of the word), my turnover is quite good for an independent retailer, and I would very much like to stock up with some of your pies - and indeed any other products of a similar nature.

Can we talk business?

Yours faithfully,

Sharon Green

Sharon G Green

Exercise 5

If you were asked to telephone Sharon Green instead of write, what would you say to her? Make a draft of the conversation you would expect to have with her.

Memoranda

A memorandum might be described as an internal note (or letter) circulating within an organisation. Quite often the memorandum will be handwritten. Each organisation will have its own design for memoranda (the plural for memorandum), but a typical format is shown below.

Alpha Engineering Co Ltd   Memorandum

To Graham Dolby   From Peter Robinson
Chief Safety Officer   Personnel Manager

25th Sept 199-

Subject: Accident to Julia Styles

I have been asked to prepare a report for the Managing Director and need to know what instructions there are for welders changing gas canisters. There seem to be conflicting accounts of what actually happened. Can you see me before Thursday if possible? Please give my secretary a ring to fix a mutually convenient time.

Memoranda are used for a variety of reasons, but tend to be informal and brief, which explains why the forms are often printed in the smaller paper sizes. They need to be addressed sufficiently to enable them to land on the right desk after going through the internal mailing system, and the date and the initials (if not the signature) of the originator are essential.

3: The written word in business

Memoranda might be used to:

1. seek information or co-operation (as in the case of Peter Robinson's note to the Chief Safety Officer);
2. give instructions or advice (perhaps from a manager to a member of his team);
3. offer ideas and suggestions;
4. notify, clarify or explain events which have occurred.

The type of memorandum shown here is an alternative to the telephone message. Most internal communication in organisations is face to face or by telephone, but when these avenues are closed for one reason or another (perhaps the person you are trying to contact is 'out of the office' or otherwise unavailable) the memorandum comes into play.

While a memorandum is often addressed to an individual, it may be reproduced and circulated to a number of different people in the organisation. For example, a manager might circulate notice of a meeting to various members of his staff.

Increasingly in modern offices desktop visual display units (VDUs) are used to convey information from one part of the organisation to another, and this has the effect of reducing the flow of paper.

Exercise 6

Peter Robinson, the Personnel Manager at Alpha has called for a meeting of his staff next Friday afternoon at 3pm. You are a member of his team but have arranged to visit a couple of local schools on Friday, hoping to recruit some new clerical staff. You are not sure how long this will take and might not be able to get to the meeting until later.

Draft a memorandum to the Personnel Manager explaining the situation.

Reports

The business report is usually reserved for the more important deliberations. The matters considered are likely to be more complex and the contents aimed at helping management to make rational decisions. Still on the subject of the accident to Julia Styles, the Works Manager has asked for a full report on the accident from the Supervisor in the Welding Section. The accident would have been reported in the official log book for accidents.

Accident Log Book				
Date/Time	Day	Department	Worker involved	Nature of Accident
22nd Sept	Monday	Welding	Julia Styles	Gas canister exploded. Worker burned face and hands. Taken to hospital.

The entries in this log are very important as the accident would have to be reported to the appropriate authorities.

For example, a formal report arising from the accident might be presented to the Works Manager at Alpha by the Supervisor in the Welding Section where the accident happened:

> ## Report
>
> To Mr C Houseman　　　　　　　　　　　　　　　From Conn McBride
> Works Manager　　　　　　　　　　　　　　　Supervisor (Welding Section)
> 　　　　　　　　　　　　　　　　　　　　　　　25th September 199-
>
> ### Re: Accident to Julia Styles
>
> As requested I have looked into the circumstances of the accident that happened to Julia. I understand the purpose of this report is to ascertain whether she can claim against Alpha Engineering (or its Insurance Company) for the injuries she received.
>
> **Cause of accident**
>
> It seems that when her gas canister ran dry Julia went to the reloading bay in compliance with the normal safety drill, but when she went back to her workstation she found the new canister malfunctioning. She then played with the fastening nut to tighten it, but instead loosened it. As a result, some of the liquid gas sprayed on to the flame of a workmate's gun.
>
> **Result of the accident**
>
> The blowback from the naked flame to the malfunctioning canister caused the casing to crack and release the rest of the gas. There was a massive explosion and, although Julia had thrust the canister away from herself just before it happened, her hair caught fire and the left hand side of her face was badly burned. A welding gun and some aluminium casings were completely destroyed.
>
> **Injuries incurred**
>
> I have visited Julia twice in hospital. The first time she was hardly able to speak, but when I saw her yesterday she was recovering. She was comforted by the news from the doctor that they would be able to repair all the damage with the aid of plastic surgery. Apparently, there will be no permanent scars.
>
> **Conclusion**
>
> I cannot see that Julia was in any way to blame for the accident, but on a strict interpretation of the rules applied in the Welding Section she should have gone to the reloading bay to adjust the gas canister.

Exercise 7

Having received the report on the accident, the Works Manager wants the supervisor to make sure all the welders follow the safety rules in future. He also wants to know the address of the hospital and the visiting hours so he can go and see her.

You are asked to draft (write) an appropriate memorandum for him to sign, following the guidelines below.

Guidelines

Conciseness

Perhaps the most important factor to bear in mind in reporting to people within the organisation is that the person receiving the report is likely to be very busy. Essentially reports are produced to give information to senior managers. The higher the managers in the organisational hierarchy, the greater the concentration of decisions in their hands. A senior manager will have to deal with many different situations during the course of a day's work. A lengthy report may have the merit of covering every conceivable issue, but the manager's time is valuable and by asking for a report he is looking for a **summary of the situation**.

3: The written word in business

Precision

Since the report is drafted with the purpose of deciding what, or whether action is required, any information provided needs to be as accurate as possible. The art is to steer a path between overburdening the report with detail and omitting data which may turn out to be significant.

Headings

The name of the person (or persons) to whom the report is addressed should be clearly stated, with appropriate courtesy titles. Managers expect to be addressed properly by their subordinates and, in any case, the report will need to pass through the normal internal mailing system.

The name and status of the author (or authors) of the report will also need to be clearly stated. Apart from other considerations, if the report is from a senior member of staff it will carry a higher level of priority.

Sub-headings

You will already have noticed how much easier it is to read a text book when the chapters are broken down into small sections. It is the same for managers reading reports. Sub-headings help them to refer back to earlier points which have been made, and generally make the report more palatable.

Title and subject

The manager should be able to see at a glance what the report is about. Other considerations apart, this will also give him the opportunity to accord it a level of priority. Managers face a daily barrage of incoming mail and have to select those items requiring urgent attention. Consider, for example, the relative importance of two reports which land on a managing director's desk on the same day. One is headed 'Proposed Improvements to Staff Canteen'. The other is entitled 'Threatened Strike Action by Line Workers'. Which do you think the managing director would read first?

The date of the report

How recent is the report? Situations in business are constantly changing. Recommendations which are valid at one time may become invalid as a new situation develops. The author of the report on the threatened strike may have recommended on 5th September offering the workforce a new bonus scheme. On 18th September the workforce were offered the bonus scheme and rejected it. For anyone subsequently reading the report these facts and dates become significant. Again emphasising the importance of dating material, the report on the canteen may be low priority when it is originally presented, but if it is disregarded for too long the conditions in the canteen may have become a cause of urgent concern. Yesterday's low priority rating may well become today's high priority.

Format

The layout of the report will vary according to the organisation's requirements, but as a general guide there should be an Introduction briefly setting out the terms of reference. Why has the report been drafted? What does it set out to achieve? The middle sections will cover the main contents of the report, be they information, explanations, ideas or arguments. The final section will be given over to conclusions and recommendations. Having produced the facts included in the report, the author is able to make certain proposals.

Tone

The tone of the report is a critical element. While it has to be objective, it is a form of communication from one person to another and should be courteous at all times, though civility rather than servility should be the order of the day. One young man wrote in a report to his office manager, 'It's fairly obvious the office has deteriorated since Mr Webster left.' Mr Webster was the previous manager. It was the young man's last report in that firm.

Appendices

In view of the need to keep the main report as brief and concise as possible it is common to include statistical data in the form of an appendix (plural – appendices) at the end of the main report.

Your task

Summarise the ground rules for writing reports in no more than 100 words using the key words and phrases technique explained in Chapters One and Two.

Annual reports to shareholders

As well as being able to write reports, one also has to be able to understand them. The key words and phrases technique can be used of course, but a second approach to the problem of comprehension is possible. This is the 'questioning approach' introduced in Chapter One. It can be used both to improve understanding and to test it.

Here is a report to the shareholders of Omega Electronics PLC by the company's chairman. Once a year Geoffrey Chalmerston accounts to them for the stewardship of his Board of Directors. This year his address (or speech) recounted on page 3 of the company's glossy illustrated Annual Report reads:

3: The written word in business

> **Omega Electronics PLC**
>
> Dear Shareholders,
>
> Our extensive measures to reduce costs and increase productivity in all company sectors have counteracted the fall in prices resulting from the enormous increase in overseas competition in the UK electronics industry. In all but one of our Divisions profits have increased slightly in spite of the fall in prices. Indeed, the Robotics Division has increased profits by a creditable 8%, though elsewhere the profit increases are much lower.
>
> The most disappointing progress is reported from the Components Division. You will recall that over the past three years we have spent close on £5 million to modernise the equipment used in this division to provide a variety of components for the world's major corporations. It was as well we did this because the UK electronics industry has had to accept competition from a barrage of cheap micro integrated circuits from the Far East. Until this happened we had been UK market leaders in this particular field, and we now have to divert our attention and our resources to new products and new markets. Inevitably, during the interim, the performance of the Components Division will languish. This year their profits have been negligible but I hope to be able to bring you better news in my next report.
>
> The value of our company's human resources has never been under-rated and during the year we have introduced a profit sharing scheme for all employees who have been with the firm for more than five years. As a result of this scheme I am pleased to report that we have been able to allocate over £1 million to the long-serving employees of this company, and this should serve as a practical 'thank you' for their loyalty.
>
> In the coming year we hope to benefit from the new plant which is being built on the outskirts of Ledbury. Belvedere Constructions, the company erecting the plant, assure us that it will be possible for it to be fully functional within the next six months. Once this new plant is in operation it will become a valuable profit-earning unit, and signal for us what I hope will be a great leap forward.
>
> Sincerely,
>
> *Geoffrey Chalmerston*
>
> Geoffrey Chalmerston
> Chairman

You will note that, since this report was in the form of a speech to the shareholders, it is in a different form to that produced by the Supervisor in the Welding Section at Alpha Engineering.

Exercise 8

After reading through the report answer these questions:

1. Which company is building the new plant?
2. When will it be completed?
3. What effect will it have on the company?
4. How are the company rewarding their loyal staff?
5. How much has been spent on modernising the equipment in the Components Division?
6. Where has the main competition come from?
7. Which Division has made most progress this year?
8. Has the company made a profit this year?

3: The written word in business

Now think of four further questions of your own, and answer them.

By asking questions and answering them you are improving as well as demonstrating your comprehension. The early questions should be the easy ones to answer. When these are dealt with the more general and searching questions can be raised. As you build up the battery of questions and answers your understanding will increase.

Report forms

Apart from Alpha Engineering's Accident Log, the reporting discussed so far has been what might be described as 'one-off'. So far we have looked at reports called for in connection with a particular non-recurring situation. Yet the bulk of reports are required on a regular basis. They tend to be routine and repetitive and call for a set format. Increasingly the details appear on visual display units (VDUs) and become part of the business's computerised memory store, the data being retrievable almost instantaneously either on a screen or on a computer print-out.

A sample of reporting forms used by one firm, Delta Food Products Ltd, is shown here. Delta is a medium sized company with a total workforce of 4,700. It produces and sells a variety of fancy biscuits and cakes, mainly serving quality confectioners and restaurants in the high streets.

The first of the reports is an Annual Staff Report Form. Its purpose is to update the records of individual members of staff so that, among other things, performance and attainments can be referred to when pay increases and promotions are considered.

Annual Staff Report
for year ended 31st March 199–

Full name Colin John Beecham **Age** 25 **Joined company** 5.4.87

Qualifications BTEC National in Business Studies **Present salary** £8050

Department Sales Office **Last increase** £500

Job Title Clerical Assistant **Times late** 21

Courses/training programmes during year None **Days absent (excluding holidays)** 13

Immediate Supervisor's Report:
Colin is a satisfactory worker. He is a good man to have around when there is a crisis. I have had to warn him a few times about punctuality, but he has a long journey to make and the buses sometimes run late.

P Petrie

Departmental Manager's Report:
Salary increase of £250 recommended.

J Jamieson

The next form to examine is the report which monitors absenteeism in Delta's different departments. The data allows comparisons to be made over a period of time, and contrasts to be made between different departments and individuals.

3: The written word in business

Departmental Absences Report Form

Department: Sales Office

Days absent third quarter of 199-

Names (alphabetical order)	Works no	July	August	September	TOTALS
Abercrombie, Jill	86/472	1	1	1	3
Beecham, Colin	87/635	0	2	0	2
Donaldson, Charles	85/471	1	2	3	6
French, Karen	87/666	0	0	0	0
Furness, Donna	83/396	1	2	0	3
Holden, Helen	84/415	0	0	2	2
Lamont, Edward	88/701	4	3	4	11
Patel, Laura	86/465	0	0	0	0
Singh, Tharampal	86/525	0	0	0	0
Thorburn, Stewart	83/406	2	0	2	4
Underwood, Clive	88/713	0	4	0	4
TOTALS		**9**	**14**	**12**	**35**

Exercise 9*

Referring to the Absences Report Form above:

1. What does the report show?
2. On this evidence do females tend to be absent more than males?
3. Which was the worst month for absenteeism in the Sales Office?
4. Which members of staff were the best (and worst) attenders?
5. What do you think the first two digits in the works numbers might indicate? (There is a clue in Colin Beecham's Annual Staff Report.)

The function of the Credit Controller is to ensure that customers do not get goods on credit (without paying for them) beyond the approved limit. If the customer has conducted a satisfactory account (paid the bills on time) the limit will be higher. The purpose of the third report form shown here is to provide the Credit Controller with useful data.

Customer Credit Report

Sales Representative Sandra Lyle
Customer's name Annie's Corner Shop
Address 13 Whitton Street, Manchester M6 5TY

Date of sale	Amount £	Payments outstanding £	Limit £	Balance of credit £
3.10.9-	1000.00	1000.00	3000.00	2000.00
14.10.9-	1600.00	2600.00	3000.00	400.00
22.10.9-		1000.00	1600.00	3000.00	1400.00
28.10.9-	1500.00	3100.00	3000.00	100.00
29.10.9-		1600.00	1500.00	3000.00	1500.00
30.10.9-				4000.00	2500.00
31.10.9-	1750.00	3250.00	4000.00	750.00
5.11.9-		1500.00	1750.00	4000.00	2250.00
10.11.9-	2000.00	3750.00	4000.00	250.00

Exercise 10

1. Explain in your own words the purpose of the Customer Credit Report shown here.
2. Explain the situation on 28th October.
3. What happened on 30th October?
4. What would have happened if the customer had wanted goods on credit to the value of £4,000.00 instead of £2,000.00 on 10th November?
5. Why do you think credit limits are necessary?

4: Grammar and punctuation

Nouns

A noun is a name for a person or object. A distinguishing feature is that it is often preceded by 'the' or 'a'. There are four different types:

Common

Common nouns are those representing ordinary, everyday persons or things such as *a director*, *an executive*, *the workers*, *premises*, *the shareholders* and *money*. The vast majority of nouns fall into this classification.

Proper

Proper nouns are the names or titles of specific people or things. They always start with a capital letter, and where there is more than one word in the title each main word begins with a capital. Examples of proper nouns include *Mr Jones*, *the Managing Director*, *Delta Food Products Ltd*, and *the Chartered Institute of Bankers*.

Abstract

Abstract nouns are those relating to things which cannot be seen or touched such as *discussions*, *participation*, *control*, *consensus*, *motivation*, *rejection* and *approval*. They are concerned with ideas and concepts, thoughts and feelings.

Collective

Collective nouns are used to identify collections of similar people or things. Examples are a **team** of executives, the **board** of directors, a **group** of companies and a **pool** of ideas.

Use of the apostrophe

When we refer to things (nouns) that are possessed by someone or something we have the choice of expressing ourselves in one of two ways. We can say, for example:

> The rules of the company *or* The company's rules.
>
> The objections of the trade union *or* The trade union's objections.
>
> The problems of the director *or* The director's problems.

The comma that is added is called an apostrophe. We are dealing with two nouns; the apostrophe is used to denote possession of one noun by another, for example of objections by a trade union. In these examples we are dealing with singular subjects, but what happens when we talk about 'companies' (note the change in the spelling), trade unions and directors? The apostrophe is then moved to the outside of the word. For example:

> The companies' rules.
>
> The trade unions' objections.
>
> The directors' problems.

So for plural subjects (the noun doing the owning), the apostrophe comes at the end of the word, immediately after the s, as in the three examples above.

Verbs

Verbs are words which signify some sort of action or thought. They are often described as 'doing' words. The root of a verb can always be preceded by the word 'to'. Examples of verbs:

to decide   to plant   to arrange   to consider   to sell

Verbs are expressed in either the singular or plural form and need to be used in the first, second or third person.

	Singular	*Plural*
First person	I plan	we plan
Second person	you plan	you plan
Third person	he, she, it plans	they plan

Verbs have different tenses, to indicate the time of the action: whether it is happening now (present tense), happened in the past (past, perfect and past perfect tenses), will happen in the future (future tense), or might happen depending on circumstances (conditional tense):

Present	The manager *plans* (or *is planning*) a sales campaign.
Past	The manager *planned* (or *was planning*) a sales campaign.
Perfect	The manager *has planned* (or *has been planning*) a sales campaign.
Past perfect	The manager *had planned* (or *had been planning*) a sales campaign.
Future	The manager *will plan* (or *will be planning*) a sales campaign.
Conditional	The manager *would plan* (or *would be planning*) a sales campaign.

We have some scope in choosing the tense we use, but we must avoid mixing tenses.

Verbs may also appear as single words or in 'verb clusters' incorporating various tenses of the verbs 'to be' and 'to have'. Examples:

The manager *was to have planned* the sales campaign.

The manager *would have been planning* the sales campaign.

The manager *is having to plan* the sales campaign.

Shall and will/Should and would

The writer of a business letter is often requesting the recipient to take some sort of action. The request can be phrased courteously using the condition tense:

I *should be* grateful if you *would* ...

Split infinitives

The infinitive of a verb takes the form 'to' followed by the root of the verb. For example: to plan, to defend, to think. It is wrong to separate 'to' and the root with an adverb; this is called splitting an infinitive. It is important not to split infinitives as this often causes ambiguity, i.e. two or more possible meanings. Consider, for example, this sentence:

The manager wanted *to simply plan* his sales campaign.

The word 'simply' comes between the verb 'to ... plan' and there is a split infinitive.

Care must be taken not to distort the intended meaning of the sentence when moving the adverb. Here a good solution would be:

The manager *simply* wanted *to plan* his sales campaign.

Exercise 1

After reading this passage you are asked to complete the table beneath it using the highlighted words and phrases.

4: Grammar and punctuation

Look at a map of the world and you **will see** the problem. There it is, this island perched in the stormy Atlantic, so close to the Arctic Circle. Life has always been a struggle for the **people of Iceland**. The piercingly cold winds have stunted the vegetation, forcing the brave **fishermen** to practise their skills of seamanship far out in the unyielding oceans.

Times **have changed**, however. Though the wild **ocean** is no friendlier, the fishing industry is booming and the islanders have one of the best equipped and most efficient fishing fleets in the world. They appear **to greatly enjoy** their improved lifestyle. Few homes are without central heating and television sets. Yet, though the **islanders'** lives are transformed, they still earn their living the hard way. In the old days the fishermen **depended** on luck and the **blessing** of God. Many would say they still do.

Example: Common noun.................. **fishermen**

i) Proper noun .... vi) Verb (present tense)...........................
ii) Abstract noun .... vii) Verb (future tense)............................
iii) Common noun........................... viii) Verb (perfect tense) ....
iv) Collective noun .... ix) Apostrophe ....
v) Verb (past tense)...................... x) Split infinitive ....

Finally, give a title to the passage.

Pronouns

A pronoun, as its name suggests, stands in place of a noun. Consider the sentence

>Geraldine is a computer programmer.

Substituting the pronoun 'she' for the proper noun Geraldine, the sentence becomes

>*She* is a computer programmer.

There are five different types of pronoun:

Personal

Personal pronouns are substituted for people who have been previously mentioned. They exist in singular or plural forms. Here are the personal pronouns:

	Singular	*Plural*
First person	I/me/mine	we/us/ours
Second person	you/yours	you/yours
Third person	he/she/it him/her/it his/hers/its	they/their/theirs

Reflexive

Reflexive pronouns are used when a particular action is related back to the person (or persons):

	Singular	*Plural*
First person	myself	ourselves
Second person	yourself	yourselves
Third person	himself/herself/itself	themselves

Interrogative

Interrogative pronouns are employed to ask questions such as:

>*Who* is responsible for losing this contract?

Which of the executives has visited Bonn recently?

What is the reason for the fall in sales?

Indefinite

Indefinite pronouns refer to people or things in general. Examples:

One cannot help admiring his nerve.

Anyone who takes on a job as a managing director will find it difficult.

Few people would turn down the chance to work in this firm.

Others may disregard environmental problems, but we will not.

None of the staff wanted to work late.

Demonstrative

Demonstrative pronouns point to some special object or quality and can be used in its place. Examples:

This is the manager's desk.

That is the cashier's office.

Those are the new word processors.

Such details are unnecessary.

Relative

Relative pronouns relate back to the nouns to which they refer. Examples:

I saw the receptionist *who* took me to the accounts office.

The committee were pleased with the ideas *which* came from the young members of staff.

'Who' is reserved for people, 'which' is usually for things but may be used impersonally for people. So:

I have not decided yet *which* desk to choose.

I have not decided yet *whom* to choose as my personal assistant.

I have not decided yet *which* candidate to choose as my personal assistant.

Use 'whom' if it could be replaced by 'him, her or them'.

Use 'who' if it could be replaced by 'he, she or they'.

Consider these sentences:

'*Who* 'phoned?'

'*Whom* did they 'phone?'

Who 'phoned? The answer might be he/she/they 'phoned, so it is correct to say 'Who 'phoned?'.

Whom did they 'phone? The answer might be 'They 'phoned him/her/them', so it is correct to say 'Whom did they 'phone?'.

Adjectives

These are words which limit, qualify or describe a noun, either linked with the noun directly, for example:

It is a *private* company.

or by means of an intervening verb, for example:

The company is *private*.

4: Grammar and punctuation

Some more examples follow:

> The filing clerk is *inefficient*.
>
> The Chief Accountant is a *worried* man.
>
> Mr Davies is an *important* customer.
>
> The *new* shop steward was elected yesterday.
>
> The *outgoing* manager bid farewell to the staff.

Two of the most common words in the language 'a' ('an') and 'the' are also strictly adjectives because they qualify nouns. 'An' takes over from 'a' whenever the first letter in the next word is a vowel – *a, e, i, o,* or *u*. So we have:

> *an* accident   *an* examination   *an* invoice   *an* idea

Adverbs

These are used to modify or extend the meaning of another word, usually a verb. Sometimes it is used to modulate a whole sentence. Adverbs should be placed close to the words they are to modify. Some examples:

> The shareholders were *exceedingly* pleased to hear of the company's record profits.
>
> The Wages Clerk checked the income tax deductions *yesterday*.
>
> Management and workers work together *amicably* in Japan.
>
> Mass production lines *sometimes* produce a bored workforce.
>
> The trade union *readily* agreed to a reduction in working hours.
>
> The exchange rates fell *overseas* when the Chancellor of the Exchequer *delightedly* announced the tax cuts.
>
> *Regrettably*, the expenditure on advertising did not halt the fall in sales.

'Regrettably' modifies the meaning of the whole sentence, making the subject a much more serious matter.

Adverbs and adjectives tend to be used rather sparingly in business where the emphasis is on factual reporting rather than 'colourful' descriptions. Perhaps the exception is in advertising where imaginative writing is used to sell the product.

Exercise 2

Fill in the blanks in the following table, using a dictionary if necessary:

Noun	Verb	Adjective	Adverb
brightness	to brighten	bright	brightly
hope			
	to appreciate		
		expressive	
			extensively
excess			
	to create		
		defiant	
			satisfactorily

4: Grammar and punctuation

response			
	to endanger		
		exclusive	
			wastefully
conclusion			
	to doubt		
		decisive	
			completely
sympathy			
	to admire		
		forceful	
			perfectly

Prepositions and Conjunctions

Prepositions

These join together groups of words or phrases to give more precise meaning. They are locating words and normally come immediately in front of the word they govern. Commonly they link a noun and a pronoun:

> He is *in* the office.
>
> They are *at* Head Office.

Or they link an adjective and a noun:

> Sam is useful *on* the keyboard.
>
> He is efficient *as* an administrator.

They may also serve as a bond between different sentences:

> Many shareholders became unsettled after referring to the company's annual report.
>
> The world has experienced a second Industrial Revolution with the advent of the microchip.

It has to be appreciated that when we are dealing with language construction we are dealing essentially with conventions. Many expressions used in business include prepositions and take a specific form. Some of the most common examples should be memorised:

distinguish between	enquire into	relate to
depend on (or upon)	in accordance with	different from
sympathetic to	confident of	unsure of
similar to	superior to	aware of
comparable to	regardless of	neglectful of
immune from	hostile to	intolerant of
agree to	rely on (or upon)	co-operate with
familiar with	conscious of	decide on

4: Grammar and punctuation

Conjunctions

The prime function of conjunctions is to link sentences. Conjunctions link two sentences each complete in themselves.

> He is a first-class storekeeper. He is close to retirement.
>
> He is a first-class storekeeper, *but* he is close to retirement.

Conjunctions used for this purpose include:

> and   but   yet   then   or   next

They also include the pairs:

> either ... or   neither ... nor   both ... and

For example:

> *Either* you take the advice which has been given *or* you accept the consequences.
>
> *Neither* the Works Manager *nor* the Chief Shop Steward were prepared to discuss the problem further.
>
> *Both* the management *and* the unions agreed to submit the dispute to arbitration.

Subordinating conjunctions are those which link a main idea or clause to another which is dependent on it. So:

> The supervisor wants to see Ann *before* she leaves.
>
> The interviewer explained *how* the test would be conducted.
>
> I will see you *when* you are ready.

This could also be written in a different order without changing the meaning:

> *When* you are ready, I will see you.

Exercise 3

Complete these sentences with appropriate conjunctions and prepositions.

1. Everybody says the firm is fair to its employees and she agrees .... them.
2. The members of the committee disagreed .... their terms of reference.
3. Andrew could not concentrate on his work .... he saw the Managing Director talking to his supervisor.
4. It was not easy to distinguish .... the old staff and the newcomers.
5. .... John had passed his examinations he was not promoted.
6. They decided to buy the new computer .... the price had risen steeply since the summer.
7. Harry agreed to drive the van only .... I had checked it.
8. The data was fed .... the computer's memory store.
9. He waited until she had arrived in the office .... showing her the new word processor.
10. Jack decided to re-order, ... the stocks of components were low.
11. The directors could neither agree .... disagree with the agency's proposals for market research.
12. At the end of the week .... Duncan and Adam were to switch to the new production line.

13. It seemed a simple breakdown .... the maintenance engineers found it difficult to trace the fault.
14. The Chief Engineer wanted to hire the equipment .... it was too expensive.
15. The distinction .... qualified and unqualified staff shows up in their monthly pay packets.

Punctuation

Punctuation is to some extent a matter of common sense. Punctuation is used to indicate rest pauses or breaks in sentences: commas, semicolons and colons for a short pause and full-stops for a longer break. Other punctuation marks are used to indicate emotions, such an exclamation mark for indignation or surprise.

Full-stops

The full-stop is used to mark a halt in the procession of thought. It helps us to put our thoughts and ideas into useful packages. The full-stop is always followed by a capital at the start of the next sentence.

Full-stops are also used to follow an abbreviation as in Capt. (Captain), Rev. (Reverend), B.A. (Bachelor of Arts), U.N.O. (United Nations Organisation), i.e. (that is) or e.g. (for example), though there is a tendency to drop the formality of a full-stop now so many business communications emerge from computers and word processors.

A series of full-stops like this ... is an indication that a word, phrase, or part of a quotation has been omitted from a narrative.

Commas

The comma suggests a shorter pause than the full stop, marking out a smaller parcel of our thought. Some basic rules should be noted:

1. Longer sentences, with a number of commas, may become confusing.
2. A succession of short sentences, without commas, tends to produce a terse, staccato style.
3. Commas should be used to separate items in a list, for example:

    The hotel's guests include old age pensioners, business tycoons, arab sheiks and factory workers.

    A comma is required after each item in the list except the last.
4. A modifying word introduced at the start of a sentence should be followed by a comma, for example:

    However, the majority of the hotel's guests are civil servants and clerks.
5. Commas in the form of quotation marks are used to indicate the reporting of the spoken word (direct speech), for example:

    'I regret to have to make this announcement,' said the Chairman, 'but this year we will be unable to pay a dividend to the ordinary shareholders.'

    If a quotation comes within a quotation it is usual to employ double inverted commas, for example:

    'I recall the Chairman saying last year, "I promise you a handsome dividend next time",' shouted one of the irate shareholders.
6. The insertion of a comma can make all the difference to the meaning of a sentence, for example:

4: Grammar and punctuation

> The leading Paris designer Pierre Bouchard says the Sunday Times is about to introduce a revolutionary fashion suitable for twenty-first-century women.

> I had no idea the Sunday Times were into that sort of thing! Paper dresses perhaps? With colour supplements?

Of course it becomes a different, and perhaps a slightly less sensational, story with the addition of commas:

> The leading Paris designer Pierre Bouchard, says the Sunday Times, is about to introduce a revolutionary fashion suitable for twenty-first-century women.

Colons

Colons are used to introduce details expanding or explaining and concluding the idea contained in the clause preceding the colon, for example:

> In business there is something more important than the achievement of policy aims: the customer.

It often precedes a list, for example:

> The following members of staff will be representing the Marketing Division at this month's meeting of the Works Council:
>
> Robert Frisby (Northern Area), Alison Catesby (London Area, Karl Schreiber (Head Office)

Semicolons

Semicolons are used as an alternative to conjunctions and full stops when writing a series of connected sentences, for example:

> He began to panic; there was no escape; this was going to be a disaster.

Question marks

The question mark confirms that you are asking a question, for example:

> What would happen next? A disaster?

Note the effect of missing out the second question mark. Disaster is no longer construed as a possibility. It is a certainty, apparently.

Exclamation marks

An exclamation mark gives you the opportunity to be emphatic, for example:

> There was going to be a disaster!

But be warned. There is danger of losing the effect if exclamation marks are over-used.

Brackets and dashes

Brackets are used to enclose some additional information such as a reference, for example:

> The instructions for changing batteries were given previously (see page 1).

Dashes are used to introduce an interruption to the sentence, for example:

> The instructions for changing batteries have been given previously – on a number of occasions – and it is assumed you will have understood them.

Paragraphs

A paragraph consists of a series of sentences, each closely related and dealing with a similar topic. There should be a sequence of thought and, ideally, a variety of length and construction in the component sentences. Good writing could be compared with a good meal.

4: Grammar and punctuation

The first course/paragraph aims simply to whet the appetite. The fish course follows. Then comes the meat. And so on, until we round off the meal with some final delicacies. It may help you to think of your written words in this way. Certainly the more 'palatable' they are, the more favourably they will be received.

Exercise 4

Rewrite the following passage with correct punctuation.

> life has not always been kind to grace morgan at 16 she lost both her parents in a car crash by the age of 23 she had been married and divorced small in stature and poor in health she decided to try her luck in business i cant be much worse off than i am now she said well she has been remarkably successful she opened a small restaurant called amazing grace in her native London she got her familys support and between them they catered for people who in graces own words weren't looking for the sometimes bizarre and always expensive food found in the trendy restaurants but still wanted something different and healthy so successful has grace morgan become over the past six years that she is just about to open her nineteenth amazing grace restaurant this time across the Atlantic im sure well be able to give new yorkers the same satisfaction weve given our customers in London she says confidently rumour has it that her companys shares are shortly to be quoted on the london stock exchange when that happens grace will have proved just how amazing she is

Spelling

A good dictionary and a working pocket calculator are the 'tools of trade' for anyone in business, from the managing director down to the humble – but important – receptionist. The general rule must be to refer to a dictionary whenever you do not know the meaning of a word or are unsure of a spelling. However, there are some pairs of words which confusingly sound alike but have different meanings, so they merit special treatment here.

advice / advise	Advice is what you give. Advise is what you do. The person who advises is either an adviser or an advisor. Both spellings are acceptable.
affect / effect	Affect is always a verb. Effect may be a verb or a noun.
canvas / canvass	Canvas is what you paint on. Canvass is what you do when you knock on doors.
companies / company	The plural of company is companies. One talks of the company's success – the company's workforce – the company's problem.
complement / compliment	Complement (verb and noun) means to make complete or that which makes complete. A compliment is a flattering remark.
council / counsel	A council is a group of administrators – called councillors. To counsel is to give advice. Those giving the advice are called counsellors.
dependant / dependent	A dependant is a person who is dependent on others.
draft / draught	A draft is an initial (rough) copy of a document. A draught is a current of air.
its / it's	'It's' represents it is. So one says, 'It's a nice day'. It is a nice day. Otherwise 'its' applies. So, a business cannot survive without its staff.

4: Grammar and punctuation

loose / lose	A nut becomes loose. A football team loses.
moral / morale	If someone is moral they have good principles and a good sense of what is right and wrong. Morale is to do with confidence and motivation.
passed / past	She has passed her examinations. History tells us about the past.
practice / practise	Practice is the noun. Practise is the verb.
principal / principle	The principal is the person in charge. A principle is a fundamental rule.
stationary / stationery	A train is stationary. Stationery is writing material.
their / there	People in work should value their jobs. There are not enough jobs to go round. 'Their' is possessive.
theirs / there's	'There's no hope' is a shortened version of 'There is no hope'. 'The choice is theirs' means the choice belongs to them.
weak / week	Weak is the opposite of strong. A week is a period of seven days.

Is it bel*ie*ve or bel*ei*ve? A useful general rule is expressed in the rhyme

'*i* before *e* ... except after *c*'.

Exercise 5

Complete the following table, giving an opposite for each word.

word	opposite	word	opposite
stationary	**mobile**	loose	
passed		theirs	
weak		lose	
past		dependent	
necessary		definite	
grateful		illegible	
consistent		intelligible	
responsible		receive	
sincerely		affected	
decent		effective	
women		advisable	
argument		changeable	
conceal		sure	
rough		acquainted	
legitimate		legal	
regular		encourage	
proper		moral	
separate		reject	
belief		credible	
practical		deficit	

Part Two

The functions

The skills to which you have been introduced will now be applied to typical business situations and for this you will need to know how the world of business operates. Each of the exercises you work on in this section will have a double purpose:

1. to give you practice in applying the skills covered in Part One.
2. to help you understand how businesses operate.

In order to achieve this, the exercises will follow a set pattern. Each chapter will examine a particular aspect of business. The first exercise in each chapter will require you to read and understand a passage on the chapter topic. You will then be expected to show your understanding of the passage by answering a series of questions. The second exercise in each chapter will provide further material in the same study area, but with words missed out: you are required to fill in the blanks from a list of words provided. The third exercise will involve the interpretation of some simple graphic and/or numerical information. The double purpose of practising the skills and learning about a particular aspect of business forms the basis of each exercise.

The remaining exercises in each chapter will have these same two objectives, using a variety of devices to develop your writing skills, to extend your vocabulary and to familiarise you with the various terms and expressions encountered in business. They will include exercises in the form of simple case studies telling you about the sorts of real-life situations which occur in business and requiring you to exercise your developing communication skills by completing various tasks. Answers for the asterisked exercises are given in the Answers section at the end of the book.

Chapters 5 to 13 look at different operations in business, for example advertising, production, administration and distribution. Chapters 14 and 15 concentrate on the way decisions are made in a variety of settings. The remaining chapters in this section (16 to 20) investigate the financial environment in which businesses operate. Studying these different topics will make you aware of how the skills you are developing fit into the general framework of business activities.

Having completed the exercises in this section of the book you should feel confident to proceed with your final preparation for the examinations.

5: Factory production

A. Comprehension

Over two hundred years ago, Adam Smith introduced some ideas which were to bring about a world revolution. If we enjoy a high standard of living in modern society, we owe much to this Scottish economist and philosopher. If we enjoy driving in sleek motor cars, wearing fashionable shoes, or flying away to distant places for exciting holidays, we should perhaps give an occasional vote of thanks to the man who made it all possible.

What then was Adam Smith's contribution? Like so many ideas which have earth-shattering effects, his was a disarmingly simple notion. He watched workers practising their craft of pin making. One man would heat the strip of metal, stretch it out, cut off an appropriate length, shape it, cool it and finally smooth and shine it. Smith drew attention to the advantages which could be gained if these various tasks were performed by different workers. Let one be responsible for keeping the brazier glowing and preparing the metal. Another for stretching and cutting. Another for shaping. Another for finishing. He described the technique as the Division of Labour, whereby workers perform short work-cycles, repeating the same actions again and again and again. Smith convinced the world that specialisation could solve the problems of poverty and want.

What was the result? The Industrial Revolution. Specialisation became the order of the day. Productivity was increased to an incredible degree. For Britain, where the revolution started, there was an upsurge in prosperity which made us the richest country in the nineteenth century world. British trains – and railway lines – spread out like a spider's web across the world, opening up the great continents of America, Asia, Africa and Australasia. British ships – built of iron and steel – were used to carry the new bountiful cargoes (including human beings) from every corner of the world, to every corner of the world.

The revolution is not over. It is still with us, but now it is a worldwide phenomenon. Everywhere, factories producing large numbers of more or less identical units are in continuous production. What were called mass-production lines yesterday are called robotic production lines today. If anything, the pace of change is increasing. And if these techniques have brought us prosperity, they have also brought us a trail of misery in overcrowded towns, boring jobs and, worst of all, unemployment.

Your task

Having read the above passage, answer these questions in your own words.

    a)   Why is the name of Adam Smith remembered?
    b)   What technique was he responsible for introducing?
    c)   Why was Britain the richest country in the world in the nineteenth century?
    d)   What do you understand by the term 'robotic production lines'?
    e)   Why do you think some jobs might be boring?
    f)   How can we blame Adam Smith for our present overcrowded towns.
    g)   How does large-scale production cause unemployment.
    h)   'We owe Adam Smith a great deal'. Do you agree? What are your views?

B. Fill in the blanks*

Fill in the blanks in this passage, using words from the list given below.

5: Factory production

The Cosmetics Factory

I was delighted to .... the invitation to visit the Diana Cosmetics factory at Winthrip Green. The .... area was very imposing and the young woman who greeted me was a good .... for the whole range of Diana products.

I soon found myself in a very .... factory watching a lot of workers in .... white overalls carrying out their .... duties. At the top of one production line I saw a .... lady working on a mixing tub in which there was a supply of very pale pink .... wax. Her workmate had just finished connecting a .... tub to a rather noisy, ... machine which spewed out an endless supply of lipsticks, now firmly .... in neat cases. As the lipsticks stood proudly, like .... soldiers, in long unbroken lines, ... girls picked out any which were .... or blemished and either threw them .... into cardboard .... or rubbed them over with a .... sponge and returned them to the line. At the end of their .... the items were transferred from the conveyor-belt to another .... of equipment from which they .... complete with their ....screw-on caps. Now I was able to .... them as the tempting Diana lipsticks which I had so often ....from my local drug store.

'Do all your .... have to wear caps?' I asked the supervisor.

'Oh yes,' she smiled, 'it's company .... We don't want any .... strands of hair in our lipsticks. We'd soon .... business if that sort of thing happened.'

'And what's he doing?' I asked as a tall slim young man suddenly appeared and with .... care dipped a long-handled .... into the tub of wax which was still being ....

The .... seemed somewhat concerned at the young man's ...., and was obviously .... when he .... as quickly as he had come.

'He's from the Quality Control Department,'she said, 'He's .... a small sample for .... You can't be too .... ' she added, 'a .... batch could lead to all sorts of claims being made against the company.'

receive	liquid	recognise	employees
loose	similar	advertisement	reception
embedded	presence	relieved	disappeared
various	distinctive	supervisor	hygienic
careful	lose	emerged	moist
extracted	infinite	receptacles	analysis
immaculate	piece	instrument	policy
mature	acquired	processed	imperfect
faulty	plastic	attentive	gyrating
	journey	contemptuously	

C. Case study

Diana Cosmetics

Don Drummond, the Personnel Manager at Diana Cosmetics, is looking at some statistics which have just been delivered to him by one of his assistants. Don has been very concerned about absenteeism at the factory. He knows that a lot of the problem stems from the routine and repetitive nature of the job, and has done his best to improve things. He has persuaded the Managing Director to pay workers good attendance bonuses and they now collect an extra £20 in their pay packet whenever they go through a month without being absent or late. He has also introduced a system of job rotation whereby people regularly change from one job to another on a weekly basis.

As he puts it, 'All the jobs on the line are pretty boring, but a change is as good as a rest.'

The workers seem to have mixed views on job rotation, but it certainly makes it easier for the Line Managers to cover absences and holidays.

Another of his ideas has been to offer flexible working hours so that staff can choose which hours they want to work between 8am and 6.30pm so long as they put in a total of 35 hours a week. It was felt this would be particularly helpful to working mothers.

Don's latest idea has been to introduce a suggestions scheme which awards prizes to workers who put forward cost-saving or profit-making ideas. The prizes have certainly been attractive to date. Last month one of the workers in the Creams and Lotions Section won a fortnight's holiday in Spain for two, for proposing a new container shape which made it easier to extract the contents. Another recent winner has been a young maintenance engineer who was rewarded with a £250 prize for replanning the workers' car park so that an additional 24 cars a day could be comfortably parked.

The figures before him cover the three quarters of the year to date:

Absenteeism
Number of whole days lost per quarter by age group and sex. (Total number of workers on payroll 1,000.)

		No of workers in age group	Jan – Mar	Apr – June	July – Sept
Men	under 21	68	57	58	57
	21 – 30	135	43	45	48
	31 – 40	56	9	7	8
	over 40	12	2	2	2
Women	under 21	165	117	135	139
	21 – 30	233	109	76	61
	31 – 40	151	123	69	57
	over 40	180	44	45	43

Your task

You are working as a personal assistant to the Works Manager, Reg Turnbull. He has just received these figures from the Personnel Department and has asked you to comment on them. Send him a brief memorandum (maximum 100 words) setting out your views.

D. Opposites and synonyms*

For each of the following words you are asked to provide a synonym (a word with the same or similar meaning) and another word which is opposite in meaning.

part of speech	word	synonym	opposite
noun	cost	expense	revenue
verb	damage		
adjective	slack		

5: Factory production

verb	weld		
adverb	acceptably		
verb	secure		
adjective	tidy		
verb	fasten		
adverb	loosely		
adjective	hard-working		
verb	conceal		
noun	employee		
verb	lengthen		
noun	pollution		
verb	release		
adjective	deteriorating		
verb	extend		
noun	imperfection		
verb	mend		

E. Join the halves*

On the left of the page are six halves of sentences. On the right are the other halves of the sentences, though not in the same order. You are required to make complete sentences.

i) The various machines in a factory

ii) When there is a pile-up of semi-processed materials

iii) Before the finished goods leave the factory they

iv) The mass production technique involves

v) When machines take over the repetitive human involvement

vi) Although mass production lines are stressful for the workers

vii) During the processing of the raw materials, handling

viii) Stocks of raw materials must be available

ix) As the materials are processed they

x) In many factories a Chief Safety Officer is appointed

xi) Machines performing the same operation are likely

a) will be checked by the Quality Control Department

b) it becomes a robotic production line.

c) will almost certainly have different productive capacities.

d) before a particular machine it is called a bottleneck.

e) continuous production of more or less identical units.

f) to be clustered together.

g) to make sure that accidents are minimised.

h) the technique has given us a higher standard of living

i) in the right quantity, in the right place, at the right time.

j) will be made to travel the shortest distance possible.

k) will be kept to a minimum so as to keep labour costs as low as possible.

Example: add (iii) to (a) Before the finished goods leave the factory they will be checked by the Quality Control Department.

F. Summarising

Give the following passage an appropriate title and summarise it in about 100 words:

> A large firm can often offer goods at a lower price than a smaller competitor. For example, thanks to bulk-buying, you can often buy a bottle of fruit squash more cheaply in a supermarket than in a corner shop. The supermarket obtains discounts from the manufacturer because they are able to buy the squash in quantity. While the squash normally costs 60 pence a bottle the supermarket get it for 40 pence, which means they can sell it at a lower price than the corner shop proprietor paid for it.
>
> The large firm also has an advantage in terms of advertising. Take two firms, A and B, which manufacture cycles. They both advertise their cycles on television and the cost of the campaign is £50,000 in each case, but firm A has 100,000 cycles to sell and firm B has only 1,000 cycles to sell. The advertising adds only 50 pence to the cost of each A cycle, while the unit cost of each B cycle has increased by £50. In such a situation firm B would almost certainly not advertise on television. However, through the advertising campaign, firm A would possibly grow even larger.
>
> Advancing technology also favours the larger firm. Consider the motor and aircraft industries. Enormous sums need to be spent on basic research if a firm is to keep up with its competitors. Prototypes have to be developed and these 'one-offs' can be enormously expensive and are often eventually scrapped to make way for modified versions.
>
> The final nail in the coffin of the smaller firm is that the industrial giants can even obtain bank loans, or funds from share issues, more easily and cheaply.

G. Write a memorandum

This cartoon was drawn by one of Kevin Benton's workmates on the production line at Formby Electrics the day after his accident. They put it on the staff notice board as a joke, though Kevin may not have been amused.

You are asked to play the role of Kevin's foreman who has to explain briefly to David Peterson, the Personnel Manager, what happened. Kevin is a fitter, responsible for checking heavy metal adapters to turbines as they move along No. 3 production line. The accident happened when one of the turbines ran off the production line. This is the second time this has happened recently and you have reported both mishaps to the Chief Engineer who has promised to find out the cause. According to Kevin it was in trying to stop the turbine turning over that he twisted his ankle. He has given you a letter from the hospital which indicates he has a badly sprained ankle and has to go back to the Outpatient's Department on Wednesday of next week.

His absence has created a problem for you because you are now a fitter short on the line and you are dealing with a very important export order.

5: Factory production

H. Meanings

First, read the passage below. Then, explain the meanings of the words and phrases which have been highlighted.

> On most factory production lines machines are laid out in such a way that the **flow of work** is maximised. **Material handling**, whether by man or machine, is time-wasting and expensive and is therefore to be avoided whenever possible. The distance travelled by the materials as they are **processed** must also be minimised.
>
> Yet, there will be a bottleneck on any **production line**. The problem arises from the fact that no two machines can be expected to have an **identical production capacity**. Consequently, where you have equipment at the first stage with a capacity to process seven units a minute, while the equipment at the second stage can only process five units a minute, a **backlog** of two units a minute is bound to emerge. Of course it would be possible to **stave off the problem** by introducing an additional machine at the second stage, but that machine would then be **under-utilised** and the bottleneck would merely have been transferred to the first stage.
>
> Since **bottlenecks seem to be inescapable**, production managers will have to ensure that they occur in front of their most expensive machines. It would be **uneconomic** to organise the flow of work so that these were left **idling**. Another way round the problem would be to allow the operatives on these key machines to work overtime. In that way the flow of work could be stabilised. **Robotisation** might also be used to solve the problem at the planning stage, though even this cannot eliminate the hazard of a machine breakdown at a **critical time**.

I. Interpretation of data

Here is a Gantt chart for three different production lines at Diana Cosmetics. As an Assistant Controller you are asked to write a brief memorandum to the Works Manager, Reginald Turnbull, commenting on the performances and comparing them over the past week.

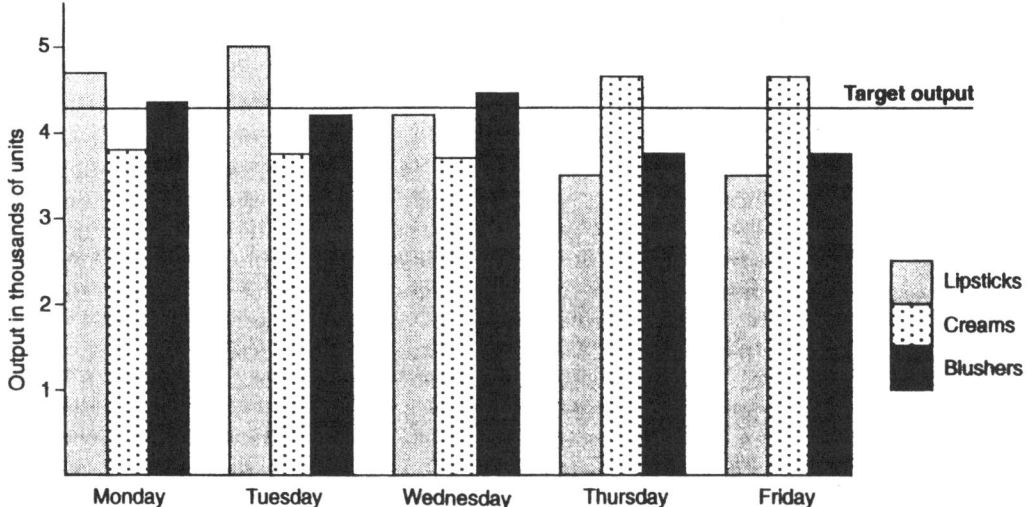

J. Complete the sentences

Complete the following sentences using your own words.

5: Factory production

1. If a machine breaks down on the production line ...
2. Large companies can usually pay their staff ...
3. Workers on mass-production lines ...
4. The Production Manager's main concern is ...
5. When one of the workers is involved in an accident ...
6. The storekeeper's job is to ...
7. Women do not usually work in heavy engineering because ...
8. A manufacturer who produces more than he sells ...
9. A manufacturer who is selling more than he is producing ...
10. One usually expects to find a factory sited ...
11. If a fire breaks out in a factory ...
12. When workers get bored at work ...

K. Vocabulary*

schedules	pollution	patent	sequence
batches	relocation	work-flow	maintenance
depot	objective	rationalisation	rejects
resources	availability	flexibility	budget
layout	overheads	prototype	buffer

Match the nouns listed above with the dictionary definitions which follow.

1. Apparatus for deadening concussion on impact at the end of a railway track, but may also refer to a reserve of stocks.
2. Since it is the grant of a sole right to make or sell it is, in effect, the granting of a monopoly.
3. A mock-up of the original design showing the expected final appearance of the proposed machine.
4. The extent to which something can be used, for example in the production process.
5. Human and financial assets which can be used in the business.
6. Costs such as the factory buildings which do not vary with output.
7. Comparatively small numbers of goods being processed at the same time.
8. What we are hoping to reach.
9. The servicing of machinery and equipment.
10. The result of an industrial activity which has an adverse effect on the environment.
11. A place for storing goods, especially vehicles.
12. Goods or materials which have been inspected and found to be of an unacceptable standard.
13. An accounting device which aims to ensure that managers do not spend too much.
14. A plan showing how the machines and equipment are arranged.
15. Documents showing how the work is being organised.
16. One thing following another without a break.
17. The movement of paper or other materials from workstation to workstation.

5: Factory production

18. Versatility and adaptability.
19. The movement of the factory (or plant) to a new site.
20. The elimination of time-wasting and unnecessary expenses.

L. Stock control card

You are a storekeeper at Highlife Shoes' factory. One of the materials used in the production of Highlife Shoes is four inch hardwood cuban heels which are made by a firm in Leicester. Below you see a stock control card which shows you have 42 of these heels in store at the present time.

Supplier:	Benton Products 6 Fenton Street, Leicester LR1 1AA Tel 2525 775439					
Commodity: Four inch hardwood cuban heels			**Catalogue no:** A783			
Reorder level: 36		**Reorder amount:** 24	**Latest price:** £5.05			
Date in or out	In from or out to	Stock in	Stock out	Balance	Reorder date	Reorder amount
5/11	Balance			37		
9/11	Line 5		5	32	9/11	24
13/11	Line 7		7	25		
15/11	Line 5		3	22		
19/11	Line 5		4	18		
23/11	Benton	24		42		

Your tasks

1. Write in the further entries shown here:

    25/11 The supervisor on Line 7 withdrew 5 of the heels from stock.

    27/11 The Chief Designer withdrew 15 of the heels from stock. He is planning to introduce a new style using these heels.

2. Make the reorder entry on the stock card and write an appropriate letter to Benton Products reordering the necessary stock.
3. Send a brief memorandum to the Chief Storekeeper suggesting the reorder level for this item should be increased to 48. Explain why.

M. Production methods

There are three main types of production method:

Job production

In this type of production specific work is carried out for individual customers. Job production is of the 'one off' variety and can range from a bride's wedding dress to an ocean-going liner. Job production is usually labour intensive and requires the employment of skilled labour which is able to interpret technical instructions. If supervisors are employed they

5: Factory production

will need to be technically competent. Unit costs will always tend to be high when small numbers of individually designed items are produced.

Mass production

This method of production is possible where the demand for a product is so great that the goods can be produced in a continuous flow. Motor vehicles and food processing are among the industries which resort to mass production techniques. Once set up the production lines are not easily changed and advertising is often necessary to ensure that stocks of finished goods do not pile up in the factory. Unskilled and semi-skilled workers can be used, though the modern tendency is to use computerised robots. By using these capital-intensive methods unit costs may be substantially reduced and higher output can be obtained by running the expensive machines over two or three shifts per day.

Batch production

This method falls between job and mass production. It could be described as repeated production runs in contrast to the continuous flow or mass production technique. The orders consist of a significant number of similar items. One industry which uses this technique is the furniture industry. A batch of teak tables of a particular design will be produced. Followed perhaps by a batch of mahogany tables. Bookprinters also use this technique. Runs of books will depend on the size of the market, but the printers switch from the production of one book to the production of another at the end of each run.

Both labour and machines have to be more versatile than in the case of mass production, but less so than in the case of job production. The production manager will have to attempt to organise the runs so that they are as economically viable as possible, but the unit costs will tend to fall as the length of the run increases.

Your task

Complete the following list of advantages and disadvantages for the manufacturer for each of the methods of production.

	Advantages	*Disadvantages*
Job production	a)	a)
	b)	b) **continual changes**
Mass production	a) **waiting for orders**	a)
	b)	b)
Batch production		

N. In-tray exercise

Most of our manufactured goods are made on mass-production lines and shoes are not generally an exception. So when one thinks of shoes which are not only hand-made but also specially tailored to suit every individual taste and foot shape, one expects to find prices exceptionally high. Yet Paula Jones and her friend Tina Patel have combined the two notions to produce a range of reasonably priced and fashionable footwear for ladies. Paula was studying for a higher degree in laser technology when she discovered a simple application of the technique to a three-dimensional measurement of the foot. After obtaining the necessary patents for the device, she set up in business with her friend, Tina, who was a talented designer of exotic footwear. The plan was uncomplicated, but surprisingly effective. They provided their customers, shoe shops and department stores, with the Laser Profiles (they called them LPs) for a modest monthly rental. They were also given a catalogue of designs so that the ladies could select the sort of 'upper' they had in mind. The

5: Factory production

designs ranged from multi-coloured fabrics to linked metallic rings: the selection was unlimited.

The business has expanded sufficiently for them to set up an office, and this is where you become involved. The Office Manager, Jason Bonham, is sick and you are deputising for him. The following items have arrived in your in-tray and you are now required to deal with them.

Futura Footwear — INTERNAL MEMORANDUM

From Paula.

Sorry to leave you on your own for a few days. I shall be back on Wednesday of next week. If there is anything too difficult save it for then, but I hope you'll use your initiative and not leave too much for me next week. I have scribbled a few notes on a couple of the letters and signed the cheque for Apex. You'll find it in the Petty Cash box. A last favour. I've been invited to give a twenty minute talk on Racial and Sexual Discrimination in the Workplace to the local Rotary Club - an all-male audience of businessmen. I don't know why I said 'yes', but will you make a list of points I might bring into the speech, e.g. discrimination is illegal. You don't need to write the speech. Just give me a list of key words/phrases in some sort of logical sequence so I can see the way your mind is working. Two heads are better than one, and I want to make them sit up and take notice.

Thanks   *Paula*

Apex Engineering Ltd

Skeffington Works, Chant Court, Stratford, London E15 9PP   Telephone 071 336 3000

Date:

Dear Sir,

Reference: Account No. 665/A7

We note your account with us, standing at £2,305.00 remains unsettled though the machinery was delivered over three weeks ago. We would like to remind you that we have recently introduced a cash discount of 3 per cent which is deducted on all bills paid within one month. You would still qualify for this discount if you paid within the next three days.

While writing, I would also like to remind you that you are entitled to a free service for the machine six weeks after installation. Although we do not expect to find any problems developing, it is a complex machine and we would like to make an early inspection to make sure that all the parts are functioning correctly. The purpose is to ensure that the machine gives you many trouble-free years.

Our engineer will be in your area during the next few weeks and perhaps you would like to make arrangements for him to call. The inspection should not take more than 20 minutes.

We look forward to hearing from you.

Yours faithfully

S. Petersfield

Mr S Petersfield
Future Footwear
Unit 8 Chase Industrial Estate
Ridley Road
Tottenham
London N17 1MM

Pay immediately.
Cheque in petty cash box.
Paula

Note: some firms put the addressee's details at the foot of the page, as in this example.

Flair Fashion Shoes
137 Oxford Street, London W1 2EN
Tel: 071 667 8888

Mr J Bonham
The Manager
Futura Footwear
Unit 8 Chase Industrial Estate
Ridley Road
Tottenham
London N17 1MM

Your Ref. JHF/KMM

Dear Mr Bonham,

We have been trading with your firm for nearly two years, and in the early days we were always impressed by the efficiency of your service and the quality of your goods. However, over the past three months we have been much less satisfied.

During that time we have ordered a total of 160 of your High Fashion shoes and have been concerned to note the increasing time taken between ordering the goods and receiving delivery. We have been obliged to monitor the time taken because a number of our customers have started to complain at the delays and we have been pressured by phone calls, letters and visits from irate customers waiting for delivery of their shoes.

Until recently we have always been able to assure customers that their orders will be completed within 14 days. Now we are lucky if we get delivery from you in one month. When I phoned up to complain I was told that you were waiting for a new machine. Unfortunately that is not an excuse I can give to my customers. They say, and I agree with them, they pay good money for shoes and they expect a good service.

From our point of view, this is a very serious matter and we are thinking of discontinuing this line unless we can look forward to a much improved service.

Yours faithfully,

Julia Harrison

Julia Harrison

5: Factory production

The Shoe Bar
357 Grove End Road, St. John's Wood, London NW8 3PR Telephone: 071 855 7791

Dear Sir or Madam,

Account Reference SB/46166

I have received your letter asking for payment of the outstanding account. First, I would like to clarify the amount involved. According to the statement you sent me last month, there is £419.65 to pay, not £491.65 as mentioned in your letter. When your Miss Jones came to see me last August, she told me that I would always be able to collect the money from my customers before you called for payment.

I have tried to telephone your office in the lunch hour - which is the only time it is convenient for me to telephone - but I have been unable to get a reply from your number. I would have explained the situation earlier if I had been able to get through. Because two of the pairs of shoes arrived late (Invoices 63457 and 63501) my customers cancelled the orders. Rather than return the shoes I put them on display in the window, but they are still there and I wish now I had sent them back to you.

I have another six pairs of shoes on order (£400 approximately in value) and I can only hope you will not let me down on delivery for these. With regard to the £419.65 outstanding I am hoping you will be generous about this, particularly since the delay was on your side.

Yours faithfully

Anna Rhodes

Anna Rhodes

Apologise for the mistake. Give her another six weeks to pay.
Paula

The Office Manager
Futura Footwear
Unit 8 Chase Industrial Estate
Ridley Road
Tottenham
London N17 1MM

Bell's Department Store

16-26 Collier Street, Palmers Green, London N13 2BN
Telephone: 071 677 7770/6/7/8

Your Ref: PJ/RJG   Our Ref: TS/DFR

Date:

Ms P Jones
Future Footwear
Unit 8 Chase Industrial Estate
Ridley Road
Tottenham
London N17

Dear Ms Jones

Laser profiles

I was disappointed when you did not turn up to the meeting you arranged with me for Wednesday last. My diary clearly shows you were to join me for lunch in our Executive Suite and everything was formally laid on for you. Perhaps you will recall we were to continue the discussion we had started regarding the possibility of offering our customers your three-dimensional measuring service and custom-designed shoes. On our side we were at the point of making a decision.

I am thoroughly disenchanted, but in fairness I feel you should at least have a chance to explain what happened.

Yours sincerely,

Gareth Davies

Gareth Davies
Chief Buyer
(Footwear)

According to my diary, it was next Wednesday.

Paula

6: International marketing

A. Comprehension

Having made a product the problem becomes to find someone who will buy it. It is the responsibility of the marketing department to promote and organise the sale of products to the purchaser. Broadly speaking, activities such as sales promotion, advertising and market research are covered. It would be possible for the factory simply to produce a motor car and then hope that it sells. However, it takes a long time to set up a production line for a car assembly plant and even minor modifications can prove difficult and expensive. It is much better to discover what people are looking for when they buy a car and then try to satisfy their needs. Do car drivers want speed – or safety? Are they looking for the power to accelerate – or comfort? Is their aim to impress their neighbours and other road users, or are they just concerned with getting from A to B and back? How important is the price, and the cost of petrol and maintenance? Which designs and colours are preferred? Who is buying the car? Is it a company or an individual? It is questions like these the marketing department will have to answer even before production commences.

It becomes obvious that making and selling are two facets of the same undertaking. The marketing manager and the production manager are two members of the same team, depending on each other in much the same way as the players in the Liverpool football team. What good does it do if our strikers are scoring goals but our goalkeeper keeps having to pick the ball out of the back of the net? This situation could be compared to the marketing team who make great efforts to find customers for their cars, only to find the cars cannot be delivered on time, or that the cars develop faults as soon as they arrive.

The problem facing any business is that the market for goods – and services – is ever changing. Take the case of a company manufacturing cigarettes. Not so long ago the market for cigarettes was assured. Then the medical researchers discovered the link between cigarette smoking and lung cancer and many other diseases. Prospects for further growth evaporated as many people decided both to save money and live longer to spend it. The government joined in by restricting advertising and sponsoring their own anti-smoking campaign. The government is also understandably involved in campaigns to discourage drinking and driving, much to the chagrin of the breweries whose sales of wines and spirits are thereby reduced.

New technologies have an even more devastating effect on the markets. Once upon a time there was a very successful company which made gas mantles. The whole country was lit by gas. Then came electric light. The sales of gas mantles plummeted. Today we look to oil for our energy. Our oil companies prosper, but for how long? The day before yesterday we used typewriters. Yesterday we used electric typewriters. Today we use word processors. And tomorrow?

The rapidly changing world is both a headache and an exciting challenge to those engaged in marketing. If they predict correctly their business will survive and prosper. If they misread the signs the business will fail and, perhaps more importantly for all of us, valuable economic resources will be wasted.

Your task

Having read the above passage, answer these questions in your own words.
    a) What is the purpose of the marketing department?
    b) Why do the marketing and production departments need to co-operate?
    c) What needs to be done before a production line is set up?

6: International marketing

d) What do businesspeople and footballers have in common?
e) In what ways do the marketing team depend on the production team?
f) Why is the design of a product so important?
g) Why is the rapidly changing world a challenge to the marketing team?
h) What does a business need to do to survive and prosper?
i) In what ways can a government help or hinder a business?
j) How do we all benefit (or suffer) from the activities of business firms?

B. Fill in the blanks*

Rewrite this passage filling in the blanks from the list of words below.

The Product Life Cycle

Much of the world about us is .... in nature. The moon circles the earth every 24 hours. The earth takes 365¼ days to circle the sun.

The flowers in the garden bloom in the summer .... in the autumn, die in the winter only to .... again the following spring. In much the same way, industrial .... have a life cycle. The original ideas may come from either the marketing or the production side. Interaction .... as the market is .... and designs are modified. Eventually the .... is ready for the market.

The first stage entails introducing the product to the market. No one will know about our wonderful new creation unless we tell them about it. So this is when we are .... to spend money on advertising. One way or another we must .... potential customers to 'taste our wares'. At this stage the people who buy the product are often aptly .... as .... or innovators. Their .... is often, 'I'll be one of the first ones to have this.'

At the second stage the sales grow and our organisation begins to .... some of the expenditure incurred .... the development stage. We also begin to benefit from .... of scale. Many of the people who buy the product at this stage will be saying, 'I mustn't get left behind.' A problem may .... as sales outstrip the supplies coming from the factory, but the .... will be keener than ever to buy because it is obvious there is a growing demand for our product. It is the same .... as when you go to the cinema. If there was a long .... outside the cinema you would think it was going to be a good film. Conversely, if there was hardly anyone in the cinema you would think it was almost .... to be boring.

In the third stage the product is said to .... maturity. At this time sales reach a peak, perhaps they even .... on a sort of plateau. People will have got used to buying the product. There will be repeat purchases. Some will say, 'We always buy these.'

However, the time will come when .... begin to decline. Customers will be .... to other products, perhaps .... by competitors. By then we should have .... a new product which we can now introduce. By .... timing of new products we can hope to maintain a steady .... of revenue and profits.

| recoup | customers | attracted | flow |
| reaction | stabilize | continues | products |

6: International marketing

provided	emerge	fade	described
develop	cyclical	product	perfected
tested	during	queue	sales
obliged	persuade	attitude	economies
bound	reach	careful	trend-setters

Market researcher: "Do you ever buy Delecto Prime Pork Sausuages?"
Woman in the street: 'I buy a large packet every week ... my little dog loves them.'

C. Pie charts

Toni Pirelli is in the ice cream business. Her company, Pirelli Perfection, sells ice cream in the form of small but attractive gateaux to up-market hoteliers in Bournemouth. There is plenty competition in this particular market, but she is encouraged by the fact that her sales have risen substantially since she started the business three years ago. However, she heard that her local competitors had also been doing well and this news prompted her to contact her trade association to find out whether she has been taking an increased share of the market for ice cream gateaux in Bournemouth. The association have now sent her the information she requires in diagrammatic form and she has asked you, as her Personal Assistant, for a brief explanation in the form of a memorandum.

Year 1: total sales £1.7m **Year 2: total sales £1.9m** **Year 3: total sales £3.5m**

6: International marketing

D. Opposites and synonyms*

Complete the following table:

word	opposite	synonym
construct (verb)	destroy	build
buy (verb)		
employee (noun)		
attractive (adjective)		
manage (verb)		
stable (adjective)		
emerge (verb)		
secure (adjective)		
careful (adjective)		
persuade (verb)		
manager (noun)		
effective (adjective)		
publicity (noun)		
powerless (adjective)		
complex (adjective)		
dismiss (verb)		
reprimand (verb)		
ability (noun)		
recruit (verb)		
adequate (adjective)		
purposeful (adjective)		

E. Join the halves*

On the left of the page are the first halves of sentences. On the right are the second halves of the sentences, though not in the same order.

Pair the halves and then write your own list of the completed sentences.

i) The salespeople in a firm which manufacturers pushchairs and prams

ii) Insurance companies offering cover against motor accidents

iii) The Traffic Manager for a company operating a cross-channel ferry

iv) The Sales Manager of a firm making hearing-aids

v) Oil company executives

a) could be expected not to welcome the news that a substantial increase in the petrol tax was contemplated by the government.

b) would be encouraged by the news that the death rate was falling.

c) will not be pleased to hear that the Meteorological Office are predicting a severe winter.

d) should approve of a long-term rise in oil prices.

e) would benefit from a rise in property prices.

6: International marketing

vi)	A publisher specialising in text books for schools	f)	would be pleased to hear of a reduction in air fares.
vii)	The Chief Buyer in a large city department store	g)	would be grateful to learn that the school-leaving age is going to be raised.
viii)	The line workers in a factory producing cigarettes	h)	would expect to be very busy after a serious gale had swept over the city.
ix)	The Marketing Manager of a travel agency specialising in holidays in France	i)	would be disappointed to learn that a new airport was going to be developed for London.
x)	A firm of London builders and repairers	j)	would be dismayed to read in the newspaper that the government was planning to prohibit the sale of all products harmful to health.
xi)	A young man who had just finished training to be a coal-miner	k)	would react favourably to the news that improvements were planned for the London Underground.
xii)	The high street banks	l)	would expect to earn more after the birth rate has risen.

F. Summarising

Give the following passage an appropriate title and summarise it in about 100 words:

> A business can only survive if it is able to anticipate the needs of consumers, and continue to do so. It could be argued that the major industrial organisation is able to produce goods without any consideration of consumers' wishes. By means of massive advertising campaigns demand is created and then the goods (or services) can be unloaded on the market. In other words, clever advertising and salesmanship can bridge the gap between the quantities produced and the quantities required in the market-place. However, there is an alternative view. The marketing concept offers the interpretation that consumers' tastes and requirements have to be taken into account if large stocks are not to be left unsold. According to this view certain questions need to be asked, such as, 'What do consumers need which they do not already have?' and 'In what form would they prefer the goods (or services) which they are presently missing?' The marketing concept acknowledges the need to approach these problems sensitively. Goods need to be available in the right quantity, at the right place, at the right price, at the right time.
>
> First, we ask what is required. Then we set about producing what is required with the human and financial resources we are prepared to commit to the campaign.
>
> It is wrong to make the assumption that someone must lose and someone must gain in a commercial transaction. Take the case of X who has something he wants to sell, say a vintage motor car. Y is an interested purchaser. X agrees to sell the motor car to Y for £15,000. X is presumably satisfied otherwise he would not have parted with the car. Y is also presumably satisfied. He prefers the car to the £15,000 he paid for it. Both parties surely benefited from the transaction, and that makes it a far cry from consumer manipulation and exploitation.

G. Write a memorandum

You work for Diana Cosmetics and are responsible for processing orders received from customers. Your Office Manager, Charlotte Amesbury, has asked you to represent her at a

6: International marketing

meeting and let her know what was said. The meeting was between Victor Powell (Assistant Works Manager), Sandra Davidson (Advertising Manager) and Julian Crawford (Marketing Manager). The main discussion went as follows.

JULIAN: I've called this meeting to find out how we're getting on with the programme for the new range of blushers for sensitive skins. The company are sinking a lot of money in this project and we've got to make sure nothing goes wrong.

VICTOR: They've got a half million budget on the promotion side alone.

JULIAN: That's true. I understand No. 2 production line will be switching over to the new range on Monday next. Can you confirm that, Victor?

VICTOR: Yes, we've got the export order for Australia to complete. We should complete the last batches for them by the end of the week and then we start on the speciality blushers.

JULIAN: Yes, that's what we're calling them isn't it – 'speciality blushers'?

VICTOR: I like it. It sounds just right.

JULIAN: It was Sandra's idea.

SANDRA: Well, I had to find a name which would make them sound different, but not too different.

JULIAN: When are you going to start the advertising campaign?

SANDRA: Well, the stocks should be reaching the warehouse by the end of the month and that's when we start our publicity campaign. We're concentrating on London weekend TV and the Sunday colour supplements.

VICTOR: Why weekends?

SANDRA: Basically because we think that's when the working girls we're after will be watching TV and reading newspapers.

VICTOR: But don't mothers wear make-up too?

SANDRA: Oh yes, of course they do, but it's the younger women who are the big spenders.

JULIAN: The point is we're aiming our promotions at that segment of the market. That gives us a chance to crystallise our advertising – to get through to the people we're after. We're using a couple of American soap stars. I can't remember their names but their faces will be familiar to everyone. We've seen the videos haven't we Julian? They come over really well. I think so anyway.

VICTOR: Why use Americans?

JULIAN: It's the glamour isn't it? The girls want to identify with the soap queens. The girls sing too. A catchy little number. You wait till you hear it, Victor.

SANDRA: It was in the top ten a couple of years ago. But we've changed the words of course.

VICTOR: How long does it last?

73

6: International marketing

SANDRA: About 30 seconds as it stands at the moment, and we're slotting it into peak viewing periods on Saturday evenings. We've got a budget of £300,000 and we'll keep running the adverts until we run out of cash. There are three different versions. I don't know which we'll choose yet. I'm not too happy about the colour supplements. We're going for the Telegraph and the People. We'll just have to see how it works out.

JULIAN: At least it's cheaper than television advertising! But we're depending on you, Victor. We need the blushers in the shops within the next month. If the girls go to the stores for the blushers and they haven't arrived yet, all our advertising budget will be down the drain.

VICTOR: We won't let you down on the production lines. My main concern is with the distribution. It's been taking a week to a fortnight to get transport organised from the warehouse. That's where I think the trouble could be (at that point he turned to you). We hope the office will deal with all the paperwork as promptly as possible.

JULIAN: We can't afford to lose any time through administrative delays. (he also turned to you). Perhaps you'll ask Charlotte to make sure orders are put through as soon as they come through. Let her know Victor's concern about the distribution. Perhaps she'll contact him in a few days to see what the problems are. This is a number one priority for us all.

Your first task
Write a suitable memorandum to the Office Manager in accordance with her instructions.

Your second task
Complete the diagram below by placing one of the following appropriate words in each of the four boxes.

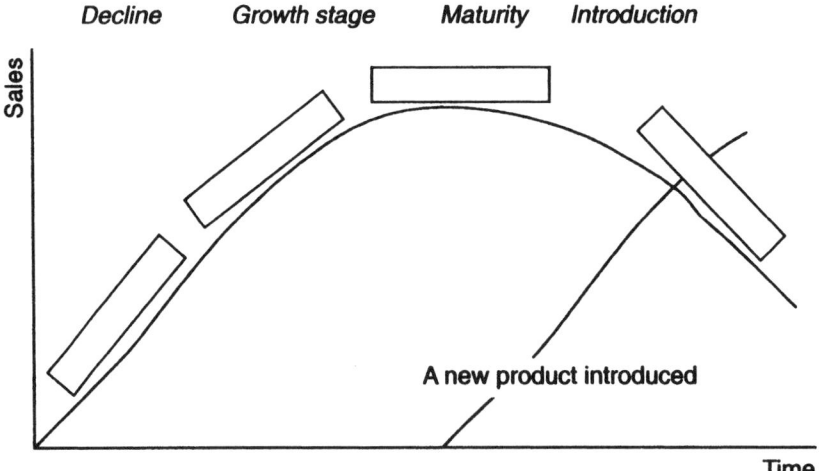

H. Meanings
First, read the passage below. Then explain the meanings of the words and phrases which have been highlighted.

6: International marketing

One of the ways of **carrying out** market research is to send questionnaires through the post to a variety of people you think might be interested in your product or service. Distance is no problem because there is a **standard postal charge**, and the people receiving the questionnaire can **take their time** to answer it.

Personal interviews are an alternative method of conducting market research. These can be carefully designed so that **set procedures** are carried out. The interviewer approaches a person in the street, or in their home or office, and asks a series of **set questions**. The answers to the questions are **carefully recorded.** However, the appearance or manner of the interviewer may influence the answers given. Thus, a **male respondent** might give an answer to an attractive female interviewer which puts him **in a favourable light.** Who makes **the major purchasing decisions** in your family could be interpreted as, 'Do you **wear the trousers?**' The male's answer could be fairly predictable. Similarly a husband and wife might give very **different versions** on how the family income is spent.

Another problem is calculating the **intensity** of a favourable or unfavourable response. For example, a company manufacturing chocolates may be asking respondents to decide which of three new chocolate centres they prefer. Having tested all three Jane comes down **strongly in favour** of the caramel centre. She finds the toffee and the nut centres quite **unpalatable.** By contrast Mary and Susan find it hard to choose between the different centres. They like them all, but **hesitatingly plump** for the toffee centre. If this pattern were **repeated throughout the sample** the company would no doubt end up by producing chocolates with toffee centres, yet by producing the chocolates with caramel centres all three girls would be **potential purchasers.**

I. Expansion

A dictionary definition of market segmentation:

> 'The breakdown of a market into separate and identifiable elements, such as age, sex, income and geography.'

Your task

You are employed by a motor manufacturer and have been asked to produce a simple questionnaire which might be sent out to a sample of drivers to find out what they will be looking for when they come to buy a new car. You have been given two examples of questions such as might be included in the questionnaire:

1. When you next buy a car would you prefer an automatic gear-box?
2. Do you rate safety as more important than speed in the design of a car?

Now you are to devise ten additional questions based on these key words:

i)	colour	iv)	economy	vii)	radio	x)	instrument panel
ii)	price	v)	boot space	viii)	acceleration		
iii)	seating	vi)	doors	ix)	cigar lighter		

J. Complete the sentences

Complete the following sentences using your own words.
1. When an older man is choosing a car ...
2. The clothes a worker chooses for the office will probably be ...

6: International marketing

3. The purpose of market research is to ...
4. If you plan to send questionnaires through the post ...
5. The marketing and production departments ...
6. When a new product is developed ...
7. The prime responsibility of the Marketing Manager ...
8. In order to maximise sales ...
9. Only when salespeople are keen and enthusiastic ...
10. All products have a life cycle and ...
11. If sales are running ahead of production ...
12. Although we reduce the prices of our goods ...
13. To increase our sales we may need to ...
14. While the Marketing Department is ...
15. A firm producing swimwear ...

K. Vocabulary*

sample	copyright	modification	quotation	franchise
exhibition	enquiry	distributor	market	segmentation
diversification	order	motivation	mark-up	survey
consumer	invoice	image	gimmick	persuade
publicity	contract	discount	turnover	salesperson

Match the words listed above with the dictionary definitions which follow.

1. To convince or induce someone to make a purchase.
2. A change in the product to make it more acceptable to the customers.
3. A widening of the product range or the entering of new markets.
4. A reduction in the quoted or list price of a product, usually in the form of a percentage.
5. Sole legal right to produce, or reproduce, a piece of work or any substantial part thereof.
6. Another name for the total sales figure for a business, over a period of time.
7. Someone whose job is to persuade customers to buy a certain product or service.
8. The securing of public attention so that a favourable impression will be created.
9. The breakdown of a market into separate and identifiable elements.
10. A request for information about a product or service prior to the placing of an order.
11. The mental picture of an organisation formed in the public's mind.
12. The ultimate user of a product.
13. The psychological stimulus behind the actions of an individual or a group.
14. A study aimed at unearthing useful information.
15. A display of products or services to stimulate public interest.
16. A firm which deals in the goods of a specified manufacturer.
17. A representative part of the whole.

18. A trading agreement whereby a manufacturer supplies and supports a retailer who sells the manufacturer's products exclusively.
19. A legally binding document in which a seller and a buyer agree to specified transactions.
20. An idea or object which is novel or unusual and has the purpose of attracting public attention.
21. A request from a customer to receive goods or services.
22. The document which lists the charges being set against the buyer and being entered on his account.
23. The amount added to a purchase price to provide a selling price.
24. A place where buyers and sellers gather together to do business.
25. A statement of the price at which a firm is prepared to supply goods or services.

L. Multiple choice*

Marketing plans are affected by a great variety of situations. Tick the box following the response which most accurately completes the statement:

1. A company in Barcelona selling ventilating and air conditioning equipment to the United States would expect their sales to increase if
    A. a new president who favours protectionism is elected in the USA. ☐
    B. the 'greenhouse effect' produces substantial global warming. ☐
    C. the value of the US dollar is falling against the peseta. ☐

2. A motor insurance company would welcome
    A. a relaxation of the laws against drinking and driving. ☐
    B. a fall in the sale of new motor cars. ☐
    C. a mild winter. ☐

3. If a government discourages smoking by prohibiting advertising or raising the tax on cigarettes, manufacturers will be likely to
    A. lower the price of cigarettes ☐
    B. step up their sales campaigns in countries where the laws are more liberal. ☐
    C. close down. ☐

4. According to marketing theory every product has a life cycle and this cannot be extended by
    A. product modification. ☐
    B. market research. ☐
    C. raising prices. ☐

5. A manufacturing company would make more profit in the long run by
    A. raising the prices of its goods. ☐
    B. cutting its costs. ☐
    C. spending more on advertising. ☐

6. Market research is necessary before going into a new market in order to
   A. publicize your product. ☐
   B. ensure sufficient finances are available. ☐
   C. gauge the nature and extent of the market. ☐

7. The breakdown of a market into separate, identifiable elements is described as
   A. market research. ☐
   B. market segmentation. ☐
   C. diversification. ☐

8. A manufacturer planning to sell tractors in other countries would be advised to
   A. contact the farming communities in the other countries by sending them letters and brochures. ☐
   B. make a tour of various other countries. ☐
   C. display his tractors at international agricultural fairs and exhibitions. ☐

M. Discussion topic

Social responsibility

The marketing function is usually seen as anticipating consumer wants and then proceeding to satisfy them. While many see evils in the capitalist system of which marketing is a part, the richest countries in the world are those which have adopted the market economy. Is that a coincidence or is it cause and effect?

It seems a fact that the people in capitalist societies are generally better dressed, less hungry and live longer. Prices are determined by the forces of demand and supply. The people choose which goods are going to be produced and, just as importantly, which goods are not going to be produced. They vote with their pounds, liras, francs, marks and pesetas. If people like a particular product or service, they will buy it, and that will encourage the suppliers to produce more of the same. If people do not 'vote' for it, production of the commodity will cease.

It seems natural that the notion of a political democracy becomes fused with the concept of consumer sovereignty. Yet we need to understand the limitations of the free market philosophy. It is dangerous to think that the price mechanism can solve all the problems which face our societies. For example, unemployment remains the scourge of capitalism and no society can be described as either fair or efficient while large numbers of our population are denied the opportunity to work. The sick and underprivileged must also be cared for, whether or not they have money of their own to spend. Those of us who begrudge giving aid to the less fortunate must expect to pay a high price for our selfishness. We may enjoy material prosperity, but the society in which we live may become ugly and unstable.

Another major criticism can be levelled at what is produced in the free economy. The quality of our lives is no doubt improved by much of what we produce, but the value of some activities are questionable.

For example, if some people want to drive sleek sports cars at 100 miles per hour on the motorways, do we allow the world's car makers to provide them with such cars, even though the lives of innocent road-users are put at risk?

Cigarette manufacturers in a market economy, facing restrictions on television advertising as a result of a government which sees their product as 'dangerous to health' may export their deadly cargoes to less sophisticated overseas markets. Nuclear waste is sometimes similarly exported to developing countries with less protected populations.

Of course it can be argued that people should be able to smoke tobacco if they want to, but do we take the same liberal stance in relation to hard drugs? Perhaps the market for heroin is after all just like any other market?

If we take the view that pornography is simply a matter of taste, do we turn a blind eye to those who hanker for young children, or have other equally bizarre sexual tastes? Is it acceptable that the ozone layer is sacrificed at the altar of short-term business profits? Should entrepreneurs be allowed to maximize their profits regardless of the social costs of pollution?

What if one state applies rigid safeguards while another fails to do so? What if one company has enlightened (but costly) environmentally friendly policies, while its competitors take profit where and how they can?

Increasingly the world is a single economic unit. In the words of the English poet John Donne (1573-1631):

> 'No man is an island, entire of itself; every man is a piece of the Continent, a part of the main.'

Questions

1. What are your views on this topic?
2. What constraints, if any, do you think are necessary in the market economy? Be as specific as possible.
3. What do you see as the major environmental problems facing the world at the present time?
4. Is it not understandable that the poorer people in the world, who are the majority, should be more concerned with improving their standard of living than safeguarding the environment?
5. In view of the highly competitive nature of international business, do you think individual firms can afford to have a social conscience?

When you have considered these problems, express your thoughts in writing.

N. In-tray exercise

Thomson Tractors have developed a new type of tractor. The TT5 is about two-thirds of the normal size and the engine is particularly reliable and easy to service. They are targetting their marketing efforts at this stage on Eastern Europe and South-east Asia and have appointed their first overseas agents in these areas. The agents are:

i) Ako Tsui, Warwick House, 384-388 Queen's Road West, Sai Yin Pun, Hong Kong. Telephone 8711369. Fax 8716739.

ii) Kenneth Li, 12, Lintang Fettes, Fettes Park, 1120 Penang, West Malaysia. Telephone 4736941. Fax 4737732.

iii) Matthias Krageloh AG, Pankower Allee 369, 1000 Berlin 51, Germany. Telephone 4923826. Fax 030 4923961.

They have recently displayed the new tractor at agricultural exhibitions in Budapest and Singapore and have received a number of enquiries. They are also planning to exhibit the tractor at an agricultural trade fair which is taking place in Berlin within the next ten weeks. The Berlin agent is organising the Thomson stand, and conducting some field-demonstrations at local farms. There is also the possibility of a trade fair in Tokyo within the next four months.

6: International marketing

All the Thomson agents have taken delivery of 50 tractors to meet immediate demand. The arrangement is to deliver additional stocks whenever the stock in hand falls below 40. To ensure that there are no maintenance problems, each of the agents is currently sending two or three mechanics to Blackburn for a four week training session.

For potential purchasers generally, the company is offering subsidised flights to England together with free hotel accommodation for three nights, but these arrangements only apply to serious enquiries, and where orders are likely to reach double figures (i.e. ten or more). Discounts up to 20% are allowed on bulk purchases from the factory in Blackburn, but where agents are involved they are responsible for determining pricing and discounts.

Your task

Play the role of the Personal Assistant to James Briggs, Sales Manager at Thomson Tractors PLC (telephone 0254 55124, fax 0254 55012) and draft replies for his signature (or otherwise deal with) the following four letters which have arrived in this morning's mail. All options should be considered.

Yap Boon Kwan Agricultural Equipment

Wisma Buildings, 135 Jalan Ampan, 50450 Kuala Lumpur, Malaysia   Tel: 03-2495111 Fax: 2419511

```
Date:

The Sales Manager
Thomson Tractors PLC
Thomson Works
North Street
Blackburn
Lancashire BB2 1LH
```

Dear Sir,

Thomson TT5 Tractors

I have received a supply of brochures describing your new mini-tractors and would very much like to see them in action. Most of the tractors on offer at the present time are over-priced for this market and the spare parts are too expensive. Your smaller version at lower cost might just allow me to find a market for them.

I heard about the exhibition in Singapore from some of my friends. They saw the demonstrations and were quite impressed with the TT5. My problem is that although I am interested in the product I could not hope to become involved in any deals without having fully tested it.

Since setting up my business in 1978 it has become one of the largest importers of farming equipment in Malaysia. I have a staff of over a hundred and import goods from all over the world. If I purchased your tractors I would do so in considerable quantities and would expect substantial discounts.

What ideas do you have?

Yours faithfully,

Yap Boon Kan

Yap Boon Kan

Hungarian Agricultural Support Agency
Vigardo u. 12, Budapest Pf: 708 P – 1399
Tel 36-1 108 6033 Fax 36-1 108 5555

Date:

Thomson Tractors PLC
Thomson Works
North Street
Blackburn BB2 1LH

Dear Sirs,

A number of our staff visited the recent agricultural exhibition in Budapest and watched the demonstrations of your TT5 tractor given by your representatives. Most of us were fairly impressed but there were questions unanswered. While your representatives were very courteous and helpful, they were required to deal with other parties as well as ourselves. The result was a general feeling that we needed to see more field trials before we could express more than passing interest. Can you help us in this respect?

While writing to you, I feel we should also point out that our Support Agency is very short of funds at the present time. We have a great need for agricultural equipment in Hungary, as do our neighbours. If we can be given long-term credit it would help us both to buy more of your TT5s and make it easier for us to pay for them. A number of our existing contacts in Italy and Germany offer us very favourable credit facilities, and we assume you could, and would, do the same.

We look forward to hearing from you.

Yours faithfully,

Karoly Barta

Karoly Barta
Purchasing Manager

6: International marketing

Marco Kee Agricultural Machinery BV
Nagalstraat 89, PO Box 71, 3770 AC Barneveld, Netherlands
Tel: 31.3550.17823 Fax: 31.3550.17804

The Sales Manager
Thomson Tractors PLC
Thomson Works
North Street
Blackburn BB2 1LH

Date:

Dear Sir or Madam,

TT5 Tractors

I have just returned from a trip to the Far East and while I was there visited the Agricultural Equipment Exhibition in Singapore. I was given various demonstrations of the TT5, and liked what I saw. In brief, I would like to come to Blackburn in the hope that you will be able to:

a) Give me some hands-on experience of the new tractor.

b) Discuss questions such as price and delivery dates with me.

c) Reassure me as to the after-sales service which is offered with these new machines.

I suggest visiting you on the second Monday/Tuesday of next month. I can get as far as Heathrow without difficulty, but I would then need help in finding my way to Blackburn. Can you please confirm as soon as possible whether the dates are acceptable and offer me some guidance on the best way of getting to Blackburn. The plane I have in mind is scheduled to arrive at Heathrow at 11.30 on Monday morning.

Yours faithfully,

Jan Van den Burgh

Jan Van den Burgh
Chief Executive

AS Agricultural Services

Proprietor Lee Tsai
Constitution Buildings, 305 Tun Hwa North Road, Taipei, Taiwan
Tel: 646 3216   Fax: 646 3370

Date:

Mr James Briggs
Sales Manager
Thomson Tractors
North Street
Blackburn BB2 1LH
England

Dear Mr Briggs,

I have recently visited the agricultural exhibition in Singapore and was given your name by the Thomson representative. Briefly, I am interested in your TT5 tractors. My interest is restricted by the price quoted by your representative at the exhibition, but he did say the price would probably be negotiable.

I am concerned too about delivery dates. The last time I dealt with an English company, goods which were promised for delivery by the end of March arrived at the end of June. By then the birds had flown. My customers had lost interest and gone elsewhere.

I obviously need to discuss these problems with someone in authority in your company. At the same time it is not the sort of thing which can be discussed suitably over the telephone. Is there perhaps an agent in this part of the world who could help me?

Your advice would be appreciated.

Yours sincerely,

Costina Soo

Ms Costina Soo
Purchasing Manager

7: Advertising

A. Comprehension

Businesses need to advertise. If they did not advertise no-one would even learn of the existence of their wares. In part, advertising is aimed at conveying information to potential customers and clients, but it is also used to persuade the public to buy. This is the area in which advertising is often criticised. Advertisements are sometimes misleading. Although it is illegal for advertisers to make untrue statements about their goods, services or prices, they still make their wares seem unduly attractive. They pander to our egos and our vanities. They create a demand which would not otherwise exist.

It is easy to say, 'I'm not influenced by the adverts!'. Everyone is influenced to a certain extent. There was recently some research on subliminal advertising. The word 'coffee' was flashed on to the television screen. It happened so quickly that no-one was aware it had happened. For just a fraction of a second it registered on the viewers' subconscious. The result? A surprising number of people chose to make coffee at that precise moment. Of course, it could have been a coincidence but it was highly unlikely.

Yet, for the typical manufacturer advertising is a form of insurance. The nature and extent of consumer's needs have to be constantly assessed. If the needs are over-estimated it is possible, through advertising, to soak up the surplus goods which have been produced. As a demand for a product sags, it can be stimulated. There are all sorts of useful by-products. Without the possibility of advertising, workforces would have to be laid off when sales fell. The warehouses would become overfilled and the stocks would deteriorate, perhaps even becoming obsolete.

An alternative to advertising would be to lower prices when sales fall. This would suit the purchasers but introduce an element of uncertainty for the manufacturers. They are always concerned to ensure that their revenue exceeds their costs, and where would they be if there were daily fluctuations in the prices of their products?

Advertising goes far beyond television and hoardings, newspapers and magazines. The manager of a clothes store is advertising by putting models wearing the store's clothes in the window. A bicycle manufacturer is advertising when he sends a new price-list through the post to his retailers. How could trading be carried on without such devices?

Some would even go so far as to say that advertising actually enriches our lives. Commercial television is able to provide us with free programmes thanks to its advertising revenues. National newspapers derive much of their revenue from advertising. Look at a typical newspaper and you will discover the proportion of the pages devoted to advertisements. We also have advertisers to thank for the free colour supplements accompanying the Sunday newspapers.

Your first task

Having read the above passage, answer these questions in your own words.
- a) What is meant by informative advertising?
- b) Why is persuasive advertising criticised?
- c) What is subliminal advertising?
- d) What should be done to counter a fall in sales?
- e) How do national newspapers benefit from advertising?
- f) How can window-dressing be seen as a form of advertising?

g) How does advertising help the workforce?
h) Why is it expensive to hold stocks unnecessarily?

Your second task

Complete the diagram below by placing the appropriate words in the four different boxes.

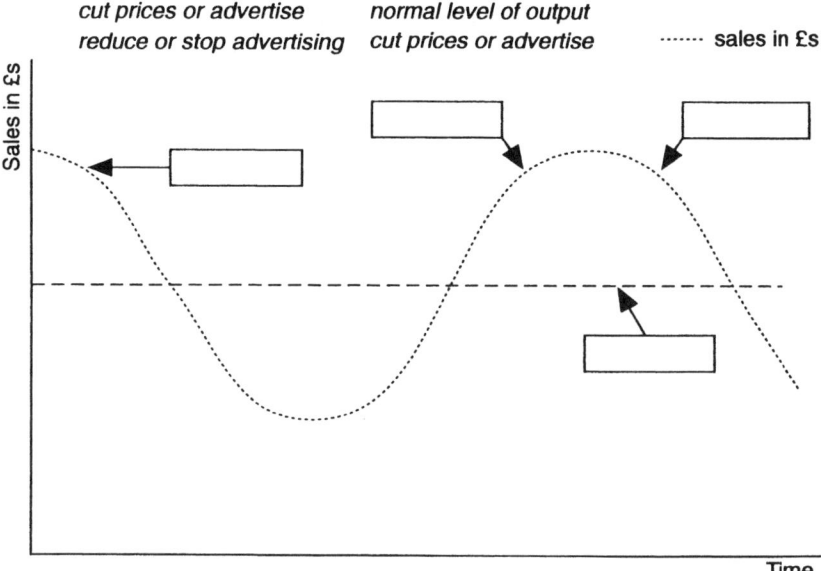

B. Fill in the blanks*

Rewrite this passage filling in the blanks from the words below:

Advertising Agencies

An agent is a person or firm with authority to act for another (the principal) in order to .... a contractual relationship between the .... and a third party. However, advertising .... are an exception to this rule, acting as principals for the services they purchase on .... of their clients. What sorts of services do they provide? They will book advertising space and .... and produce material for them. A business may generate and control the .... of its advertisements, or it may use the services of an agency. Some firms find it easier not to .... their own advertisements. Take the case of an engineering firm. No doubt they have a talented staff, but their training will .... be in the .... of engineering. They could not be expected to .... an eye-catching advertisement any more than the advertising agency staff could be expected to .... a bridge or design a gas turbine.

The advertising agency will have developed its own .... of expertise which it then makes available to its clients. There will be various .... of scale. Commercial artists can be employed. They will do nothing else but create .... called for in advertisements. The agency's managers will be able to develop an .... strategy for their clients – and .... it. They will be able to produce a media schedule setting out a .... of planned insertions, showing .... costs, timing, nature of media and the bookings to be reserved. They will know the basic .... made by advertising .... for use of their services or facilities. Furthermore, because they are big .... of the newspapers and .... and the television networks, they will be able to

7: Advertising

.... favourable commissions which they can pass on, in part at least, to their principals. For these reasons the agency fees will usually be amply covered by the savings they are able to achieve for their clients.

Among the .... staff in an advertising agency will be the media buyer who is responsible for timely and .... purchasing of media time and space to discharge the requirements of a client's media schedule. Another .... in the agency, the media planner, will be charged with formulating plans .... all types of media in such a way as to enable a client to reach out to the potential markets with.................. efficiency and minimum expense.

economies	obtain	brand	design
prepare	build	involving	maximum
artwork	detailed	create	establish
principal	agencies	production	behalf
normally	executive	customers	charges
economical	specialist	programme	magazines
media	implement	field	advertising

C. Case study

Wessex Tobaccos

This company is one of Britain's leading cigarette manufacturers with factories in Bristol and London. Until June last year they had entrusted their advertising to Mendoza Inc., an American agency with offices in London, but from July onwards they switched to Carson & Green, an English firm based in London.

Carson & Green are changing the image of the company, concentrating their attention on the younger elements in society, since they regard this segment as the least concerned with the health hazards.

The following data covering last year's results for Wessex Tobaccos has now become available and allows the relative performances of the American and English advertising agencies to be compared.

Wessex Tobaccos sales revenue and advertising costs for last year

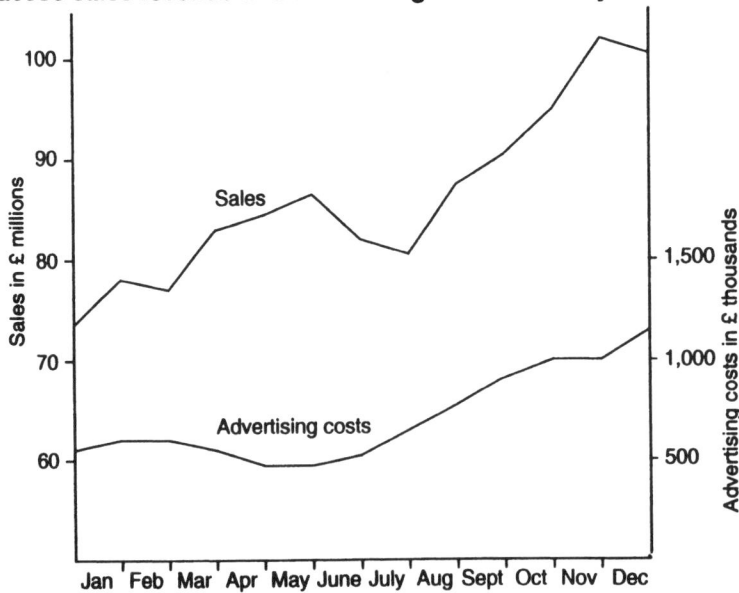

7: Advertising

Your task

You are the Personal Assistant to the Office Manager, Adrian Slaney. He has asked you for a brief memorandum interpreting the results for last year and commenting on the results generally. He has intimated that he would like you to deal with three specific questions:

1. Which of the advertising agencies have been more successful?
2. Which other factors might have affected the results?
3. What are the dangers to the company in the new advertising strategy?

D. Opposites and synonyms*

Complete the following table.

Word	Synonym	Opposite
profit (noun)		
condense (verb)		
expensively (adverb)		
gather (verb)		
agent (noun)		
gloomily (adverb)		
approximately (adverb)		
revenue (noun)		
concentrate (verb)		
encourage (verb)		
consequential (adjective)		
attack (verb)		
irrationally (adverb)		
prevent (verb)		
popular (adjective)		
demand (noun)		
conceal (verb)		
persuasive (adjective)		
totally (adverb)		
distinguished (adjective)		
sensitive (adjective)		

E. Join the halves*

On the left of the page are the first halves of sentences. On the right are the second halves of the sentences, though not in the same order. Pair the halves and then write your own list of the completed sentences.

7: Advertising

i)	If money were not spent on advertising it would give manufacturers the opportunity to	a)	communicate between those with goods and services to sell and those who might benefit from those goods and services.
ii)	Some firms spend large sums of money on advertising to	b)	make large numbers of their workers redundant.
iii)	Many manufacturers see advertising as an insurance policy which gives them the opportunity to	c)	which the advertising message of a television or radio commercial is sung.
iv)	Advertising can be seen as the means to	d)	ensure that advertisers do not make false statements about their products and services.
v)	The advent of satellite television has opened up possibilities for international advertising agencies to	e)	restrict the entry of competitors into the market.
vi)	If manufacturers do not advertise when sales fall they might have to	f)	substantially reduce the cost of the goods to the consumer.
vii)	A jingle is a short tune to	g)	whom the advertisement is intended to appeal.
viii)	A hoarding is a site for poster advertising which some firms use to	h)	remind the public of the name of the product.
ix)	The Trade Descriptions Acts were passed to	i)	protect themselves against their own too-optimistic forecasts.
x)	The purpose of much advertising expenditure on established brands is to	j)	advertise throughout the world with a single commercial.
xi)	The target audience is the section of the population to	k)	flatter the target audience by pandering to their self image and making them more receptive to the advertising message.
xii)	Ego bait is intended to	l)	attract the attention of people such as pedestrians and motorists.

F. Summarising

Give the following passage an appropriate title and summarise it in about 150 words:

> The art of advertising is to persuade people to buy your product or service. This requires a basic understanding of psychology, the needs of human beings and how those needs can be satisfied. An American psychologist, Abraham Maslow, has suggested those needs can be compartmentalised and arranged in the form of a hierarchy. At the lowest level people need food, shelter, warmth and sex. When these needs are largely satisfied, people begin to think about the safety of themselves and their personal possessions. Squirrels, when they have had their fill of nuts, begin to bury nuts in their winter larders. Human beings have the same tendency, much to the relief of the insurance companies. Insurance appeals to those who would feel the loss of personal possessions, through burglary, flood and fire, and those who seek pensions and financial security generally.
>
> Even when a human being does not feel under threat at the safety level, a new need emerges according to Maslow. There is now a need to be approved by other people, a need for love and respect. The advertising industry finds this a very useful area for its machinations.

7: Advertising

'If you want people to look at you admiringly, or enviously, you have to wear Jayboy Jeans – no-one else's will do! ' That is the message, in effect.

Or the advertiser might be trying to persuade you to buy a new car. 'This is the latest and the best sports car in the market. It is faster, sleeker, more enviable, than anything else in the world. If you haven't got one, or don't get one pretty soon, the rest of the world is going to see you as a dead duck!'

And when we are largely satisfied at this social level, according to Maslow we simply move on to egocentricity. We all have egos, but what is an ego? It is a love of self. We look into the mirror and hopefully like what we see. Of course, not only in physical terms. We hunger for self-respect now that our lower level needs have been largely satisfied. Another happy hunting-ground for the advertising agencies, for example 'Diamonds are forever', or 'Use Real Results from Diana Cosmetics – fights wrinkles fast!'

According to Maslow the ultimate need is for fulfilment. This would no doubt come when we have all that the advertisers say we so desperately need. For most of us it seems that day will never come!

G. Reply to a letter

You are the Personal Assistant to Helen Christie, Senior Partner in the Ascot Advertising Agency. Mrs Christie has received the following letter from a client.

7: Advertising

ASD Limited
Thetford Industrial Estate, Thetford, Suffolk IP5 6JT
Tel 0606 424211

Ref KDC/JP

Date as postmark

Dear Mrs Christie,

I was very disappointed that you did not turn up to the meeting you arranged with me for Friday last. My diary note clearly shows you were to join me for lunch on that day and I reserved a table at the Golden Pheasant. I was hoping to introduce you to Mr Lander, our Chief Executive, who came in specially from Ipswich for the meeting.

You will recall we were going to discuss ways in which we might conduct the publicity campaign for the European Carrier project. I shall be in Paris for the next five days but would like to hear from you as soon as possible.

Yours sincerely,

A. Bellamy

Andrew Bellamy
Marketing Manager

Mrs H Christie
Ascot Advertising Agency
Greencoat Road
Arlington
Berkshire RG4 BB2

Mrs Christie has asked you to prepare a letter for her signature. She wants you to offer her apologies but explain that according to her diary the meeting was for this Friday. She will contact Mr Bellamy as soon as he comes back from Paris.

H. Meanings

First, read the passage below. Then explain the meanings of the words and phrases which have been highlighted.

In many ways a business organisation has the **same complexities** as the human body. For example, the production department can be compared to a person's hands. Human hands **in conjunction with tools** are used to make things, and it is the production department which is **entrusted** to make the motor cars and washing machines we have come to expect in our **affluent society**. The salespeople and advertising managers can be **likened to the voice of the organisation**. If they are **unconvincing**, the goods will stay on the factory floor as they reach the end of the **production line**.

Once a **bargain** has been made the goods have to be carried to their **destination**. Maybe the organisation will have its own **fleet of lorries**. Maybe it will pay for other carriers to deliver the goods. In any case this is where so-called distribution **comes into play**. The transport and distribution functions could well be described as the legs of the operation. Without transport the finished goods would **stay put**.

How does management fit into this **analogy**? The managers are the brains of the outfit. It is they who receive information from the **outlying parts** of the body and make **appropriate decisions** in just the same way as the human brain **reacts to various stimuli**. How does the data reach the managers? Through the office which is at the centre of a vast **communications network**. Messages are received, modified and relayed. **Data banks** are maintained and **made accessible** to management as and when required. The office can therefore be compared to the **nervous system** of the human body.

I. Expansion

You work for an advertising agency, and have been asked by your old school friend Colleen O'Grady to help her promote her new clothes shop. Colleen recently left the Central London Fashion School with a prize as Student of the Year. In partnership with her boy friend, Shaun, she has now taken a 14 year lease on a town-centre shop. The shop will be called 'The Cave' and will be set out like Aladdin's Cave.

The local newspaper has agreed to offer some free publicity for the new enterprise. They will print a photograph of them together with a short article explaining what makes their shop 'different'. The photograph has been taken but a copy is not available at present. It will apparently show Shaun behind the counter and Colleen wearing one of her own outfits.

Colleen and Shaun are on holiday in Europe at the present time, but you have been asked to draft a 150 word article which might accompany the photograph in the newspaper, bearing in mind that Colleen has mentioned the following points she wants covered:

- Clothes designed for individuals.
- Choice of materials but specialising in Thai silks (a friend at college came from Thailand).
- All accessories available.
- Fashion shows every Saturday (midday and afternoon).
- Both of them went to local comprehensive school.

You may make any assumptions necessary because Colleen will vet the article before it is handed over to the newspaper, but you are expected to make as much as possible out of this free publicity.

J. Complete the sentences

Complete the following sentences using your own words.

1. Advertising can help a business to ...
2. If you have goods or services to sell ...
3. The Trade Descriptions Acts make it an offence for a trader ...
4. A good advertising agency will ...
5. While advertising on national television is ...
6. If a retailer has a good window-display ...
7. Local radio is often used to ...
8. When stocks are building up ...
9. Although newspapers and magazines ...
10. One of the weaknesses of human beings is that ...
11. It is essential that the packaging of a product should be ...
12. When you design an advertisement for a women's magazine ...

K. Vocabulary*

audiovisual	publicity	hoarding	artwork	gimmick
feature	exhibition	ego	exclusive	persuasion
audience	bulletin	brand	tabloid	teaser
stimulus	sponsor	presentation	slogan	dry-run
leaflet	logo	media	showcase	profile

Match the words listed above with the dictionary definitions which follow.

1. A cabinet made of glass or clear plastic used to display products while protecting them against deterioration and pilferage.
2. The art of making people do what you want them to do.
3. A combination of visual art forms, such as film and video, with sound in the form of record, tape or cassette.
4. An idea or object which is novel or unusual.
5. An individual's conception of himself/herself.
6. An established product name which is usually registered with the Registrar of Patents.
7. A display of a company's products to bring them to public notice.
8. A story or photographic material which is supplied to one publication alone.
9. A group of people exposed to any form of persuasion.
10. A company symbol, badge or name style.
11. Catchwords, phrases or sentences associated with a particular product or company, putting across a selling point in an entertaining fashion.
12. A site for poster advertising.
13. A printed piece of paper, single or folded-over to make four pages.
14. Someone who is prepared to finance an operation so long as their name will be featured in the publicity.
15. A brief description of a product or person which amounts to a character sketch.
16. A brief mailing announcement, issued periodically.
17. A newspaper with a small page area.
18. An advertisement which makes people curious because some information has been withheld.
19. The art of claiming attention.
20. A story or article written in some depth for a particular publication.
21. An action which provokes a response.
22. The pictorial or illustrative part of an advertisement.
23. A planned meeting at which attempts are made to sell ideas or products.
24. The intermediaries used by the business fraternity to advertise their wares.
25. A rehearsal for a tv/video presentation where action, lines and cues are practised.

L. Correspondence*

New Dimensions Media Specialists

Solent House, Harbour Approach, Southampton, Hampshire S02 9JP   Tel: 0452 373700

Date:

Mr Ulrich Kerber
Kerber GmbH
Hardofweg
D-7921 Heidenheim
West Germany

Dear Mr Kerber,

Following the instructions you gave us last week we have drafted a few advertisements for the local press and enclose some samples produced by our copywriters and designers. They are rough sketches at this stage to minimise costs but if you like any of them we can easily refine the artwork.

I would suggest that we take a weekly spot in both the Evening Echo and the Western Gazette for a continuous period of sixteen weeks. My thought is that we should go for the Saturday editions of the Echo since the circulation tends to be higher. Our research has also shown that the average readership per copy and the average time spent reading each copy also go up for the Saturday editions.

The Western Gazette is a weekly paper so these considerations do not apply. Its advantage for us is that its readership tends to be in the country areas not covered by the Echo.

I think we should use the same material for the whole of the sixteen week period. This has two beneficial effects. On the one hand it educates or familiarises our audience, and on the other hand it gives us a 25% discount on the advertising fees.

The other dimension to our campaign at this stage would be a regular morning slot on local radio (Radio Solent). I propose a 25 second slot repeated within the hour.

Please let me know your reactions to these proposals as soon as possible.

Yours sincerely,

Dominic Haigh

Mr Dominic Haigh
Senior Partner

Some people **work** to be warm!
(others prefer to live in comfort ...)

It's no joke trying to keep warm on a budget. Eskimos survive in the Arctic but only because they eat lots of blubber. Maybe you should change your diet?

Take it from us – blubber is horrible!

Alternatively take the advice of Kerber, the central heating experts. Complete the coupon below and we will send you our free booklet.

Name..

Address..

....

Post to Kerber Central Heating Ltd, Unit 4, Ilchester Industrial Estate, Ilchester IR1 1XX

Keeping warm the Kerber way

AN INTELLIGENCE TEST

(for homeowners with a sense of humour)

Another cold winter is forecast with lots of ice and snow. How are you planning to keep warm in your home?

A. Buy a smaller car so you can park more easily, while you spend a few days searching for more gas and electric fires.

B. Invite all your friends to live with you so you can sit close together and keep each other warm.

C. Give up your job and take a vacation in a sunnier climate until the weather at home improves.

D. Look for an efficient, cost-saving central-heating system which allows you to be as warm as you want to be.

If you chose D you have passed the test and can send for our free booklet.
Just fill in the coupon below.

Name..

Address ....

....

Post to Kerber Central Heating Ltd, Unit 4, Ilchester Industrial Estate, Ilchester IR1 1XX

Keeping warm the Kerber way

7: Advertising

Some people keep warm by chopping wood ...

It's back-aching and dangerous. Even Red Indians and Boy Scouts have stopped chopping wood. Relax in comfort and let the experts do the hard work for you. Kerber combine the technology you are entitled to expect with the price you can afford.

Please send me without obligation a copy of your helpful booklet.

Name..

Address...

....

Post to Kerber Central Heating Ltd, Unit 4, Ilchester Industrial Estate, Ilchester IR1 1XX

Keeping warm the Kerber way

Your first task

Find synonyms for the following words used in Dominic Haigh's letter:

a) drafted (line 1) b) samples (line 2) c) sketches (line 3)
d) suggest (line 5) e) thought (line 7) f) circulation (line 8)
g) considerations (line 11) h) areas (line 13) i) beneficial (line 15)
j) fees (line 17) k) dimension (line 18) l) reactions (line 21)

Your second task

Play the role of Ulrich Kerber and reply to Douglas Haigh's letter. Let him know your reactions to his proposals.

8: Transport and distribution

A. Comprehension

The world of business needs a transport system if it is to function effectively. On the one hand, raw materials have to be brought to the factories for processing. Very often those materials need to be imported from other countries. There are so many different materials called for that few countries are able to cater for the needs of their industries. Some countries are rich in one commodity. Other countries are rich in other commodities. The resources of all the countries in the world can be made available to all – so long as there are the necessary means of transport.

For a typical person in an industrialised country there is nothing that he or she consumes, from food to cars, which is not imported from abroad or made at least partially from imported raw materials. The world is economically interdependent. A car may be assembled in England from parts made in Japan or Germany, which are in turn made of raw materials such as rubber from Malaysia, iron ore from Sweden and chrome from Zimbabwe. The petrol which fuels it may well come from Saudi Arabia. The total miles travelled by all the various materials before they become a car which can be used is astronomical.

Even during the production process transport is important. The work flow will be designed to ensure that the materials being processed travel the shortest possible distance along the factory floor.

However, it is after the goods have been produced that transport becomes a major issue again. Between the factories and the final consumers will be a battery of professional carriers. Fleets of lorries and vans will now be brought into play. In many cases the factories will use the services of a wholesaler. The wholesaler buys in goods from a variety of manufacturers and then distributes them to the retailers, or shopkeepers, as they are more generally called.

The wholesalers reduce the amount of transportation required since they collect supplies in bulk from the factories and provide a cost-saving delivery service to the retailers. Additionally, the wholesalers justify their existence by giving advice and information to retailers in relation to new products, changes in tastes and fashions, and complaints.

For those who look for a more flexible arrangement, cash-and-carry warehouses have been developed so that the smaller shopkeepers and hoteliers can collect supplies whenever they are needed. With outward transport costs eliminated and immediate payment for the purchases being called for, the cash-and-carry warehouses are able to reduce their prices, which goes some way towards meeting the transport costs incurred by their customers.

Whenever goods need to be loaded or unloaded, additional costs are incurred. One way of reducing such costs is through the use of containers. The containers vary in size and shape but the principle is always the same. Loading and unloading between point of departure and destination is minimised. The containers are normally made of steel or aluminium. They are usually enclosed and tend to be of a standard height and width, though some are open-topped with a fixed tarpaulin cover. With standard units stacking is easier and identification is also facilitated. In general, containerisation helps to speed up the turn-around of vehicles, reduces losses through pilferage and careless handling, and gives protection against the elements. The latter point can be critical when goods are carried on a ship's deck.

It is interesting to note that since containerisation was introduced, the workforce employed in the docks has fallen significantly.

8: Transport and distribution

Your task

Having read the above passage, answer these questions in your own words.

a) To what extent is Great Britain economically independent?
b) What methods of transport do you think would be used to bring the raw materials into a typical factory?
c) What different methods of transport are available to businesses?
d) Why would line managers be interested in methods of transport within the factory?
e) What functions do wholesalers perform?
f) How are goods generally carried between wholesalers and retailers?
g) What is the purpose of the container?
h) What are the benefits of having standardised containers?
i) How have the containers affected the work of the dockworkers?
j) How do you think containers help to stop pilfering?

B. Fill in the blanks*

Rewrite this passage filling in the blanks from the words below:

Transport by Air

If the customer wants the goods .... they can be sent by aircraft. It may be that important machinery has broken down and .... parts are required to avoid an .... hold-up in production. Or it may be that medical supplies are called for to .... an epidemic. In such a situation time might be of the essence. Promptly dealt with .... diseases can be contained, but once they have .... beyond a certain point they will become out of control.

Another case where air transport will be used is where the goods are .... Flowers are grown in the Scilly Isles off the south-west coast of England. Because of the .... climate the flowers bloom in the Scillies before .... in Britain. Cut flowers are in great demand in the Spring, especially on Mother's Day, when all .... children are expected to .... their mothers with flowers. The flowers are flown from the Scilly Isles to London so as to catch the lucrative market. If they were sent by ship they would arrive too late and be in poor shape. The condition of racehorses is also of concern to the owners. Before a big race the horses need to be brought to a .... of condition. If they had to spend days and even weeks on the ocean their .... would be interrupted and they could be .... disturbed. Of course an air trip is also likely to .... them, but they will soon be back on firm ground and the .... will be quickly forgotten. In this way they can be raced on .... tracks and win big prizes for their owners. Obviously horses need to be carried in .... horse boxes, and even tranquilized, because if they kicked out in .... they could cause the aircraft to crash.

Though air freight rates are comparatively expensive, they will be less of a .... when the goods are small in .... but high in value. Items like gold bullion and .... gems might be flown to their destinations. In the case of .... ingots, if they were sent by sea, for example, there would be many weeks during which the .... was at risk. By contrast, when an aircraft carries gold to its destination, the costs of .... guards and insurance policies are .... reduced.

8: Transport and distribution

Perhaps the major weakness of air transport, apart from its expense, is that there are a limited number of .... running the services which are required. It is usually necessary to start and .... the journey on some sort of motor vehicle.

unsettle	foreign	security	urgently
burden	consignment	panic	peak
training	elsewhere	caring	contagious
spare	spread	present	precious
airports	bulk	reinforced	gold
finish	experience	favourable	expensive
combat	perishable	emotionally	greatly

C. Case study

Solent Carriers

On Monday of next week there is a fashion show at the Kaiserlich Hotel, Herzogstrasse 15, 6800 Mannheim, West Germany. The show is to be televised internationally and will include contributions from most European countries. While most of the models will be German or French there is a small British contingent and they will be displaying high couture evening wear. One of London's most famous jewellers has agreed to provide some expensive jewellery for the British models to wear. The jewellery will have to be personally delivered by courier to Lisa Faversham (who is managing the group for this presentation) in Room 12 at the Kaiserlich any time after midday on the Sunday, and returned immediately after the show finishes at 21.00 hours (9.00pm).

You are the courier who has been given the assignment. You are to deliver the jewellery in person to Lisa Faversham and fetch it back to the London jeweller. Lisa will arrange an escort for you when the plane lands at Frankfurt, the nearest international airport to Mannheim.

Other facts you need to know:

i) You can arrange to pick up the consignment from the jewellers at any time between 0900 and 1800 hours either on the Saturday or Sunday before the show.

ii) The jewellers are a 30 minute taxi ride from Heathrow Airport in London and you are expected to be at the airport at least half an hour before the flight departure time.

iii) Customs procedures at Frankfurt may take up to 20 minutes. It usually takes another 20 minutes to get to the station.

iv) Rehearsals for the show will start at midday on the Monday.

v) Emil Zurcher, the escort who will meet you at the airport is known to you from previous assignments.

vi) There is a time difference of one hour between Germany and Britain. When it is midday in Britain it is one o'clock in Germany.

vii) The flight times from Heathrow to Frankfurt and the train times from Frankfurt to Mannheim are shown below.

Daily flights from Heathrow to Frankfurt (all times shown are GMT i.e. British times)				
Flight times	08.00	11.30	16.00	23.30
Estimated time of arrival	09.25	12.55	17.25	00.55

8: Transport and distribution

Timetable for trains between Frankfurt and Mannheim		
Frankfurt	Darmstadt	Mannheim
06.15	06.50	07.35
(and an hourly service thereafter – last train at 23.15)		

Your task

The arrangements are generally up to you so long as you keep within the prescribed limits. Having planned your itinerary you are now asked to complete the telex message started below, letting Lisa Faversham know as much as possible of your plans in no more than 40 words.

Telex 654329 Kaisermann K For Lisa Faversham Room 12.

D. Parts of speech*

i) Add an appropriate **adjective** to each of the following sentences where indicated:

a) Air transport is the .... method of travel.

b) Most of the .... airlines offer regular flights from London to Frankfurt.

c) The .... maintenance of aircraft is essential if flying is to be safe.

d) Aircraft are invaluable to tourists because they make for .... holidays.

e) While aircraft are the fastest form of transport, they are not suitable for .... freight.

f) One of the problems of transporting goods or passengers by air is that there are .... terminals.

ii) Add an appropriate **adverb** to each of the following sentences where indicated:

a) Passengers can be picked up .... at bus stops.

b) Coaches can carry passengers more .... than buses.

c) Heavy lorries are .... more damaging to the environment than other forms of transport.

d) Buses are normally employed most .... in congested urban areas.

e) One problem facing bus companies is that they are often not .... viable.

f) Motor vans and small lorries can now be hired by those who need transport .... and are prepared to 'do it themselves'.

E. Multiple choice*

Choose the phrase, A, B or C, which **best** completes each sentence, and tick the appropriate box.

1. Because a train runs on fixed tracks
   - A. it can be timetabled to stop at more stations. ☐
   - B. it can carry more passengers. ☐
   - C. it is not subject to traffic jams. ☐

8: Transport and distribution

2. If a railway only has a single track
   A. a breakdown will probably not cause serious problems.
   B. a breakdown will definitely cause serious problems.
   C. a breakdown is likely to cause serious problems.

3. When a particular railway service becomes unprofitable
   A. it may help the situation if fares are lowered.
   B. it will help the situation if fares are lowered.
   C. it will not help the situation if fares are lowered.

4. Because most journeys do not start and end at railway stations
   A. support transport is not normally required at the terminals.
   B. support transport is usually required at the terminals.
   C. support transport is occasionally required at the terminals.

5. Times of arrival and departure for trains can be given with greater accuracy than
   A. for lorries or coaches because road transport is slower.
   B. for aircraft because airports are congested.
   C. for other forms of transport.

6. One of the attractions of inter-city travel by rail for executives is that they
   A. will reach their final destination more quickly.
   B. will have the option to do some work while they are travelling.
   C. will not need a taxi at the end of their journey.

7. Heavy and bulky freight can be carried overland comparatively cheaply by rail because
   A. bigger loads can be carried in a single haul.
   B. the loads can be conveyed at night.
   C. railway workers wages are low.

8. When railway lines are closed down because they are uneconomic
   A. the workers will have to find jobs in other industries.
   B. the workers will not be able to find jobs in other industries.
   C. some of the workers may lose their jobs.

9. If the government spent substantially more on the development of motorways
   A. they would also have to subsidise the railways.
   B. it would probably make the railways less profitable.
   C. it would encourage more freight to be sent by rail.

10. A Eurotunnel between England and France

100

A.	will make French goods more expensive in England.	☐
B.	will encourage more Britons to go abroad for their holidays.	☐
C.	will improve the British economy by encouraging tourism.	☐

F. Summarising

Give the following passage a title and summarise it in about 120 words.

Transport by sea is bound to be comparatively slow, but it is also comparatively cheap. A typical ship's speed is about 25 knots (less than 30 miles per hour), so it can take about six days for a cargo ship to cross the Atlantic Ocean. One of the problems associated with carriage by sea is that the cargoes can only be landed at ports, so trains and/or lorries may be required as support transport. This adds to both the cost and the time taken.

The great advantage of sea transport is that tens or even hundreds of thousands of tonnes (a tonne is a weight of 1000kg) can be carried at one time. Bulk oil tankers can deliver three or four hundred thousand tonnes in a single journey. There are considerable economies of scale in this, for the amount of the fuel required by the vessel and the size of the crew do not increase in proportion to the capacity of the ship.

One of the original defects of long sea voyages was that cargoes would be harmed. For example, meat carcasses would deteriorate, especially when ships had to cross the tropics. Modern refrigeration has changed that. It allows meat to arrive at distant ports in prime condition, much to the advantage of farmers in places like the Argentine, New Zealand and Australia. Containerisation has also helped in that it reduces the damage likely to be caused in the process of loading and unloading.

Of course, ships of all kinds have to run the gauntlet of storms at sea. Many ships still sink with their cargoes every year and insurance against loss is covered by Lloyd's of London, the traditional market for marine insurance. As long ago as the seventeenth century Edward Lloyd ran a coffee house near the London docks. It became a popular meeting place for ships' masters and merchants to meet. There they obtained insurance for a trading voyage, for both ships and cargoes. To encourage business Lloyd began to provide shipping information from around the world, and this eventually became the famous Lloyd's newssheet, giving the whereabouts of virtually all the ships in the world.

G. Reply to a letter

You are working in the office of a London merchant who buys and sells a great variety of goods from all over the world. You have just received the following letter from a new customer in Malaysia:

8: Transport and distribution

Thomas Tan & Son
51 Jalan 92199, Damansara Jaya, 47400 Petaling Jaya, Selangor, Malaysia
Telephone 033 262626   Fax 033 252525

```
date as postmark

Messrs J P Hall Ltd
Import and Export Merchants
Finsbury Square
Carbury
Berkshire RG33 8QP

Dear Sirs,

I was pleased to receive your order for my company's livestock and I will
be pleased to send these on to you in six weeks time as arranged. It
would help me to know how you would like the current order of small trop-
ical fish to be transported. As explained in our catalogue the fish are
packed in specially insulated plastic containers which should keep them
in good condition for up to twenty days after leaving here. We can send
them by air or by sea, as you wish, but by air the cost of carriage which
we will invoice to you, will be increased by 25% - from £60 to £80.

As you will know you have also ordered some pythons for later in the
year. These will travel much more easily in the large reinforced crates
we provide, they simply go to sleep if the temperature falls, unlike the
fish. Perhaps while writing you will let us know the method of transport
preferred for both these consignments.

Yours sincerely,

Sebastian Tan

Sebastian Tan
```

Your task

You are to reply to the letter having been given the responsibility for choosing the mode of transport to be employed. You are also asked to question the apparent error in the increased cost of carriage by air.

H. Meanings

First, read the passage below. Then explain the meanings of the words and phrases which have been highlighted.

> The Railway Age dates from about 1840 to the end of the **nineteenth century**. During this time British **rolling equipment and tracks** were introduced to every continent of the world, **invariably purchased on credit** or financed in some other way by the **increasingly affluent** British. British engineers went all over the world to supervise the building of the railways. Many of them stayed in the **host countries**, which explains why there are still colonies of expatriates in the Argentine, Belgium and even Russia, though of course they are now almost **completely integrated**. British railways **covered the face of the earth**. The Canadian Pacific Railway **stretched almost endlessly** from the Atlantic in the East to the Pacific in the west. And in what was to become the United States of America, British railways carried the European immigrants to take up their free grants of **virgin land** in the American **hinterland**. Even the Russian Tsars wanted to benefit from the miracle of steam power which could haul immense loads at **hitherto unheard of speeds** across continents. The Trans-Siberian Railway was built **painstakingly** from the centre of Moscow through the **barren steppes** to the far, far east of Asia – at Vladivostock. The world was truly opened up by the railways in the nineteenth century. **Like an oyster!**

8: Transport and distribution

The transport revolution was not limited to trains. Iron ships powered by steam were **infinitely more efficient** than the wooden sailing ships. No longer was it necessary to wait for **favourable winds** to carry cargoes to their destinations. No longer were there those **long dry waits in the doldrums** with sailors **whistling for the wind**. The new vessels could carry greater cargoes, longer distances with **more predictable timing**. They were even safer since they were not required to **flirt with the wind**. They carried the hundreds of thousands of migrating Europeans to the **lands of promise** in the United States. In the 1840s a failure of the potato crop **drove** the Irish to the New World. In the 1890s it was a currant crop failure in Greece which had the same effect. In between and after these dates the **land-hungry immigrants** from Europe poured into America. Italians and Germans even **found their way** to countries like the Argentine and Chile in South America, but always through the new ocean-going, iron-clad giants. The world would never be the same again.

The invention of the internal combustion engine was the **end of the beginning** for the new age of scientific transport. Even before the arrival of the twentieth century, the **newfangled** motor cars and aeroplanes had appeared and were **heralding the age of the legless man.**

Of course, there were also implications for war. Empires were **never so far flung**. Armies were **never so mobile**. The world had suddenly become **small and vulnerable**. Yet with the new threats to mankind there were also the opportunities. The affluent part of the world was becoming a giant factory – **a single economic unit**. Even those areas which remained **primary producers** began to feel some benefits from the new way of life.

Nor has the transport revolution ended. Man has already reached the moon and it is only his **own psychological limitations** which are delaying his final journey into space.

I. Expansion

You are a member of the team which is setting up a new firm offering a courier service to businesses in your vicinity. The firm will be called Wings Unlimited. There will initially be a team of seven young couriers (none over the age of twenty) who will carry parcels and documents etc to the destinations given by the clients. The difference between this courier service and many others will be that Wings Unlimited are prepared to offer services beyond mere delivery of packages, but this concept has not been clarified so far.

There will be a scale charge of 20p per mile over any distance up to a weight of 100 kg, with delivery guaranteed on the same day up to a radius of 100 miles. The leader of the team, Kelly Barton, has asked you to draft a suitable advertisement for the local weekly newspaper. It should contain no more than 60 words, mixing larger and smaller print. The key words he has asked you to bear in mind in drafting the advertisement are as follows:

      price   willingness   reliability   civility   discretion

You will need to include the address and telephone number in the advertisement but, as these are not known with certainty yet, Kelly has asked you to simply indicate where they will be displayed in the advertising copy. He wants you to include an idea for the firm's logo, and also to think up a one minute patter for the local radio station. Although he has not specifically said you will be expected to perform personally on the local radio station, that seems to be the implication.

Send Kelly a brief but formal memorandum responding to his requests.

8: Transport and distribution

J. Complete the sentences

Complete the following sentences using your own words.
1. When goods are sent by air ...
2. If bulky goods need to be sent overseas ...
3. Storms at sea can cause loss or damage to cargo ...
4. When commuters' trains run into London late ...
5. An aircraft has a long way to fall so the maintenance of the aircraft ...
6. When perishable items such as tomatoes and flowers ...
7. When there is only a single line railway track ...
8. If the government raises the tax on petrol ...
9. There will always be a demand for luxury liners because ...
10. Many of the new large oil tankers are built in Japan because ...
11. There has been a slump in shipbuilding in recent years because ...
12. The really heavy lorries are called juggernauts and they ...

K. Vocabulary*

peak	wreckage	terminus	freight	ferry
carrier	tachograph	commuter	congestion	diesel
freighter	tourist	tanker	capacity	haulier
conveyance	exporter	draught	merchant	consignee
consignor	hovercraft	airship	manifest	log

Match the words above with the dictionary definitions which follow.
1. A shuttle service, usually waterborne and crossing a river or channel.
2. A person or firm carrying goods as a business.
3. A cargo carrying ship or aircraft.
4. Abnormal accumulation of people or traffic.
5. The person who is arranging for goods to be delivered.
6. The highest point in a curve recording statistical fluctuations.
7. Another name for cargo or goods being carried commercially.
8. A device fitted to a vehicle which records on a disc the time and distance travelled during a journey.
9. A vehicle used for carrying liquid, usually oil.
10. The depth of water a ship draws or requires to float her.
11. A wholesale trader especially with a foreign country.
12. The person to whom goods are being delivered.
13. All that is left after a ship has sunk.
14. A person who travels by train or car to and from their daily work.
15. A fuel used to drive trains and heavy lorries.
16. A permanent record of events occurring during the voyage of a ship or aircraft.
17. A list of cargo for use by customs officers etc.

8: Transport and distribution

18. The end or start of a bus or coach route.
19. A person or firm who sells goods abroad.
20. A machine which uses lighter than air gas to travel through the air.
21. A person who travels for recreational purposes.
22. A vehicle riding on a cushion of air.
23. One who is engaged in transporting goods by road.
24. A device for carrying goods or people from place to place.
25. The maximum amount that can be contained in a vessel.

L. Missing phrases*

Fill in the blanks in this passage, using phrases from the list below.

The chain of distribution

Between the manufacturers and the consumers will be a variety of carriers, wholesalers, stores and shopkeepers, making up a complex chain of distribution. When retailers (stores and shopkeepers) are operating on a sufficiently large scale, they .... purchase goods directly from the manufacturer. Bulk buying will reduce their unit costs and this will .... charge lower prices to their customers. From the manufacturers' point of view the direct contact with their customers (the retailers) give them .... the market and allow them to adjust their products and policies to the changing markets.

The wholesalers often become an intermediary in this, the traditional pattern of distribution. They obtain goods from many different manufacturers and sell them to .... retail outlets in their own catchment areas. By .... and selling comparatively small quantities to retailers they greatly reduce transport costs, as shown in the diagram below:

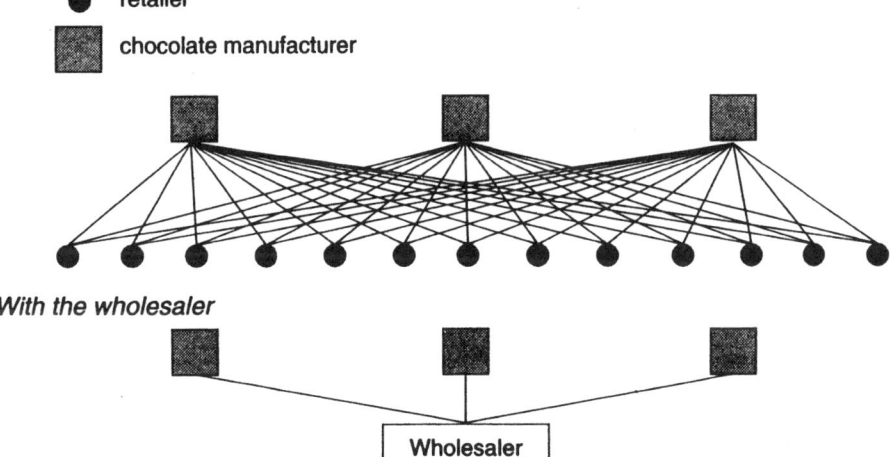

Without the wholesaler

● retailer

▓ chocolate manufacturer

With the wholesaler

Wholesaler

The retailers keep small quantities of .... goods, thus giving the consumer as much choice as possible. They provide .... for the customers, particularly

8: Transport and distribution

where there is a parade of shops as in a typical high street. Customers .... for information and advice, and they provide .... to the wholesalers and manufacturers.

i)	a multitude of	ii)	a better picture of	iii)	a pick-up point
iv)	allow them to	v)	turn to them	vi)	a useful feedback
vii)	may be able to	viii)	a wide variety of	ix)	buying in bulk

M. Join the halves*

On the left of the page are the first halves of sentences. On the right are the second halves, though not in the same order. Pair the halves and then write your own list of the completed sentences.

i) Department stores

ii) Retailers sometimes sell goods at a loss

iii) Discount stores concentrate on a limited range of products

iv) Automatic vending machines have the advantage that they

v) the shopfronts of chain stores are easily recognisable

vi) Mail-order retailing allows people to shop from glossy catalogues

vii) Bulk purchasing allows the large retailers to keep their prices low but

viii) Small shopkeepers in large cities may find customers are discouraged by

ix) Many visitors to Britain are surprised

x) A quick turnover of perishable foods

xi) Shops and stores increase the manufacturers' sales

xii) The larger supermarkets and hypermarkets are being built outside the towns

a) without leaving the comfort of their homes.

b) so that ample car parking facilities are available.

c) restrictions on the parking of cars outside their shops.

d) may limit the range of choice to the consumers.

e) because the shops close so early.

f) usually offer a wide range of services including restaurants and hairdressing salons.

g) allows shopkeepers to offer fresh produce to their customers.

h) to encourage people to come to their shops and buy other products.

i) by advertising the products through their window displays.

j) so as to maximise price.

k) reductions through bulk buying are available 24 hours a day.

l) so that customers know what to expect to find inside, wherever the store is.

9: The office

A. Comprehension

One way of describing the function of the office is the administrative back-up for the organisation. Everyone involved in a business operation has to refer to the office from time to time. Even in the first few minutes of the day the office comes alive. The salesperson telephones from a customer's shop to find out some details about prices, or discounts, or delivery dates. A customer telephones to find what has happened to the order he sent in last week. The short-listed applicants for the new Quality Control Manager's job turn up for their interviews with the Personnel Manager. The Company Secretary arrives earlier than usual to ask whether the Agenda for the Board of Directors' Meeting later in the day has been typed yet. And the office junior brings in the morning mail which he has opened and sorted, and which now needs to be distributed to the various managers. There is a great variety of tasks undertaken in the office and the staff engaged in these operations need to know a great deal about the business. For example, when customers visit the office, or telephone, they naturally expect the staff who deal with them to be knowledgeable. They expect their enquiries to be dealt with courteously, promptly and competently. Receptionists may occupy a comparatively lowly position in the organisational hierarchy, but they create the vital first impression which often determines whether we get the order or not.

The importance of the office is obvious. It is the hub of the communications network for the whole organisation. Technology affects the whole of business, not least the office, and the concept of a completely paperless office is beginning to emerge. Already on many executives' desks there are keyboards or other devices to communicate with the computers which control all the electronic devices in the office. Electronic files are replacing conventional filing cabinets, and intelligent facsimile and copying machines are appearing together with a variety of printers able to print anything from letter-quality characters to four-colour diagrams. Telephone systems are now incorporating a host of facilities from an answering service to video-conferencing.

Video-conferencing involves executives separated by hundreds and perhaps thousands of miles, discussing problems face-to-face on television screens. This in turn conjures up the notion of clerical workers performing many of their daily tasks away from the office, so that offices of the future are not only going to be paperless. They are also going to occupy less space, require fewer staff and allow much shorter working weeks.

These changes will affect a large number of people. The introduction of robotic production lines in factories and new technology in offices will change the way men and women work, and the roles they expect to fulfil. There have already been great changes in the traditional patterns of employment due to new technology, and this seems likely to continue, with implications for both sexes.

Whatever happens as a result of the new technologies, the role of the office will be changed rather than diminished. Most office workers of the future will find themselves seated at multi-function work-stations able to exercise control over routine purchases, sales, market research, production runs and accounting procedures. In other words, we can expect a centralisation of decision-making powers, with the office becoming even more emphatically the very hub of the business.

Your task

Having read the above passage, answer these questions in your own words.
    a)   How would you describe the function of the office?

9: The office

b) To what extent do you think office work is boring?
c) Why do you think the receptionist has a responsible job?
d) What do you understand by the term a paperless office?
e) What sorts of equipment would you expect to find on the desk of an executive in a modern office?
f) Why do office workers need to know a lot about business operations?
g) What would be the effect if office workers were inefficient or poorly motivated?
h) What is 'video-conferencing'?
i) What social implications do you see resulting from the impending changes?

B. Fill in the blanks*

Rewrite this passage filling in the blanks from the list of words below:

Communication

The first requirement in communications between two .... is that they should be on the same wavelength. Thus, when messages are .... by a radio station on a .... of, say, 530 metres, receivers will only pick up the message if they are also on a .... frequency. This explains why it is that people of widely different .... persuasions have difficulty in carrying on meaningful conversations and discussions. A devout person would no doubt have the same difficulty in .... with an atheist. Certainly someone who speaks only Swahili would have great difficulty in communicating with someone who only speaks English, though even this problem could be .... in part by sign-language.

From a business point of view these problems are important when one .... the relationship between management and workers in many firms. It may well be that management and workers are virtually on .... wavelengths. Managements will .... on things like cash flows and return on capital employed which are outside the .... of the workers. There is also a danger that management will fail to read the .... correctly from their customers. Something like market .... represents an attempt to obtain a .... or response which indicates people's.................. to a product or service.

If communication is to be effective, conditions need to be conducive. For example, noise may act as a .... Few people who have used the telephone will not have experienced the .... which occur when there is a .... on the line or when a voice is coming over, but faintly. In much the same way a letter may be sent, but if it goes .... in the post the communication is ....

Psychology is another important factor in communication. When you transmit .... to other people you are dealing with highly .... human beings. The words may give them pleasure as when you .... good news or pay them a .... The words may make them angry as when you are .... or critical. You may make them feel threatened, ... or co-operative, depending on your choice of words or the .... of your voice. In brief, words have to be .... with care.

handled	signals	language	problems
crackle	embarrassed	astray	messages
impart	compliment	considers	concentrate

108

feedback	attitudes	aborted	research
frequency	similar	parties	sensitive
transmitted	different	rude	political
tone	barrier	overcome	conversing

'Can any of you think of one more reason why communication with other people is sometimes difficult? WAKE UP, HOPKINS!'

C. Interpreting data: invoices and statements

When goods are sold on credit (in other words they are to be paid for at a later date) an **invoice** is sent by the seller to the buyer. This document details the goods purchased and shows the price (less any discount) to be charged. There are two basic types of discount allowed to purchasers. **Trade discounts** are given to purchasers as an incentive to buy larger quantities of merchandise. The larger the quantity the higher the rate of discount. **Cash discounts**, by contrast, act as an incentive for the purchaser to pay the account within the stated time span. **Value added tax** is a government tax which the seller has to add on to the bill and pay over to the tax collector in due course.

Monthly **statements** are sent by the sellers to their customers to remind them of any outstanding amounts.

9: The office

An example of each of the documents is given here:

Tomorrow Fashions Ltd
Glengarron House, Petworth, Yorkshire YO9 7KK   Tel 0204 424242 Fax 0204 562211
INVOICE 22nd November 199-   Account No. 2543
Ultra for Men, Westover Road, Barchester BR1 1QQ

Description	Catalogue Reference	Quantity	Price £	Amount due £
Blue Ridge Jeans	P89A	16	18.00	288 00
Paul Duvalier Ties	X77	30	6.50	195.00
Trueleather Belts	Z112	12	12.00	144.00
				627.00
	less 25% Trade discount			155.00
				472.00
	add VAT			82.60
Terms: 5% Cash discount if paid within 28 days				554.60

Tomorrow Fashions Ltd
Glengarron House, Petworth, Yorkshire YO9 7KK   Tel 0204 424242 Fax 0204 562211
STATEMENT 31st November 199-   Account No. 2543
Ultra for Men, Westover Road, Barchester BR1 1QQ

Date		Debit £	Credit £	Balance £
Oct 31	Balance b/f			575.00
Nov 7	Goods	235.00		810.00
Nov 15	Goods	300.00		1,110 00
Nov 22	Goods	554.60		1,664.60
Nov 27	Returns		10.35	1,654.25
Nov 29	Cheque		575.00	1,079.25
E & OE				

Your first task

Study the documents and then answer these questions.

a) What was the total charged to Ultra for Men's account on 22nd November?
b) How much does Ultra for Men owe to Tomorrow Fashions at the end of November?
c) Why might goods have been returned to Tomorrow Fashions on 27th November? Give three possible reasons.
d) Will the entry be on the debit or credit side of the statement when Ultra for Men settle the 22nd November bill?
e) How do the monthly statement and the invoice relate to each other?
f) When comparing the two documents can you spot any apparently trivial errors? Why do you think it is important to correct any mistake?
g) E & OE is an abbreviations of the words Errors and Omissions Excepted. What do you think this phrase means ?

9: The office

Your second task

On checking the Ultra for Men statement you find that they have not claimed the cash discount they were entitled to when they sent in their cheque on 29th November. Write to them on behalf of Tomorrow Fashions explaining how you propose to deal with this situation.

'I don't care what the computer says Miss Harman – your salary for this month is £556.50 and not £999,443.50.'

D. Prepositions and verbs*

Add an appropriate **preposition** to each of the following sentences where indicated.

a) No matter whether the filing system is technologically advanced or based .... traditional methods, records will normally be sorted and stored .... alphabetical order.

b) Material is often microfilmed or fed .... the memory of a computer for future reference.

c) .... the data to be stored will be incoming letters, copies of outgoing letters and a variety of internal memoranda.

d) Stocks need to be available .... the right quantities, ... the right form and place .... the right time.

e) It does not matter .... of the juniors collects the mail .... the mornings.

f) It does not matter .... takes the mail .... the post office .... end of the day.

Add an appropriate **verb** to each of the following sentences where indicated:

a) In designing a filing system it is necessary to .... the costs of keeping the records to the benefits to be gained.

b) A filing system should allow the user to .... information with certainty and without unacceptable delay.

c) When deciding how to file the less obvious items it is useful to .... to the telephone directory to see how they have .... with the problem.

d) Letters need to be .... for errors before they .... the office.

e) The purpose of a form such as an invoice is to .... information in a simple, concise and uniform manner.

f) Forms need to be .... from time to time to .... whether any modifications are required.

E. Correct a letter

You run the office of a local nurseryman and have taken on a young school leaver. She has written her first letter for you to sign. It includes a number of errors, though the facts are as stated. Rewrite the letter in a better style and with the corrections made.

```
                                                        Conway Nurseries
                                                              Highbridge
                                                           Oxford OX6 2WQ

   Garonne & co ltd.
   14/18 Spencer street
   Liverpool L15 6BJ

   Dear sirs,         Ref 1356/67

   The dahlias we ordered from you last month have just arrived and their
   definately not the ones we ordered. We want cactus types because theirs a
   great demand for these among our clientel. You've sent us the wrong ones
   what's more you've charged us 40p each the rate for 100 instead of 35p
   the rate for 500 or more. We ordered 750 so we're entitled to the cheaper
   rate. What's even worse you charged us for carrage although with the
   quantety we ordered you should pay for carrage. We might as well keep the
   dahlias I expect we'll sell them but I'm returning your invoice so you
   can correct your mistakes.

   I still want the cactus dahlias.

   Yours truly



   managing Directer
```

F. Summarising

Your first task

Summarise the following dialogue as briefly as possible without losing any of the essential meaning.

Robert joined Wilkins and Deans, a firm of city stockbrokers just yesterday. This is his first day in the office. He always wondered what it would be like and now he is beginning to find out. Across the room there is the executive to whom he has been assigned, Jeremy Deans. He is one of the junior partners. He is talking on the telephone to a very important client.

    JEREMY: I think you were wise to buy the bonds, Sir George. They've gone up seventeen points since September. If you want to sell I'd advise you to do so soon... ah yes, the Midland stock ... I'm sure we wrote off again for the certificate ... I'll just get the file *(he puts his hand over the mouthpiece and calls to Robert)* ... Fetch me Sir George Donnington-Smythe's file.

Robert looks frantically through the Ds: there is nothing between the file of Alexander Doe and R L Dunne and Co. In the background Jeremy's voice is becoming increasingly agitated.

JEREMY:	It's most unusual. Their registrar's department is usually very efficient. My secretary's fetching the file now ... *(he calls to Robert agitatedly)* Donnington – Donnington-Smythe – look under the Ds!
ROBERT:	I *am* doing. It's not here. *(He tries the Ss – perhaps someone has filed it under Smythe.)*
JEREMY:	I won't keep you waiting, Sir George ... I'll ring you back when I can get my hands on the file. I've got a new secretary and I'm afraid he's not up to the usual Wilkins and Deans standards ...

Robert is furious too because he can hardly be expected to conjure the file up out of thin air. Jeremy leaves him to keep looking for the missing file and almost as soon as he leaves the room a cheerful woman appears.

WOMAN:	Hello, you must be the new assistant. I'm Lynda Mackay. How are you enjoying your first day? Oh by the way I've just been borrowing the Donnington-Smythe file. I'd better put it back before someone needs it.

Your second task

Draft a memorandum such as Jeremy Deans might address to all clerical staff to ensure that this sort of situation does not arise again.

G. For the notice board

It is Robert's second day at Wilkins and Deans. The telephonist is having her coffee break and has switched the line through to Robert. Robert is taking his first call.

ROBERT:	*(Phone to ear)* Wilkins and Deans. Good morning ... Mr Deans, yes, certainly. I'll put you through ... It's a call for you Mr Deans.
JEREMY:	Who is it?
ROBERT:	I didn't catch his name. It's a man, that's all I know.
JEREMY:	You'd better put him through... Jeremy Deans here. Who's that? Oh yes. Well I told you yesterday we're not really interested in a new photocopier at this stage... Yes I'm sure it's an excellent machine ... I'll let you know if I have any second thoughts on the subject.

Jeremy is an important executive, a junior partner. His time is very valuable, and because Robert did not bother to find out who was on the other end of the telephone his new boss was obliged to endure an unwelcome telephone conversation. But Robert is about to make a second blunder as he takes his next call.

ROBERT:	Wilkins and Deans. Good morning ... Mr Deans ... Who is it calling? *(He learns quickly. Mr Deans obviously wants to know who it is calling.)* He doesn't seem to be in the office at the moment. Can you hold the line please. *(He puts the 'phone down and Lynda Mackay appears.)*
LYNDA:	Did you see the late night movie last night?
ROBERT:	*(Wanting to be friendly)* Which one was that?
LYNDA:	The Third Indemnity. There was this great scene on the cliffs at the end when ...

9: The office

ROBERT *(Listening patiently ... then suddenly ...)* Oh my goodness I've forgotten Mrs Hathaway ... Hello Mrs Hathaway ... I'm afraid I haven't been able to trace him ... *(Mercifully Jeremy appears just as he is about to put down the 'phone.)* Oh he's here now Mrs Hathaway ... *(he turns to Jeremy)* It's Mrs Hathaway for you.

After he has dealt with the telephone call Jeremy complains bitterly to his new member of staff:

JEREMY: Mrs Hathaway was ringing from Aberdeen. She was fuming when you put her through to me. Do you realise how much it costs to 'phone from Aberdeen at this time of the day? Another time take the caller's number and I'll ring back. I'm sorry if I lost my temper. You're not alone in making mistakes like that. In fact I think it's worth putting up a notice on the Staff Notice Board about some of the pitfalls in dealing with 'phone calls.

Your task

Draft a brief notice covering as many points as you think important with regard to telephone calls, such as Jeremy might have placed on the staff notice board.

H. Case study

An in-tray exercise

You work in the office of Martin Bright, an estate agent trading under the name of Homehunters, and in the absence of your boss until Wednesday of next week you are required to deal with the day's mail which includes the following offerings. Note that Mr Bright expects you to use your initiative. The only other person in the office is the receptionist.

```
                                                   46 Railway Sidings
                                                            Blimthorpe
                                                  Lincolnshire BE1 1AA

                                                     (yesterday's date)

Homehunters
65, Cathedral Close
Lincoln

Dear Sir,

I am looking for a four bedroomed house for my son who is shortly leaving
the army. He has a wife and three children and is going to work for the
Civil Service in Lincoln. He will have a gratuity from the army of about
£15,000 which he can use. There must be a double garage as both he and
his wife have a car. Do you have any suitable properties?*

Yours sincerely,

Celia Croft

Celia Croft
```

*You have seven or eight properties on your books which might suit Mrs Croft's son.

> The Gables
> Pennington
> Lincoln LN0 0TT
>
> (yesterday's date)
>
> Mr Martin Bright
> Homehunters
> 65 Cathedral Close
> Lincoln LN5 6GA
>
> Dear Martin,
>
> The client you brought round last week seems very interested in the house. He has gone back to London for a few days but he said he will be coming back next weekend to make an offer. I do not wish to lower the price below £85,000 but he kept on about the place needing decorating and I suppose I have to be realistic with the price.
>
> Incidentally his name is Ponsford* I think and he seems to have been in to see you at some time. I do hope you can get a sale for me. It has been three months since The Gables went on the market.
>
> Best wishes,
>
> *George Fry*
>
> George Fry

*Mr Ponsford and his wife came to the office after they visited Mr Fry. They also seem to be interested in another property they visited.

> **R.E. Stephenson & Sons Ltd**
> Renton Works, Dewsbury, Yorkshire Y022 9LL   Telephone 0924 662211
>
> (yesterday's date)
>
> Homehunters
> Cathedral Close
> Lincoln LN5 6GA
>
> Dear Sirs,
>
> Thank you for your recent letter and judging from the details given, our Universal Model would be ideal for your requirements since it is particularly good at reproducing photographs. About six weeks ago we supplied a similar machine to one of your competitors in Lincoln and the feedback is very favourable.
>
> We understand you are looking for an urgent replacement for your photocopier and it so happens that our Mr Henderson will be in your neighbourhood on Monday of next week and could give you a full demonstration at that time. He could leave the copier for up to seven days without obligation. This would give ample opportunity to put the machine to the test and I am sure you will be delighted with it.
>
> Please let me know by return whether you are interested.
>
> Yours sincerely,
>
> *Francis Caton*
>
> Francis Caton
> Sales Manager

I. Write a letter

You work for a firm of grocery wholesalers, Allardyce and Grimble Ltd of 16 Castle Way, Edinburgh, Scotland EH1 9HG. You have been given a list of overdue accounts and asked to prepare a standard letter reminding these customers of the amount outstanding and asking them for prompt payment. You are also asked to remind them of the availability of a 5% cash discount if they pay their accounts within 28 days of the date of the invoice You can address the letter to the first customer on the list but the letter should be suitable to send to all similar customers, with just names, addresses and amounts changed.

Name & Address	Period Overdue		Total
	1 month £	2 months £	£
Sandy McTavish & Co Blackfriars St., Edinburgh EH8 8JT	500.76	200.00	700.76
Blakes Superstores 6-8 High Reach, Edinburgh EH8 6JP	2,675.80	1,700.00	4,375.80
McDougall & Green Riordan Street, Edinburgh EH2 4FG	135.66	200.00	335.66
Paul Singh Bennett Street, Edinburgh EHI 3SS	905.00	133.66	1,038.66

J. Complete the sentences

Complete the following sentences using your own words.

1. Office equipment and machinery often ...
2. A letter with finger marks on it ...
3. We have been very patient in allowing ...
4. If office workers are given comfortable seating ...
5. If you quote the lowest possible price ...
6. When you plan to buy new office desks ...
7. A monthly statement of account ...
8. The invoice is a very important document because ...
9. Incoming registered letters should be entered in a special register and a signature obtained from ...
10. In some offices all incoming letters are opened before ...
11. Letters marked 'Personal' or 'Private' should not be opened ...
12. When an incoming letter is received, check that all enclosures are included, then ...

K. Vocabulary*

reminder	catalogue	retrieval	archives	summary
excess	minute	colleague	signatory	emphasis
agenda	stereotype	complaint	feedback	receptionist
docket	tidiness	document	diary	acknowledgement
recipient	supervisor	impolite	query	telecommunication

Match the words above with the dictionary definitions which follow.

1. Stress laid on words, facts or ideas, to indicate the relative importance attached to them.
2. Formal written evidence of a transaction, such as the title deeds to a property.
3. A form of receipt.

9: The office

4. A person employed by an organisation to receive clients, find out what they want, and generally cater for them until they are taken over by someone else.
5. A response to a communication which indicates how effective it has been
6. A habit of arranging work in a neat manner
7. A person who receives goods, information or services
8. Lacking in common courtesy
9. An expression of doubt or disagreement.
10. The place in which a business stores those records which no longer need to be immediately accessible.
11. The recovery of stored data.
12. A list of goods usually in alphabetical order or under headings, for easy reference.
13. Someone with whom you enjoy a professional relationship in your workplace.
14. Information transmitted over long distances by cable, telegraph, telephone or radio.
15. The expression of a grievance
16. The person who has added his or her name to a letter or document
17. A replica, reproduction or facsimile.
18. A brief account which dispenses with details.
19. Items of business to be conducted at a meeting.
20. The essence of the discussion at a meeting, formally recorded.
21. A book used by executives for planning future activities.
22. A voucher recording payment for work done, customs duties paid etc
23. A person in charge of a group of workers.
24. Beyond the stated limits.
25. Something to prod the memory.

L. True or false*

Tick the column according to whether you think the statement is false or true.

		True	False
1.	A large open plan office ...		
a)	gives more natural lighting than an equivalent area of enclosed rooms.	☐	☐
b)	gives more privacy than enclosed rooms.	☐	☐
c)	allows managers and supervisors to keep an eye on their staff.	☐	☐
d)	makes it more difficult for staff to get to know each other.	☐	☐
e)	could create problems when staff are being interviewed.	☐	☐
f)	is preferable to enclosed rooms when important clients are being entertained.	☐	☐
g)	allows artistic and pleasant environments to be introduced.	☐	☐
h)	is more difficult to clean than closed rooms.	☐	☐

9: The office

2. Office equipment

   a) When you use a paper-clip to hold papers together they cannot work loose. ☐ ☐

   b) Important papers should be placed in the wastepaper basket. ☐ ☐

   c) When you arrive at the office in the morning you can expect to find incoming mail in your in-tray. ☐ ☐

   d) If a file is missing from the filing cabinet it is probably being looked at by someone else. ☐ ☐

   e) In many offices if you want to transfer an incoming 'phone call to another department you have to get back to the switchboard operator. ☐ ☐

   f) Having a fax machine in the office means you can convey a message to any company in the world at any time of the day or night. ☐ ☐

   g) Armed with staples and a stapler a mail clerk can fasten loose papers together so they do not become parted. ☐ ☐

   h) Photocopiers offering colour facilities are essential equipment in every office. ☐ ☐

3. Documentation

   a) When goods are sold on credit it is usual for the seller to send the purchaser an invoice giving details of the transaction. ☐ ☐

   b) An invoice will give details of any trade and cash discount given. ☐ ☐

   c) Suppliers are usually provided with a monthly statement showing details of any amounts due from them. ☐ ☐

   d) A delivery note usually accompanies the goods when they are sent to the purchaser. ☐ ☐

   e) Paperwork is often in duplicate or triplicate to avoid unnecessary repetition of form-filling. ☐ ☐

M. Response to telex

You are Office Manager for Jiminez SA, a Toledo company which buys animal skins. It converts these into leather then makes them up into high quality belts, clothing and furnishings which it exports all over the world. This morning you received the following telex from London, where the Chief Executive, Luis Jiminez, has been for the past month:

```
Arriving Madrid Monday next 09.30 accompanied by Mr George Baker
Head of Universal Stores Inc who wants to see our stocks of leather
fashion goods. Is bringing his wife. Arrange meeting with marketing
team am lunch with self and my wife midday and dinner for six at
Alvaro's in evening. Warn all staff. Baker wants to see factory and
meet people. Could lead to big order from Universal. We must quote
best prices. He is also visiting other factories before he places
orders.

L Jiminez
```

Your tasks

1. Make a list of the staff you would expect to notify.
2. Who would you expect to be invited to the dinner at Alvaro's restaurant? What arrangements would you make with them?
3. Draft a memorandum you would place on the staff notice-board.

N. Discussion topic

The grapevine

While the office the hub of the official communications network for the organisation, informal channels also exist. The word 'grapevine' is applied to the lines of communication in this informal network, a network which will include friends and acquaintances meeting in the canteen or travelling home on the bus or train together. There is a multiplying effect as one person talks to others, who in turn talk to others. In a comparatively short space of time a large number of people can be informed – or misinformed. Why does the grapevine exist? First, because people at work will want to talk to each other; there will be social as well as professional interaction. People want to impress each other with information they have – important information. It is sometimes known as the jungle telegraph – a network of channels for rumour and gossip.

Many of the stories are likely to emerge from the office, which is both the source and the destination of most information. The communication, essentially verbal, is prone to distortion by its very nature. Added to which it is liable to embellishment to make it more interesting to the recipients. Half-truths and outright falsehoods are sometimes added by accident or design and these can be harmful to the organisation.

Another feature of the grapevine is that bad news is more likely to be repeated than good news. The same feature is found in the press. The public will buy newspapers which offer sensation rather than dull, routine news. It is difficult to trace the source of the rumour and gossip, and so it is likely to prove difficult to halt a flow of harmful misinformation.

Managers are not always the victims. They may sometimes use the grapevine for their own ends, feeding in unfounded but carefully devised rumours of their own. An example would be where a manager leaves copies of letters 'accidentally' lying around for a certain member of staff to see, or mentions something 'in confidence' knowing that the news will spread through the organisation like a forest fire.

The best way to deal with the problems of the grapevine is to keep the staff as fully informed as possible about management's intentions and decisions. The subversive activities of the grapevine can be largely eliminated if staff become involved in management's plans and participate in the decision-making process.

Questions

1. How would you deal with the problem of the grapevine in the office?
2. To what extent do you think staff should be informed of management's plans and decisions?
3. In what circumstances, if any, do you think employers should let employees see the firm's accounts?
4. Do you think there are some things which employees should never be told? What are they?
5. Do you think the grapevine is also found in political life, and that the game of politics is also sometimes played in the office?

9: The office

6. Over a cup of coffee one day a respected colleague gives you some alarming news about some new appointments which are to be made. It appears that some outsiders are to be brought into the organisation and this would effectively block any promotions for you – at least for the immediate future. He has told you 'in strict confidence'. How would you react?

10: Business meetings

A. Comprehension

A committee normally comprises between three and twenty members. It is headed by a chairperson who has the power to control the discussion. The abilities of the chairperson are likely to be reflected in the effectiveness of the committee. He (or she) will be expected to identify the problem for the committee members, consider the available facts with them, and encourage them to express their views.

The use of a committee in business can be advocated whenever the normal chain of command is inappropriate. The committee allows people from different departments and specialisms to come together to deal with problems of common concern. They also allow people from different levels in the organisational hierarchy to meet and confer, for example in a joint consultation committee where representatives from the management side can consult directly with worker representatives.

The committee is essentially a communication device. The problem in a large organisation is to ensure a two-way flow of instructions (downwards) and feedback (upwards). It is often possible for a management to delegate the responsibility for making decisions in non-critical areas to committees, though it is important to remember that the Board of Directors (at the apex of the organisational hierarchy) is also a committee and functions accordingly. Minutes are required to be kept of the decisions taken at the meetings which become a record of the business transacted and the decisions reached. The proceedings are required to follow the order set out in the agenda which is distributed to the members before the meeting.

Under no circumstances can voting take place unless a quorum (a minimum number of members) is present. The quorum will be laid down in the committee's terms of reference. A motion (or resolution) is the term used to describe the point in the meeting when a decision is being considered. One of the members will normally make the proposition and will then need to find a seconder – someone who supports it. The wording of the resolution is very important as the committee will be bound by it if more than a half of the members present vote in favour. The only way a member can avoid the collective responsibility for the decision is by resigning.

Another form of meeting used in business is what is sometimes described as a 'command meeting'. In this case the manager calls his subordinates together and uses the occasion either to tell them what he wants from them or to listen and exchange ideas with them. It is a very effective way of ensuring that the team is kept fully informed. Some managers have these meetings on a regular basis, say every Friday afternoon at three o'clock, so that the coming week's programme can be discussed. The meeting can coincide with a tea break and this gives the group an opportunity to socialise before getting down to the serious business. These meetings are in no way comparable with the committee meetings since they are very much a vehicle for the individual manager. He can use the time to sell ideas to his team, seek their aid in finding solutions to problems, or simply inform and instruct them.

From the workers' point of view perhaps the most important meetings are those conducted by their trade unions. As well as the local branch meetings there are regional and national executive committee meetings which are all conducted on a formal basis. Shop stewards committees operate at factory level and play an important role in communicating workers' grievances to management.

10: Business meetings

Your task

Having read the above passage answer these questions in your own words.

a) Why does the chairperson of a committee need to be chosen carefully?
b) When is the formation of a committee justified?
c) Who would you expect to find in a Joint Consultation Committee?
d) In what sense is the Board of Directors a committee?
e) How does the committee reach a decision?
f) How is the decision recorded?
g) What is a command meeting? How does it differ from a committee?
h) What options are available to the member of a committee who strongly disagrees with a resolution passed by the majority of the committee's members?

B. Fill in the blanks*

Rewrite this passage filling in the blanks from the list of words below.

When a manager invites his subordinates to a meeting and .... to exchange ideas with them, certain .... can be expected. Almost inevitably they will show a greater interest in, and .... with, the things that are happening around them. People generally like to be involved. The .... to participate is .... for their egos – flattery which will harm no-one. They like to feel 'in on things' and in any case they will probably have .... contributions to make to the discussions. They can be expected to know more about their .... jobs than the manager and should be able to help improve the .... of the decisions he finally makes.

One of the problems faced by the manager is that in choosing .... alternatives he has to .... the reactions of the subordinates to the decision. If they are highly motivated even a bad decision may work out favourably, and conversely, if they lack .... for the actions they are asked to take, even an otherwise .... decision may turn out to be wrong. By bringing his subordinates into the decision-making .... the manager is able to learn what their .... would be before 'taking the plunge'. He should find there is a greater willingness to .... his authority and .... grievances. He might also find that any changes will be more readily accepted.

The benefits attaching to subordinate .... might even show up in the statistics. One could expect the more .... atmosphere to be .... in the figures for absenteeism, lateness and .... turnover.

There are however certain dangers .... in inviting subordinates to participate in decision making. Some may feel that the manager is paid to make decisions and has no right to .... ideas from them. Others may have little to .... or take up a great deal of time making .... irrelevant points. Furthermore such meetings can be expensive.

pleasant	labour	proceeds	benefits
invitation	particular	fewer	identification
poach	predict	reactions	enthusiasm
sound	between	valuable	participation

10: Business meetings

quality	involved	contribute	irrelevant
reflected	routine	food	accept

C. Case study

Permaplastics Ltd

You are Personal Assistant to James Pike, Works Manager at Permaplastics Ltd. The company make a variety of plastic containers for the pharmaceutical industry. Mass production techniques are generally in use but some lines are reserved for small batch production, coping with specialty products for hospitals. At a recent meeting of the Joint Consultation Committee it was suggested there should be more women supervisors in the factory. Mr Pike has asked you to let him have a brief but formal report on the subject (maximum 200 words) setting out your views. He has asked you to consider the following points specifically:

1. Seven of the present supervisors are due to retire during the coming twelve months.
2. There is a closed shop arrangement at Permaplastics (i.e. all the workers have to belong to a trade union).
3. Over the next two years the production lines are likely to become fully robotic and one in four of the workforce is likely to become redundant. This information has not so far been made public.
4. He is going to have to speak on the subject of women supervisors at the next Works Council and is hoping your report will give him some help.
5. The only statistics available are shown below.

	Totals	*Aged under 30*		*Aged 30 and above*	
		Men	*Women*	*Men*	*Women*
Line workers	276	37	153	69	17
Supervisors	33	4	1	23	5

D. Their, there and they're*

Fill in the blanks in the following sentences with words in the heading, then rewrite the sentences with the words included.

i) .... is a deep-rooted democratic tradition that people have a right to speak on matters which affect .... interests.

ii) The union representative said, '................ entitled to express .... views.'

iii) When people come together to discuss problems .... may be a development of cliques in which case .... objectivity could suffer.

iv) 'I don't see the point of asking them for .... opinions if .... not interested' said the supervisor.

v) '................ is still no news from Headquarters,' said the union branch secretary, '................ certainly taking .... time.'

vi) .... are some chairpeople who tend to dominate committees.

10: Business meetings

'Mr Chairman, as my train leaves in ten minutes, I propose we accept the amendment.'

E. Multiple choice*

Choose the phrase, A, B, or C, which **best** completes each sentence, and tick the appropriate box.

1. Of course the costs incurred in staff meetings may be justified
   A. but that is no excuse for wasting the staff's time.
   B. but at least management should be aware of them.
   C. but that is no excuse for wasting management time.

2. Decisions reached in committees may sometimes be compromises
   A. which is another way of saying they are useless.
   B. and that is always a good thing.
   C. or, as it is sometimes said, a camel was a horse designed by committee.

3. The careful recording of decisions and the writing of minutes involve time and expense
   A. even after the formal meeting has ended.
   B. only before the meeting has started.
   C. and a great deal of effort by everyone.

4. A number of different ideas can be put forward in a meeting
   A. but too many cooks can spoil the broth.
   B. and everyone will be satisfied with that.
   C. but that will satisfy no-one.

5. The interaction between members from different sections of the organisation
   A. will ensure that people understand each others' problems.
   B. should help people to understand each others' problems.
   C. will lead to frictions and discontent.

6. While each member has an equal say in committee proceedings
   A. none of them want to contribute.
   B. they will all want to say more than their share.
   C. they do not necessarily have an equal stake in the outcome.

7. In a business setting the committee is often used to
   A. bridge the gap between departments.
   B. encourage people to get to know each other.
   C. communicate with people outside the organisation.

8. Since committee decisions are collective
   A. there is no need to record them.
   B. they can be reached quickly.
   C. no single individual can be held responsible for them.

9. The board of directors constitutes a committee
   A. elected by management.
   B. elected by shareholders.
   C. chosen by management and workers.

10. Everywhere in life it is to be seen that progress depends on
    A. the exchange of ideas.
    B. the demolition of one group by another.
    C. bitter conflicts between those with opposing ideals.

F. Summarising

Summarise the following dialogue as briefly as possible without losing any of the essential meaning.

Unitcare PLC are a national firm of builders producing luxury apartments. Four of their senior executives, Tom Fenton, Victor Freer, Colin Webster and Laura Blanchard are meeting to discuss plans for a new retirement village in Blackpool.

TOM: It sounds a great idea. People are living longer these days. There are plenty of senior citizens who would like to keep their independence as long as possible. You could say it's an opportunity to grow old with dignity. I think we could start with a SWOT analysis. Strengths – weaknesses – opportunities – and threats. Perhaps I could bring you in at this stage Victor. What are your ideas?

VICTOR: Well, as you say, there are more and more retired people. I suppose one of the strengths is that retired people don't want big living rooms or lots of bedrooms. We can get more apartments into a building and get a better return on our investment.

COLIN: Some of the companies down south are offering this sort of accommodation for the lifetime of a retired couple

10: Business meetings

LAURA:	How does that work?
COLIN:	The purchasers have to be over sixty-five. The older they are the less they have to pay for the lease. When they die the title to the property reverts to the developer.
LAURA:	You mean they lose their capital.
COLIN:	They don't, but their families do. You've got to remember they get the accommodation for a lower outlay when they first move in. The generally save about 20% on the price.
LAURA:	I'm surprised the old people go for that.
COLIN:	Oh they do! It's quite popular.
TOM:	I believe they provide a warden service too.
COLIN:	Yes, they do.
VICTOR:	That'll make it rather expensive.
COLIN:	Well, they pay a service charge for that sort of thing.
TOM:	That's certainly one of the options open to us. Another idea is to include a couple of rooms where they can meet socially.
LAURA:	That sounds a good idea. I think you have to accept that loneliness is one of the curses of old age. I think a social club – or something like that – would be attractive.
VICTOR:	We might even find it's self-financing if we can get some reasonable bar takings.
COLIN:	Hold on, Victor. We're talking about retired people. They're not the original big-spenders.
VICTOR:	No, but that doesn't mean they're paupers. The sort of people we're catering for will often be getting good pensions.
TOM:	I've got an appointment in a few minutes so we need to wind up for now. You all seem reasonably enthusiastic. Laura, can I ask you to prepare a discussion paper for the next meeting. Consult with Colin and Victor of course. Thank you.

G. Write a speech

You have been asked to make a short speech at the next meeting of the Works Council of Sunacre Laundries Ltd. There will be nine workers' representatives and three managers at the meeting. Your manager has asked you to put forward the case for the introduction of creches at the laundry so that mothers with young babies can bring them to the laundry and hand them over to professional child-minders while they are at work. He does not expect the speech to last for more than five minutes but he has given you some key words (shown below) which he hopes will help you in your preparation. You may add any further ideas of your own. You are required to draft a speech so that you could, if necessary, read straight from your draft. Bear in mind he has asked you to speak in favour of the scheme.

convenience	*warm and safe play areas*	*more young mothers can be recruited*
less absenteeism	*qualified staff in attendance*	*rooms available in annexe*
less stress	*staff's views requested*	*payment for the service?*
	less lateness	*children between two and five*

10: Business meetings

H. Meanings

First read the passage below. Then explain the meanings of the words and phrases which have been highlighted.

> The effectiveness of any committee is inevitably determined by the actions of its chairperson. The chairperson is responsible for **compliance with the technicalities.** For example, the meeting must have been **properly convened** and a **quorum of members must be present**. Furthermore proper notice of the meeting must have been given.
>
> The **charisma** and skill of the chairperson will decide to a large extent how much work the committee does and whether relationships are **harmonious or strained**. A good chairperson will insist that when any members speak their remarks are **addressed to the chair**. This is not simply a matter of **extending** courtesy to the chairperson. The chairperson is **deemed impartial** and should not take sides in any dispute other than with regard to a matter of **procedure**. Disagreements will be less personal when the arguments have to go through an **intermediary** and there will be less chance of **personality clashes.**
>
> In any meeting there will be some members who find it easy to **interpose their arguments.** Others will find it more difficult. It may be a matter of experience in committees, strength of character, age and **status** compared to other members. The good chairperson will **spot the difficulties being encountered** and bring these members into the discussion at an appropriate moment.
>
> 'Yes,' the chairperson might say, 'I can see you feel very strongly about that particular matter, Mr Hughes. Does anyone have a **contrary opinion**? What about you Miss Latimer?'
>
> **The ball is in Miss Latimer's court.** The chairperson has ensured that everyone will listen to what she has to say.

I. Prepositions, conjunctions and pronouns

Add appropriate words where there are blanks in the sentences below. Rewrite each sentence indicating (in brackets) against each word whether it is a preposition, conjunction or pronoun.

i) In most factories a worker is .... no obligation to join a union .... the shop stewards may try to persuade

ii) If young executives wish to be successful .... business they should be able to communicate confidently .... that is what is required.

iii) It was the chairman .... cast his vote against the motion, ... he regretted his action later.

iv) It is difficult for a junior member of staff to stand .... to a senior manager in a meeting .... it may sometimes be necessary.

v) Sometimes in a group discussion .... order .... courtesy prevail.

vi) I took my courage .... my hands, stared .... the table at the managing director and told .... I disagreed with her suggestion.

J. Complete the sentences

Complete the following sentences using your own words.

10: Business meetings

1. The purpose of a committee meeting is to ...
2. The chairperson of a committee ...
3. When two members of a committee disagree ...
4. Sometimes a manager calls a meeting of his subordinates ...
5. ... because it is necessary to conclude the meeting.
6. ... when a personality clash is looming.
7. Communication involves the transmission of ...
8. One can see the committee as an instrument of democracy because ...
9. A motion becomes a resolution when ...
10. ... elected by the shareholders.

K. Vocabulary*

interview	proposer	referees	relevant	adjournment
resolution	grievances	neutral	quorum	command
co-option	adequate	audience	agenda	casting
amendment	seconder	minutes	liaison	procedures
apologies	motion	auditors	convene	report

Match the words listed above with the dictionary definitions which follow.

1. The company chairperson will be expected to give this at the Annual General Meeting.
2. The breaking-off of a meeting. The postponement of further discussion.
3. A detailed list of items to be discussed.
4. Notices of meetings must always be this.
5. The sort of meeting which might lead to the offer of a job.
6. Those whom you would be concentrating on when making a speech.
7. A firm considering employing you would contact them before inviting you for an interview.
8. Might be reduced if people are allowed to participate in the making of decisions.
9. An abbreviated record of what was said during a meeting.
10. A proposition to be voted upon.
11. Someone who makes a formal recommendation at a meeting.
12. What the chairperson of a committee meeting should strive to be.
13. A formal decision reached at a meeting.
14. The minimum number of members needing to be present to make a committee meeting legal.
15. The sort of meeting called by a manager who wishes to face his subordinates.
16. Discussion in a meeting should always be this.
17. A suggestion to alter the wording of a motion.
18. Will need to be appointed at a company's Annual General Meeting.
19. Someone who supports a formal proposal in the meeting.
20. To call an Annual General Meeting.

21. This will be necessary between the secretary and chairperson in a committee meeting.
22. Should be conveyed to the chairperson if you cannot attend a meeting.
23. The power available to a committee to ask others to attend or serve on the committee.
24. The chairperson's vote when the committee is undecided.
25. The rules governing the conduct of a meeting.

L. Executive discussion*

Alvaro Garcia's family have produced furniture for the Spanish domestic market for generations, but within the last decade operations have been extended to other European markets, particularly the UK, and Alvaro's company have now set up a large factory for assembling furniture in South London.

Alvaro recently flew over to London to give his subsidiary the once-over. His report has now been made available to his London team who are wondering what the outcome is going to be. Alvaro's son, Felipe, has come over to find out how the London subsidiary is responding. His first meeting is with the Chief Accountant, Adrian Trigg, in Mr Trigg's office.

FELIPE: My father's report seems to have created a bit of a stir here in London.

ADRIAN: It certainly does.

FELIPE: His main concern is the spiralling costs.

ADRIAN: I'm only too aware of the problem. We've got to try to contain expenditure. If our costs rise, our prices have to rise, and that puts our sales team under pressure.

FELIPE: I understand you've got a budgetary control system in operation. How does it work?

ADRIAN: Like all control systems. We set standards – or targets. Then decide how much we can spend on new machinery, on advertising, and pay. It's pay which is tending to be the problem for us.

FELIPE: Why's that?

ADRIAN: Well, the unions expect to get pay increases in line with inflation.

FELIPE: It's much the same in Spain.

ADRIAN: But your inflation is less than ours.

FELIPE: I believe it is.

ADRIAN: We try to follow the guidelines you lay down, but our expenditure on labour is usually over the limit and that puts pressure on the other cost centres.

FELIPE: How?

ADRIAN: We're always trying to keep the other areas under tight control, but what do you do when the Production Manager says, 'One of the sanding machines has broken down!' Do I stand firm and say, 'Sorry that's just too bad'? Or the Marketing Manager says, 'I need to spend more on advertising.' Am I supposed to say, 'You can't do that, you've already spent all you're entitled to spend this month, and the contingency reserve has been used up to meet the latest pay claims'? 'We've got to

10: Business meetings

advertise!' he says, 'The market leaders have started an enormous advertising campaign. We're beginning to lose our market share.'

Felipe now meets Oliver Haines, the Chief Executive of the subsidiary, in his office.

FELIPE: ... My father was also concerned about communication problems here. What did you think about his comments?

OLIVER: Whenever you get a company as large as this you're going to have communication problems. I'm always getting frustrated about the time it takes to get replies from Madrid, even with fax and telex.

FELIPE: You should be able to get replies within 24 hours. I realise there's a problem when neither my father nor I are at the office. We are the only ones who speak English.

OLIVER: I remember one case recently when I was trying to find out how to tender for some furniture for the Burlington Hotel Group, and when I did get a reply it was too late ... the bird had flown.

FELIPE: Yes, I heard about that. It was unfortunate – unavoidable – but I think there are some things you can do to improve the communications between Madrid and London.

OLIVER: Of course, the obvious area for improvement is language. Out of 70 sales and administration staff only one can speak Spanish... and she's Isabel Thornton, the Spanish Office Manager ...

FELIPE: ...and none of the senior executives can speak a word of Spanish. My father feels especially concerned about this.

OLIVER: Understandably ... I've been discussing this with the staff and they've come up with a number of useful ideas. One of them was that we exchange staff between London and Madrid ... People at the same level... with language improvement as the objective.

FELIPE: That sounds interesting. Of course, it assumes they already know enough of the language to benefit from the exchange.

OLIVER: I've got four or five fairly senior members of staff who would be willing to act as guinea pigs.

FELIPE: You'll have to give me their details. Maybe I could meet them before I go back ...

In the canteen, an informal discussion is going on between a number of the staff (Connie, a Designer, Nicholas, the Data Processing Manager, and Michele, a Personnel Officer) who have heard rumours about the invitation to spend six months in Madrid – learning Spanish.

CONNIE: I've started taking Spanish at evening classes. I haven't got very far – but it's very interesting. The trouble is I can't see the company letting me go to Spain for six months until I am more fluent.

NICHOLAS: If I thought I could have six months in Spain, I'd go on a crash course tomorrow.

MICHELE: I don't see why Isabel Thornton can't start Spanish classes here.

CONNIE: Of course, she *is* Spanish, isn't she?

10: Business meetings

MICHELE   She's lived in England for the last five years, so her English is good, too, and I think she could really help us. I know she's taught her children to speak Spanish. Her daughter went on to university to study languages.

NICHOLAS: If Isabel is the teacher, I'll be the first student to enrol!

Your task

Tick the box following the statement which answers the question most accurately.

1. What does Adrian Trigg see as the main difficulty in keeping in line with the financial targets set by Madrid?
    A. They do not allow for the fact that prices are higher in the UK. ☐
    B. They do not allow for the fact that the UK workers are claiming higher wages to meet rising costs. ☐
    C. They are unrealistic. ☐

2. How should the success of the UK subsidiary be judged?
    A. By its expenditure. ☐
    B. By its revenue. ☐
    C. By its profit. ☐

3. Why should the senior staff of the Spanish subsidiary in the UK learn Spanish?
    A. So they can interact more effectively with the parent company. ☐
    B. So they can have a six month trip to Spain. ☐
    C. So they can understand the instructions given to them. ☐

4. What would be the best justification for switching staff between London and Madrid?
    A. It would help them to improve their English (or Spanish) ☐
    B. It would give them a break from their routine jobs. ☐
    C. It would reward those with ambition. ☐

5. What is meant by a 'crash course' in Spanish as referred to by Nicholas, the Data Processing Manager?.
    A. A short intensive course. ☐
    B. A long intensive course. ☐
    C. A dangerous course. ☐

11: Personnel management

A. Comprehension

The Personnel Department is concerned with the provision and maintenance of a workforce. There are two dimensions to the task. The first is to ensure that employees are available in the right numbers, at the right time and with the necessary skills for the jobs that need to be done This is the dimension of quantity. The second dimension relates to the quality of the workforce and is evidenced by the workers' enthusiasm and motivation. Highly motivated workers will be more productive.

The personnel function in an organisation has many facets. There will have to be contact with line and departmental managers to ascertain staffing requirements. Applicants for jobs will need to be interviewed and recommendations made for appointments. Procedures will need to be developed for upgradings and promotions as well as selection. After staff have been appointed induction programmes will need to be organised so that the new recruits can fit in as efficient members of the team as soon as possible Further training may be necessary, either in the firm (on-job) or at college (off-job). Such programmes need to be arranged to fit in with the normal work schedules.

The whole framework of pay is obviously of concern to personnel, including salary scales, overtime and bonus payments where appropriate. The calculations are complicated somewhat by flexible working hours which give staff the opportunity to choose their own attendance times within certain limits. There is generally a core time during which all staff are expected to be present

The records maintained for all employees will show the remuneration paid, together with tax deductions, and will include details of training, examination successes, lateness and absences There is, in effect, a personal profile for every member of staff

In the United Kingdom, there is a legal requirement that every employee must receive a written statement setting out the terms and conditions of their employment The statement will include a job title which could be relevant if the employee is subsequently dismissed for refusing some task for which he was not employed. Modern employment law accepts that the employee's job cannot be taken from him unfairly. Any employee who is dismissed unfairly may be entitled to compensation where an industrial tribunal considers the dismissal was wrongful or unfair. When a worker is no longer required he or she is made redundant and this entitles him or her to compensation depending on his or her length of service and pay. Workers cannot be discriminated against either because of their race or their sex, by law.

The Personnel Department has an overall responsibility for carrying out the policies of the Board of Directors in relation to staffing, but is also expected to help in the formulation of that policy. A vital area of involvement would be the negotiations with trade unions and the shop stewards, listening to grievances and attempting to cope with them, but also attempting to anticipate them. The Department should be concerned with all matters of welfare, from lighting and heating through to safety and personal hygiene.

No matter how automated production becomes, the roles of people are central in every business. The most expensive equipment is ineffective in the hands of careless or disgruntled workers and the Personnel Department carries the main responsibility for ensuring that morale is high in the organisation.

Your task

Having read the above passage, answer these questions in your own words.

11: Personnel management

a) According to this article what are the prime objectives of the Personnel Department?

b) What needs to be done after staff have been appointed?

c) How is the Personnel Department involved in the payment of wages and salaries?

d) How does the law protect the employee?

e) What do you think might be included in an induction programme?

f) What problems would you expect if an off job training programme was to be arranged?

g) What do you think would be the purpose of interviewing candidates for a job?

h) What does an Industrial Tribunal do?

i) Why should the Personnel Department be concerned about the employees' attitude to work?

j) How do you think grievances should be dealt with?

B. Fill in the blanks*

Fill in the blanks in this passage, using words from the list given below:

From time to time it is necessary to check the performance of staff, both .... and collectively. A manager will need to appraise performance so that he can see how best it might be .... There is always likely to be a gap between what could be .... and what is actually attained and the manager's aim should be to ensure that this .... is minimised. It should be borne in mind that the business organisation is normally hierarchical – like a family tree – and the manager's performance is itself subject to surveillance by superiors.

The appraisal often takes place as a .... to the annual salary reviews. Where there is a pay .... the question might simply be, 'Has this person worked well enough to .... the next increment?' Or where there is a possible .... the question would be, 'Has this person done enough to .... promotion?' In these instances the .... of appraisal is to provide a yes or no response. However, there may be a need to choose between .... for promotion. This can be a .... problem for a manager because, where he has a number of .... on his team, he risks demotivating a number of them when he chooses someone else.

Various factors such as workrate and .... of work will need to be brought into account. In some jobs these are easy to .... A salesperson who has sold £100,000 worth of goods in a month has obviously done .... better than a .... who has only sold half as much. For other jobs the .... is much more difficult if not impossible. For example, how does one assess the performance of a hotel .... or a chef?

The manager should also reckon with .... and punctuality. If someone stays away from work it is not only a .... of whether or not they should be paid for their absence. It is .... to a goalkeeper in a football match deciding not to turn out for the second half. Of course when a person is seriously .... they cannot go to work, but there are sometimes very .... reasons offered for absence. Lateness also needs to be .... Continuing the football analogy, it is like the centre back who turns up to the match fifteen minutes late with his side already three goals down. It is not .... to compare a business with a football team,

133

11: Personnel management

firstly, because .... clubs are businesses anyway, and secondly, because we are talking about .... and team effort in both cases.

flimsy	teamwork	unreasonable	receptionist
thorny	deserve	individually	shortfall
prelude	attendance	professional	upgrading
akin	indisposed	judgement	hopefuls
quality	candidates	merit	purpose
scale	achieved	improved	colleague
question	measure	discouraged	significantly

C. Case study

EDU Plastics

This company produces a variety of plastic toys for young children. The range of products includes bendy dolls, toy computers and construction kits. The company is having to contend with a lot of competition from overseas, particularly from Taiwan and Korea. All the senior executives have just attended a meeting with Gordon Mansell, the Managing Director, at which he impressed upon them the need to lower costs by at least 10% in the coming year.

'It's a matter of survival,' he had said, 'If our toys are dearer, people aren't going to buy them. If people don't buy our toys we are going to have to close down the factory. If the factory closes down we will all be out of a job.'

Bill Miller, the Personnel Manager at the Tring Plant, could see his point, but felt the ball was mainly in the court of the marketing people and the accountants, but he changed his mind when he got back to his office He pored over some statistics which had just been presented to him in the form of bar charts. They showed the absentee rates at the company's two main plants since they were set up just over four years ago. During this time the average number of workers employed was about 100 at each of the plants, and the nature of the work was such that there were always about the same number of women and men employed. The female workers tended to be unskilled and under the age of 30, while about half the men were engineers or craftsmen

One of the only differences between the Trenton and Tring Plants is that flexible working hours were introduced at the Trenton Plant at the end of the first year of operation Bill finds the scheme for the other plant is contained in a small section of the company's Staff Handbook. It reads:

Flexible working hours

Each employee on the production line is able to choose the starting and finishing times each day, so long as prior approval of the appropriate line supervisor is obtained. Employees must attend during the coretime each day, but the remaining hours can be absorbed within the flexbands.

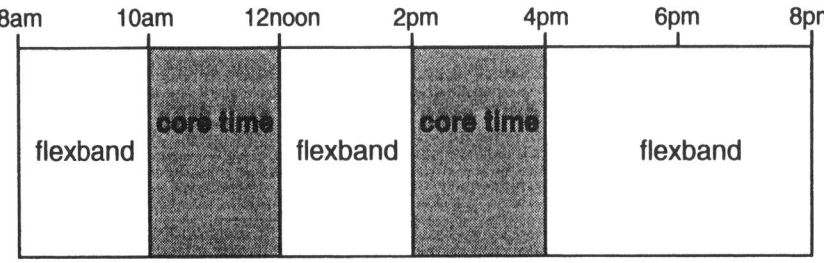

134

11: Personnel management

Absenteeism at EDU Plastics Ltd for the past four years

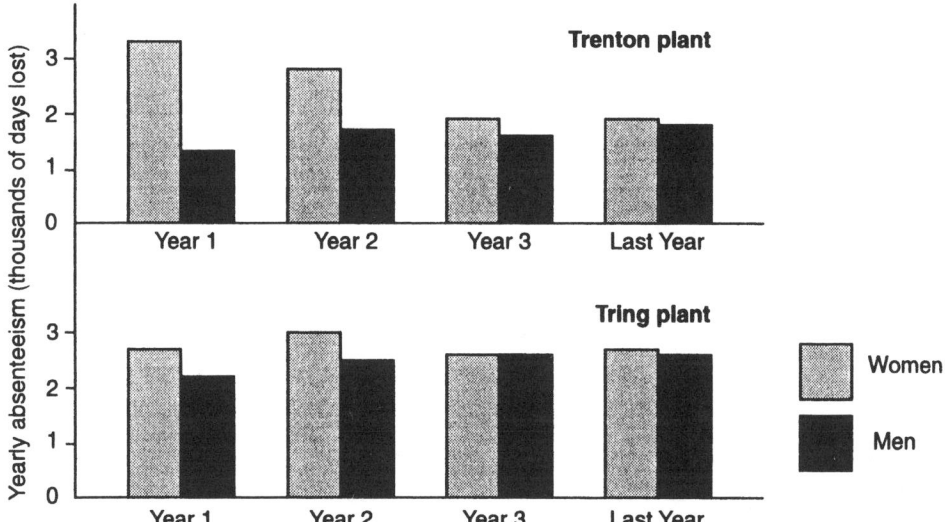

Your first task

Answer the following questions:

1. A line worker at Trenton, Jean Trelawney, who is a single parent, wants to take her children to school in the mornings before she goes to work. This means she cannot get to work until 09.30 in the morning. She also wants to take an hour for lunch to do her shopping. She will take this between 12.30 and 13.30. What time will she be able to finish work if she has to work an eight hour day?
2. Do you think the idea of flexible working hours is paying off at the Trenton plant, bearing in mind that absenteeism is expensive for the company?
3. Do women or men tend to be absent most? What explanations might there be?
4. How do the records of the Trenton and Tring plants compare?

Your second task

Bill Miller has decided to write a brief report to Robin Farnes, the Works Manager at the Tring Plant. Produce a report such as he might have written (limit 200 words).

D. Opposites and synonyms*

Complete the following table

word	synonym	opposite
motivate (verb)		
promotion (noun)		
usually (adverb)		
satisfying (adjective)		
compliance (noun)		
relevant (adjective)		
recruit (verb)		
ability (noun)		

11: *Personnel management*

casual (adjective)		
select (verb)		
feasible (adjective)		
redundancy (noun)		
agree (verb)		
intelligence (noun)		
frequently (adverb)		
skilfully (adverb)		
personal (adjective)		
efficiency (noun)		
apprentice (noun)		
dynamic (adjective)		
extrovert (noun)		
locate (verb)		

E. A job application

The following advertisement has appeared in your local press and you decide to apply for the job. Write a suitable letter to the advertiser.

Looking for an interesting career?
We offer 20 new posts for trainee managers

Over the next two years those chosen will be given experience in various aspects of the leisure industry. At the end of that time we would expect you to be capable of handling a responsible job – in the largest hotel, holiday and entertainment group in Europe. Age/experience no bar, so long as you are prepared to make your contribution enthusiastically.

If you think you have something special to offer write to us now with full details of your record to date and your future intentions. Only the 100 most promising candidates will be interviewed.

Adrian Marshall, Staff Manager, RGD Group, PO Box 78, London W1 9YY

F. Summarising

Summarise the following dialogue as briefly as possible without losing any of the essential meaning.

Jeremy Deans, Junior Partner with Wilkins &Deans, a firm of City stockbrokers, yesterday called Peter Hartley, Supervisor of the European equities trading desk, into his office.

JEREMY: Thanks for coming to see me Peter. I wanted to talk to you about a couple of disciplinary problems that I have noticed with your team.

PETER: Sounds serious.

JEREMY: Well I think so. The first one is swearing. I accept the dealing room is a tense place and they are under a lot of pressure, but it is all at top volume. I was taking an important Japanese client out last week and as we walked past I could see that he was clearly surprised and embarrassed.

PETER: It's very difficult to handle. I mean the dealers do tend to get completely involved in the situation and a no-swearing rule would be very difficult to enforce.

JEREMY: I think you should have a word with the team. Remind them that I could cut their bonuses if I really saw no improvement.

PETER: OK, if you think it will help.

JEREMY: I do. What they say in the bar is up to them, but here it's different.

PETER: Is there anything else?

JEREMY: Yes, I'm afraid so. Punctuality seems to be slipping. I've noticed dealers coming in after eight several times this week. Are there any reasons you know of?

PETER: I know that Michael and Sarah take the train and there have been delays this week.

JEREMY: Well I feel there is a general slackness. You were not here when I arrived at eight this morning.

PETER: Yes, sorry. I got stuck in traffic.

JEREMY: Alright. I accept that. These things happen, but I am sure the reasons are not always genuine. Imagine what they'd say if their pay cheques were late.

PETER: It starts with one person being a bit late and then someone else joins them. Before you know where you are it's a major problem. I've spoken to a few of them, but I'll let them know you are aware of the situation.

JEREMY: Please do, Peter. And say I shall be checking up on them for the next few weeks. If any of them come in late they are to account to me. We can't afford to let this attitude take hold. We've got some promotion opportunities coming up shortly, and I was hoping to look to your team for candidates.

PETER: Michael has made a record profit on his portfolio this month.

JEREMY: That's good. It's up to you to see the others do the same!

PETER: One last thing. You mentioned a few days ago that personal 'phone calls seemed to be on the increase. Well I've made a rule that no-one is to make personal 'phone calls during trading hours except in an emergency.

JEREMY: Excellent. Clients get a bad impression if they see dealers just chatting on the phone, and it wastes good trading time.

G. Write a report

Refer to the previous exercise. In his role as Chief Administrator, Jeremy has now asked Peter for a short but formal report (maximum 150 words) on discipline on the equities desk. Draft a report such as Peter might have submitted to him.

11: Personnel management

H. Meanings

The following memorandum was recently circulated to staff in a firm of London stockbrokers. Having read the memorandum, explain the meaning of the words and phrases which have been highlighted.

Wilkins & Deans

Memoandum

To All Office Staff   From J. Deans,
                                       Chief Administrator
                                       (date)

                    Letter-writing

As a number of new staff have joined us recently I have thought it **expedient** to make clear the firm's policy on this important subject.

Whatever has to be written in a letter **the tone should always be courteous**. No matter what has been said or written by the customer, rudeness can never be justified. **By the same token** curtness should be avoided, no matter how overworked you might be. The aim should always be to act in **a professional manner**.

Incoming mail should be dealt with promptly. Delays do not **reflect favourably** on the organisation or the individuals concerned. There has to be **a system of priorities**, with the more important customers receiving attention first. However, there is no merit in **maintaining a backlog** of unanswered mail. With a suitable effort the backlog could be eliminated. Of course there will be **peaks of work** from time to time which create temporary difficulties.

In replying to a letter or **writing in response to a telephone call** you should always make sure you have covered all the **points at issue**. If it is going to take time to look into some of the questions raised it would be polite to **briefly acknowledge** receipt of the message and explain the reason for the delay. **A diary note a few days hence** would help to make sure that any promises made are kept.

I. Reply to a letter

Your Manager, Donald Formby, has asked you to reply to this letter he has received from a Mrs Jane Crampthorne. He has asked you to explain that the Personnel Manager had great difficulty choosing between the candidates and there were a number of factors to be brought into account, apart from qualifications. He understands from Mr Skelton that Mrs Crampthorne's name has been kept on file in case there are any further vacancies in future.

```
                                          16 Wyndham Street
                                               High Ercall
                                        Shropshire WE16 6SS
                                                     (date)
Mr D Formby
General Manager
Diatron Products PLC
Lembroke Square
Chester CH1 2WW

Dear Mr Formby,
Last week I attended an interview for a post as secretary in your
Crewe branch. I was met at your head office by a Mr Skelton, who I
understand is your Personnel Manager. He was rather off-hand but I
felt I came out of the interview well. Then yesterday I received a
letter which told me I had been rejected. Much worse, I also dis-
covered that the post had been offered to a Ms Webster whom I spoke
to while I was waiting to be interviewed. She had less experience
and fewer qualifications than myself. Apart from which, she was
badly dressed and badly spoken. In comparing us I cannot see why
you chose her rather than me.
I would very much like to know your explanation.
Yours sincerely,

*Jane Crampthorne*

Mrs Jane Crampthorne
```

J. Complete the sentences

Complete the following sentences using your own words.

1. Some workers receive a Christmas bonus when ...
2. When an employee works more than the scheduled hours ...
3. If you are given luncheon vouchers ...
4. Tax has to be deducted by an employer ...
5. It is not easy to obtain job satisfaction ...
6. When someone stays away from work ...
7. An ideal job would be one where ...
8. When you are being interviewed for a job ...
9. An interviewer should always ...
10. A personnel department ...
11. Work would be more interesting if ...
12. An induction programme ...

11: Personnel management

An example of job satisfaction? The combined wine taster and television critic.

K. Vocabulary*

referee	applicant	interviewee	induction	dismissal
aptitude	overtime	morale	bonus	questionnaire
redundant	participation	personal	personnel	courtesy
discretion	remuneration	personality	frustration	environment
counsellor	militant	moderate	foreman	representative

Match the words listed above with the dictionary definitions which follow.

1. Someone in charge of a group of people in a factory.
2. A payment made to employees when the firm's results are good.
3. A payment made to an employee when he or she works longer than normal hours.
4. Pent up fury or emotions.
5. A person who does not hold extreme views.
6. A fanatic who is prepared to do battle in pursuance of his beliefs.
7. The act of terminating employment from the employer's side.
8. Referring to an individual. Private and confidential.
9. The people who work in and for an organisation.
10. A person who is seeking appointment to a particular post.
11. The degree of enthusiasm shown by a workforce.
12. Someone who gives advice.
13. The procedures which help a new member of staff to fit into the organisation more quickly and efficiently.
14. The person who is being examined orally as part of a selection process.
15. The distinctive character of an individual.
16. Allowing subordinates to share in the making of decisions.
17. Suiting one's actions or words to circumstances.
18. Treating other people with respect.
19. What someone becomes when they are no longer required at work.
20. Another description for pay, usually applied to directors and senior executives.
21. The physical surroundings of a business.

11: Personnel management

22. A person who gives an opinion about someone who is applying for a job.
23. A talent for doing a particular task well.
24. A survey to find out people's reactions to a proposal.
25. Someone who is chosen to speak for you and generally look after your interests.

L. Write a report

Two daily newspapers in the Manston Group, the *Morning News* and the *Southern Star*, are being amalgamated to form a new paper, the *Southern Belle*, in order to combat rising costs and falling circulation and advertising revenue.

The Morning News

This paper sells mainly in London and the south-east of England. The average daily circulation over the last six months has been less than 200,000 which is well below the breakeven point.

General layout of the paper:

Pages 1 and 2: national and international news

Pages 3 to 6: local news (there are three varied editions for different geographical areas).

Pages 7 and 8: special features.

Then follow the pages given over completely to advertising, the final pages covering sport and entertainment.

The target audience is primarily male.

The printing works and offices are in Finchley in North London and there are 1,200 employees of whom nearly half are female part-time workers.

75 of the 115 journalists, however, are males over the age of 45.

The Southern Star

This paper concentrates on national and international news, but also has six centre pages catering for a family audience. There are regular features on fashion and cookery, holidays and family problems. The circulation last year averaged 400,000 but there has been a serious decline in recent months.

The printing works and offices of the *Southern Star* are sited on the outskirts of Croydon in southern London. The workforce of 750 (all full-time) have known for some months that the existing works would be closing down when the lease expires at the end of next year.

The majority of the journalists on the staff are female, mainly under the age of 40.

The Southern Belle

These two papers are to be amalgamated to make a completely new paper, the *Southern Belle*. It is to be published as soon as possible. Following market research, the Manston Board have decided on the new format.

According to the research, the public absorbs the main news items through television media, so the *Southern Belle* will concentrate less on the news and more on features, particularly those of general interest to the family.

It is hoped to keep the circulation around the half-million mark, but 400,000 will be the breakeven point.

By using the latest technology the number of technical operators will be reduced to 250, with 45 on the editorial staff. Redundancies are inevitable.

The *Southern Belle* will be produced from the Southampton works and offices – 75 miles to the south-west of London. These will need to be modified to house the new equipment.

11: Personnel management

Your task

Play the role of personal assistant to Alan Crawford, Personnel Manager at the *Morning News*. He has asked you for a brief report (about 200 words), covering specifically the staff problems you anticipate at the *Morning News,* and how these problems might be dealt with.

12: Finance and accounting

A. Comprehension

The purpose of any business is to make a profit. Profit is not a dirty word. It simply means that the resources which have been entrusted to us have been used effectively. The more effectively the resources have been used, the more profit will be made. If all the businesses in a country were making a loss there would be an economic disaster. The government taxes business profits and uses the proceeds to pay for free education, the National Health Service, unemployment pay, old age pensions and national defence among other things. So one of the reasons the business managers need to keep a record of their transactions is to allow the Inspector of Taxes to calculate how much tax is due. However, there are other reasons why the business managers want to keep financial records. They want to know whether the policies they are applying are proving to be successful or otherwise. They want to know whether modifications are called for. They also want to know who owes them money (debtors) and to whom they owe money (creditors). They want to make sure they collect all the monies which are due to them, and they also want to make sure they are not suddenly confronted by a creditor they had forgotten about.

Apart from retail business the majority of sales are for credit. When manufacturers sell goods to their retail customers, the retailers will not be expected to pay for them until they have had a chance to sell them to the public. That is the way business normally operates. By giving their customers, say, two months' credit, the manufacturers are giving them ample time to raise the funds from the proceeds of the sale.

The manufacturers' suppliers – the people who provide them with the raw materials – will in turn give the manufacturers time to raise the funds. A considerable degree of interdependency is thus developed. The cash flow – payments in and out – are vital to a business. An adequate supply of working capital is essential if insolvency is to be avoided. A firm is said to be insolvent when it is unable to meet its financial commitments.

Since almost all of the business conducted between firms is on a credit basis, credit control becomes significant. Specific credit limits will be allocated to each customer. Thus a new customer, John Turner, might be allowed to have an outstanding account of £5,000 for three months, while Evelyn Corbett, who has been a satisfactory customer for more than a year, has a limit of twice that amount.

Before any order is passed through to the Despatch Department in the factory, it will be checked against the customer and the credit rating. The salespeople are not allowed to give customers credit when these limits would be exceeded, unless there is a special clearance from the Sales Manager.

The drive for increased sales will make the large influential customer particularly attractive and for this reason they are likely to receive preferential treatment when credit ratings are determined.

Firms may attempt to reduce the risk of loss through bad debts by a variety of devices. They usually offer cash discounts for prompt payment and often operate a credit control department to monitor the granting of credit and the collection of debts. It is also possible to resort to a practice known as factoring (or invoice discounting) whereby specialist companies are approached with a view to their purchasing the book debts at a discount. They will collect the debts and keep any accounting records required.

Your task

Having read the above passage, answer these questions in your own words.

12: Finance and accounting

a) Why are the tax authorities interested in the accounts of a business?
b) Who benefits when a business makes a profit?
c) Why is cash flow important to a business?
d) How are credit ratings determined?
e) What should a salesperson do before selling goods on credit?
f) What does a credit control department do?
g) How does factoring operate?
h) Why do you think a sales manager and a credit control manager might sometimes come into conflict?

B. Fill in the blanks*

Rewrite this passage filling in the blanks from the list of words given below.

The Accounting Function

The ...... function of the Chief Accountant is to ensure that .... funds are available for such capital .... on new plant and equipment as is required in the Corporate Plan. Adequate working capital will also be required to meet revenue expenditure such as .... and salaries, purchases of raw materials and the inevitable administration expenses. Whenever .... or sales are made records will need to be kept. In many ways the accounts are like a .... telling you what has happened since the business commenced. On 3rd April we purchased a new mainframe for £750,000. On 11th May we spent £15,000 on a new motor van, and so on. The data tells management what .... are at their disposal and what commitments they have to be prepared to meet. By .... the accounts managers can see how much cash is available, how much they owe to their ...., and how much they are owed by their .... They must always be in a position to meet their commitments if .... is to be avoided.

The accounts make a contribution to the decision-making process. Once .... have been identified, alternative .... have to be considered and evaluated. The evaluation will very often be centred on .... data provided by the accounting departments. If we chose Option A how much would it cost? What would be the net revenue (after .... of the expenses)? How much would labour costs amount to? Would it be .... to use more capital intensive methods of production? It is this type of question which can be .... by the accountants.

When the decision is implemented there will be a need for feedback. Control ...... will be necessary to ensure that any deviations are speedily noticed so that .... action can be taken. The .... flow of accounting information will be the means by which the deviations are spotted. The use of computers will make it .... to improve the feedback both in terms of .... and speed.

mechanisms	corrective	solutions	insolvency
expenditure	primary	assets	deduction
adequate	wages	possible	purchases
cheaper	debtors	storybook	examining
statistical	vital	answered	problems
continuous	accuracy	computer	creditors

12: Finance and accounting

C. Pie charts

The following charts show a breakdown of the costs of production in three similar companies which build 16 to 18 metre racing yachts. You work for the British company and have been asked by the Cost Accountant, Gladys Garwood, to write a brief memorandum for her setting out your findings. She has given you a few brief notes indicating the sort of information she is looking for.

How income/revenue is disposed of in three international companies (% of total)

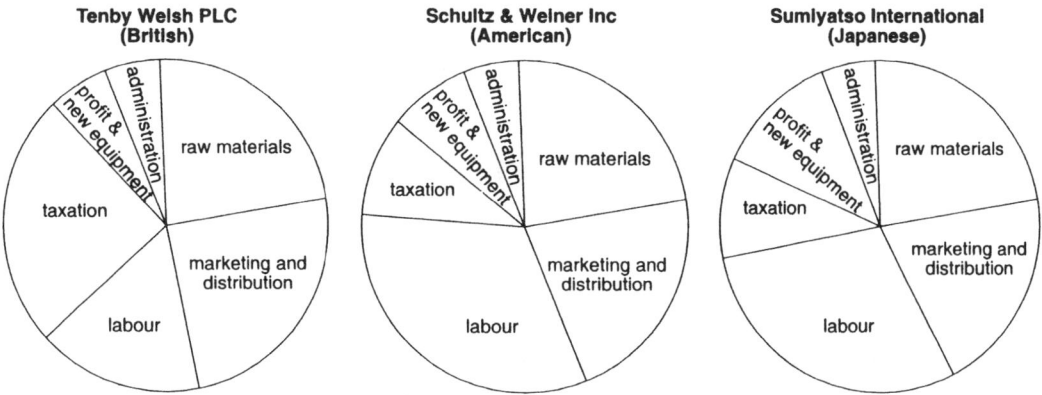

Comparisons – Japanese labour? American labour? Possible explanations?
Thanks Gladys

D. Adjectives and adverbs*

Add an appropriate adjective, adverb or preposition from the lists below to each of the following sentences where indicated:

a) People who go into a business for the first time will ………… appreciate the help of a ………… bank manager.

b) Funds will ………… be required to purchase equipment.

c) Chief Accountants will not ………… agree to spend money even though the equipment is regarded as ………… .

d) Capital outlay will ………… be called for to replace ………… machinery.

e) Almost all business conducted ………… firms is on a ………… basis.

f) While ………… payments can be deferred, others are due for payment ………… .

g) Sometimes when a business expands ………… it encounters cash flow problems.

h) ………… rates of tax make it ………… difficult to succeed in business.

i) Income minus expenditure during a ………… year equals profit.

Adjectives: *credit   high   co-operative   obsolete   some   new   essential*
Adverbs: *immediately   probably   invariably   always   between   often   increasingly*

12: Finance and accounting

E. Multiple choice*

Choose the phrase, A, B, or C, which **best** completes each sentence, and tick the appropriate box.

1. When a trader buys goods on credit he does not have to
   A. pay for them immediately. ☐
   B. pay for them until the end of the month. ☐
   C. pay for them. ☐

2. The purpose of keeping accounts is to
   A. see how much has been spent. ☐
   B. find out why the business has lost money. ☐
   C. determine whether the business has made a profit or a loss. ☐

3. The tax authorities want to know how much profit a business has made
   A. during the financial year. ☐
   B. in order to calculate any liability for tax. ☐
   C. since the business was set up. ☐

4. It is expensive for a manufacturer to carry a high level of stocks
   A. and the danger of pilfering is increased. ☐
   B. but the danger of pilfering is decreased. ☐
   C. but less storage space is required. ☐

5. A manufacturer may hold stocks of finished goods with the purpose of
   A. reducing the expense of advertising. ☐
   B. reducing the possibility of machine breakdowns. ☐
   C. improving the delivery time to customers. ☐

6. A firm is said to be insolvent when it
   A. cannot meet its commitments. ☐
   B. is making losses. ☐
   C. is making profits. ☐

7. The credit rating given to a customer will depend upon
   A. his willingness to buy goods. ☐
   B. the time he takes to pay for the goods. ☐
   C. his reputation. ☐

8. By giving customers two months to pay for the goods they buy the manufacturer is
   A. making it difficult for them. ☐
   B. giving them time to sell the goods before they have to pay for them. ☐
   C. making sure they pay for them. ☐

9. A firm can encourage their customers to pay more promptly by
   A. increasing cash discounts. ☐
   B. reducing cash discounts. ☐
   C. eliminating cash discounts. ☐

10. The people who owe money to the business are called
    A. creditors. ☐
    B. debtors. ☐
    C. suppliers. ☐

F. Summarise

Give the following passage a title and summarise it in about 100 words.

Many businesses are owned and controlled by a single person (called a sole trader). There would not be much capital required and he would no doubt be given credit by his suppliers. This would give him the opportunity to sell goods to his customers before having to pay for them. He would no doubt turn to his bankers for temporary loans if, and when, these were required. If he wanted to increase the size of his business he would either turn to the bank for longer-term support or 'plough back' some of his profits. The attraction for the sole trader is that he has maximum control over the business, making decisions without reference to others.

Other businesses are organised in the form of a partnership. Each partner provides a part of the capital, and the profits and losses are shared on an agreed basis. The amount of capital which can be raised is restricted by the personal wealth of the partners and is likely to be inadequate for the modern large-scale enterprises. Partnerships tend to remain relatively small, predominating in retailing and the professions. Solicitors' practices are often in the form of partnerships, one of the partners concentrating on conveyancing (property sales), another on litigation (lawsuits), while a third deals with probate (wills and trusts).

The problem with partnerships is that all partners are liable for the debts of the firm, irrespective of the amount of capital they invested. So it would be possible for an extremely rich person to have a small stake in the enterprise, but to lose all his personal assets if the business fails.

A business which is drilling for oil or producing motor cars will obviously need extensive funding and they will be able to obtain money more easily from the public if they are in the form of a limited company. This is because if the company becomes insolvent the shareholders only stand to lose their original stake, the price they paid for their shares.

An enterprise requiring large amounts of capital would probably have its shares quoted on the stock exchange and this would give its shareholders the opportunity to dispose of their shares more easily, if they so wished. Different classes of shares may be issued but, in general, the ordinary shareholders have voting rights which give them power to elect the board of directors who will organise and control the company's activities.

12: Finance and accounting

G. Reply to a letter

You are working for an accountant, Peter Dolby, and in his absence you are required to answer the following letter. Mr Dolby is on holiday until a week on Monday.

---

63 The Boulevard
Bournemouth
Dorset BH5 6PH

(date)

Peter Dolby Esq
Chartered Accountant
6 Poole Road
Bournemouth
BH7 7HH

Dear Mr Dolby

I have just started up in business as a restaurateur here in Bournemouth and I have been advised to seek the services of an accountant. Mr Dobbs of Shelley's Amusement Arcade has recommended your good self and I am wondering whether you would be prepared to look after my interests, of course assuming the fees are reasonable.

Apart from dealing with my accounts I am also considering the possibility of forming a limited company and would welcome your advice on this. My wife's family might be prepared to help with the finances. I think I should warn you that although I consider myself a first-class chef, I have no experience of keeping accounts.

Yours truly

George Lazemby

George Lazemby

H. Meanings

First, read the passage below. Then explain the meanings of the words and phrases which have been highlighted.

If you are considering **setting up** your own business, an accountant is the best person to give you financial advice. It is a **legal requirement** that proper financial records are kept and the **basic principle** is to record every single transaction. One of the purposes is to ascertain whether you have made a profit or loss during a **given period**. Profit could be described as the difference between the value of the business at the start of a trading period and the value of the business at the end of that period.

Before deciding whether we have made a profit or loss we need to consider the extent to which our **assets have depreciated**. Our assets are those things we own which could be converted into cash, **in contrast to** our liabilities which are debts which we owe whether or not they are due immediately. Perhaps we bought a motor vehicle for £10,000 when the business started, but it is very unlikely that we would be able to sell if **for anything like that figure**. The general rule is that we estimate the life of the asset and if the life of the motor van is, say, five years, we then **write down** its value by 20% per annum so that by the end of the five years it is showing nil value in our books.

A deduction also has to be made for bad debts. This is a **normal hazard** in business, especially since so many transactions are for **credit** rather than cash. We have supplied goods to a particular customer who has now become **bankrupt**. He cannot pay the money he owes us and so the profit we thought we had made from the transaction has **proved illusory**.

12: Finance and accounting

I. Interpretation of data

It is the last day of November and the computer print-out below shows amounts owed by various debtors of K J Spry & Co of Taymoor Works, Wentworth Green, Lancashire BL5 3TP. Draft suitable letters to any whose accounts have been outstanding for more than one month.

	Date	Sales	Payment received		Balance
			Cash	Cheque	
Dove Aldridge Ltd Brent Works Blackpool BL3 6HH	11.10 19.11	£160.00		£160.00	£160.00 Nil
J V Dredging Equipment Ltd 11 Station Road Wyndham BL9 6WY	16.10	£995.00		£995.00	Nil
Percy Grimes & Partners Barley Cross Blackpool BL1 9AS	24.10	£800.00			£800.00
Sanderson & Wright 16 Crompton Road Bolton BN7 1BB	28.10 6.11 13.11	£65.50 £750.00	£65.50		£65.50 Nil £750.00
Peter White Blenheim Road Bolton BN8 9RJ	28.10 29.11	£99.95		£60.00	£99.95 £39.95

J. Complete the sentences

In each of the blank spaces below write any one of the following words:

a) company's   b) companies   c) its   d) it's*

*Note: This form is used in formal prose or letters only when reporting direct speech.

1. When .... buy goods from you on credit the transaction has to be recorded in your accounts.
2. The .... accounting department will prepare the annual Trading and Profit and Loss Accounts.
3. When .... are short of working capital usual for them to turn to their bankers for assistance.
4. .... not uncommon to find a company making substantial paper profits but being unable to pay dividends to shareholders.
5. If a company cannot meet .... commitments an Official Receiver may have to be appointed.
6. .... a legal requirement that a .... annual accounts are audited by a professional accountant.
7. A company may declare a dividend if .... accounts show that a profit has been made.
8. A .... share capital will be shown on .... Balance Sheet.

12: Finance and accounting

K. Vocabulary*

bankruptcy	invoice	revenue	ledgers	equities
assets	overheads	debtors	liabilities	budget
investor	returns	balance	fixtures	depreciation
creditor	capital	drawings	goodwill	expenditure

Match the words above with the dictionary definitions which follow.

1. The spending of money, on advertising for example.
2. Articles such as display cabinets which would be difficult to remove.
3. A payment to shareholders when a company has made a profit.
4. A person whose affairs are in the hands of an Official Receiver.
5. Another name for ordinary shares.
6. The person who takes on the responsibility for checking a company's accounts.
7. Possessions which can be converted into cash.
8. A deduction made from the price of goods when payment is made promptly.
9. Debts which will have to be paid either now or in the future.
10. A list of goods which have been sent to a customer indicating the amount charged to their account.
11. The situation when the two sides of the accounts are equal.
12. The books of account showing how much we owe and are owed.
13. Goods which are not wanted after all, usually because they are faulty.
14. The proprietor's withdrawal of funds from the business.
15. The proprietor's stake in the business.
16. People who owe us money.
17. The fall in the value of an asset as a result of waste or usage.
18. A person to whom we owe money.
19. Something which is valuable yet intangible.
20. The situation facing persons who cannot pay their creditors.
21. Money received from sales.
22. The device which aims to control expenditure.
23. The costs attached to maintaining fixed assets such as plant and machinery.
24. An asset such as a share certificate which can be offered as a safeguard when a loan is received from a bank.
25. Someone who buys something in the expectation that it will rise in value.

L. Annual accounts

When Andrea Brigadini's daughter, Laura, married an Englishman and moved to England, he thought he would now see very little of her, and when his wife Sophia died a few years later his future looked bleak. Then Laura invited him for a holiday in England. She and her husband had just moved into their new home in the New Forest and Andrea went to stay with them for a month. While he was there he visited a number of gift shops and realised there was a market for fashionable leatherware such as he had been making in Italy for the past forty years. Taking the opportunity to be closer to his daughter and her young family he bought a small gift shop in one of the New Forest villages frequented by tourists. There was a small workshop to the rear and he now spends his time making up leather jackets, handbags and belts which he then sells in the shop with the help of his daughter and one of her friends. He has just completed his second year in the business and the accounts for the two years are shown below and overleaf.

Your task

After studying the accounts, complete the following sentences:

1. Andrea's profits have risen ...
2. The explanation for the increase in the value of stocks he is holding could be that ...
3. The money he has withdrawn from the business – described as Drawings – is shown in the ...
4. If he withdrew less from the business for his personal spending ...
5. Andrea's working capital ...
6. After two years of trading, the business ...
7. His payments under the heading of 'Other outgoings' might include ... and ...

Andrea Brigadini trading as Burley Leathercraft
Trading and Profit and Loss Account for year ending 31st December 199-

	First year (£)		Second year (£)	
Sales		78,288		88,215
Less cost of sales	51,455		54,251	
Opening stock for year	–		12,337	
			66,588	
Closing stock (end of year)	12,337	39,118	18,897	47,691
Gross profit for year		39,170		40,524
Wages	15,268		19,878	
Depreciation	750		750	
Other outgoings	2,653	18,671	1,109	21,737
Net profit for year		20,499		18,787

12: Finance and accounting

Balance Sheet as at 31st December 199-

	First year (£)		Second year (£)	
Fixed assets				
Freehold shop		35,000		35,000
Fixtures and Fittings	3,000		3,000	
Less provision for depreciation	<u>750</u>	<u>2,250</u>	<u>1,500</u>	<u>1,500</u>
		37,250		36,500
Current assets				
Stock at end of year	12,337		18,897	
Debtors	125		6,350	
Cash in hand and at bank	<u>265</u>		<u>1,325</u>	
	12,727		26,572	
Current liabilities				
Creditors	<u>3,926</u>		<u>18,325</u>	
Working capital		<u>8,801</u>		<u>8,247</u>
		<u>46,051</u>		<u>44,747</u>
Represented by				
Capital		40,000		46,051
Add net profit for the year		<u>20,499</u>		<u>18,787</u>
		60,499		64,838
Less drawings		<u>14,448</u>		<u>20,091</u>
		<u>46,051</u>		<u>44,747</u>

13: The board of directors

A. Comprehension

The board of directors of a limited company is primarily responsible for determining the objectives and policies of a business. It is the directors who determine the direction the business is going to take. They will need to ensure that the necessary funds are available and will appoint key staff to whom they will delegate the authority to run the business on a day-to-day basis. They will need to design an effective organisation structure so that there is both a chain of command linking one level of management with another and an effective communication network so that instructions can be passed downward and information passed upward.

The directors are appointed by the shareholders, normally at the company's annual general meeting, at which the chairman of the board will be expected to account for their stewardship during the previous year. The company's accounts will be presented to the shareholders at that time so they can judge for themselves whether or not the board has been successful.

Direction in business is like strategy in a war situation. The strategic decisions determine the areas in which the company's resources will be employed. Above all it involves planning to ensure that the business first survives and then flourishes. Strategic decisions, made by the board of directors, are concerned with the disposition of resources. These contrast with the tactical decisions by means of which the senior executives (appointed by the directors) carry out in detail the plans conceived or approved by the board of directors.

The fact that boards of directors tend to meet rather infrequently, say once a week, means that part-time directors can be elected to the board. Since they will not have departmental responsibilities within the company they are often described as non-executive directors. There are arguments in favour of such directors though they may lack a detailed knowledge of the company's activities. They may bring expertise to the board. Some are lawyers, or experts in tax affairs. Some represent influential groups of shareholders whose support is necessary if the board is going to carry out its plans, while others are directors in a number of companies and are used to interlock boards within a group of companies. For example, a holding (or parent) company may appoint a director from their board to serve on the board of a subsidiary company, with a view to keeping a watching brief on the directors' activities.

Your task

Having read the above passage, answer these questions in your own words.

- a) How would you describe the role of the board of directors?
- b) And the role of the senior executives?
- c) What happens at the annual general meeting?
- d) What is the difference between a strategic and a tactical decision?
- e) What part can non-executive directors play in the proceedings?
- f) What objections might be raised against the appointment of non-executive directors?
- g) What is meant by an interlocking board of directors?
- h) How is it that a board of directors can control a company though they only meet, say, once a week?

13: The board of directors

B. Fill in the blanks*

Fill in the blanks in this passage, using words from the list below.

Executive Directors

A modern business enterprise is often a .... system requiring a lot of ...., which is provided by the public when they .... shares in the company. Since they have .... the capital, it is appropriate that they choose the people who are to .... the company for them, namely the board of directors. Many of the .... also have executive responsibilities. Thus, a marketing director might be a full director of the board, ... by the shareholders at the annual .... meeting like the other directors. Yet he might also be responsible for the day-to-day .... of the marketing department. Most of his time will be .... on administrative matters, organising market research, dealing with .... and generally ensuring that the .... sales are maximised. But he will function as a director when the board of directors meets. The .... of managing director also .... the roles of chief executive with membership of the board and this allows him to act as a vital .... between the board of directors and their .... management team. The managing director is often also chairman of the board of directors.

Executive directors have the advantage that they are .... involved with the .... affairs. If the board of directors wish to move in a .... direction the executive directors will know whether such a .... of action is practicable. For example, the board might wish to .... their products in a particular .... market. The market would be profitable for the company, but the .... director knows that his team of salespeople lack the experience to take advantage of the situation. Or perhaps the board would like to .... the advertising expenditure during the .... year but the .... director knows that the company will have to meet some heavy commitments during the .... months and it would be better to .... the campaign.

Perhaps the best board is one which contains a .... of executive and non-executive directors. In this way the board has the .... of some directors who know the practical problems .... by the business, while others bring their own .... of expertise to the boardroom discussions.

link	company's	actively	coming
increase	delay	sell	company's
capital	provided	run	spent
certain	mixture	brand	overseas
combines	course	coming	faced
benefit	appointed	marketing	financial
general	advertising	complex	buy
directors	management	post	appointed

C. The organisation chart

Romford Engineering is a public limited company and its shares are quoted on the London Stock Exchange. The chart below shows the lines of communication and command between the company's senior officials.

13: The board of directors

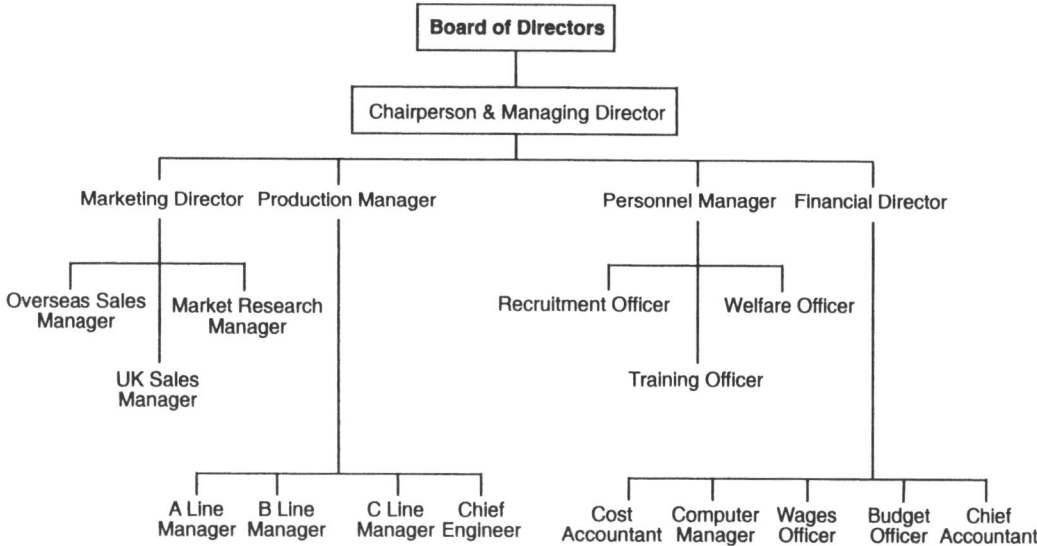

After studying the chart you are required to answer the following questions:

a) From whom do the Marketing Director, the Production Manager, the Personnel Manager and the Financial Director in (other words the Departmental Heads) take their orders?

b) From whom do the Line Managers and the Chief Engineer take orders?

c) If the Managing Director and the Production Manager had a meeting, what do you think they might discuss?

d) How many executive directors are there in Romford Engineering?

e) If the Computing Manager was sending information to the Managing Director should he send it through the Financial Director? Why?

f) How many immediate subordinates do each of the Departmental Heads have?

g) In what circumstances do you think the Marketing Director and the Production Manager might have conflicting interests?

h) Would you expect the Chief Engineer to be paid more or less than the Production Manager? Why?

i) What sort of work would you expect the Wages Officer to do?

j) If there was a dispute between one of the line managers and the Chief Engineer how would you expect it to be settled?

k) If there was a dispute between the Marketing Director and the Financial Director how would you expect it to be settled?

D. Nouns and verbs*

Add an appropriate noun or verb from the lists below to each of the following sentences where indicated:

a) The .... of a company have the responsibility to .... that the legal requirements are complied with.

b) The directors of a company must .... a copy of the company's annual .... to the Registrar of Companies.

13: The board of directors

c) The directors will .... decisions by passing resolutions at the .... meeting.
d) Each of the directors will normally have one vote when a .... is ....
e) Resolutions are .... when there are a majority of .... cast in favour.
f) Executive directors are those who .... departmental
g) The directors are .... by the .... at the annual general meeting.
h) The managing director .... to the board for the performance of his management ....

Nouns: accounts   board   responsibilities   directors   votes   shareholders
       resolution   team
Verbs: make   proposed   elected   answers   passed   ensure
       undertake   send

E. Multiple choice*

Choose the phrase, A, B, or C, which **best** completes each sentence, and tick the appropriate box.

1. When the directors are discussing the problems facing the company they primarily have to consider
   A. the interests of the public. ☐
   B. their own interests. ☐
   C. the interests of the shareholders. ☐

2. When a proposal is made and a vote taken the usual arrangement is that
   A. each director has one vote no matter how many shares he holds. ☐
   B. only the chairperson can vote. ☐
   C. the directors with most shares have the most votes. ☐

3. Key members of staff will be chosen by the managing director because
   A. he is more knowledgeable than the other directors. ☐
   B. he has got to answer to the board for their performance. ☐
   C. he earns more than the other directors. ☐

4. Non-executive directors will often be appointed because
   A. they have valuable contacts with potential customers. ☐
   B. they have departmental responsibilities. ☐
   C. no-one else is available. ☐

5. Directors are usually required to have shares in the company so they can
   A. be seen to have a personal stake in the business and thus be affected by their decisions. ☐
   B. receive share certificates from the registrar's department. ☐
   C. take on administrative duties. ☐

13: The board of directors

6. Strategic decisions are concerned with

    A. the details of day-to-day administration.
    B. the disposition of the company's resources.
    C. the payment of wages.

7. While decision-making powers are commonly delegated to senior executives

    A. the directors are not responsible to the shareholders for any mistakes which might be made.
    B. they are not responsible for any errors of judgement.
    C. the directors remain responsible to the shareholders for any mistakes which might be made.

8. The further ahead one plans

    A. the more troubles there are likely to be.
    B. the more one can anticipate problems and thus avoid them.
    C. the less one can anticipate problems.

9. Tactical decisions are those by means of which the senior executives

    A. carry out their own plans.
    B. destroy the opposition.
    C. carry out the plans prescribed by the board of directors.

10. The directors have to initiate long range plans with a view to ensuring

    A. the achievement of the company's objectives.
    B. the maintenance of good relations with the senior executives.
    C. compliance with the law.

F. Summarising

Give the following passage an appropriate title and summarise it in about 100 words.

Top management is often under heavy pressure so that immediate problems often absorb much of their efforts. Time to analyse complex data and project future trends is likely to be limited. To combat this problem a long-range planning department might be set up to act in an advisory capacity. The long-term planning team would be directly responsible to the managing director, but freed from routine duties. Such a department would be small and made up of top quality generalists, trained to see the wood as well as the trees.

It is difficult to decide how far ahead to plan. An accurate long-term forecast is most advantageous to the firm, but the further ahead one looks, the less certain one can be of the outcomes. To overcome this problem a flexible approach needs to be adopted. Long-range plans for, say, three to five years might be mapped out, but there will have to be frequent reviews and re-appraisals so that the direction of the firm can be changed as and when the need arises.

Firms may want to enter new industries, launch new products, enter new markets (perhaps overseas) or acquire new subsidiaries. Existing activities may be expanded, consolidated or cut back. Whatever the requirements, careful planning is called for. The production side of the business has to be geared to keep pace with changes in the

13: The board of directors

market. At the same time stocks must be kept at just the right level. If the stock level is too high, capital is tied up unproductively. If the stock level is too low, an upsurge in demand will lead to potential customers being turned away, possibly permanently.

There is also a difficult choice to be made between a policy of diversification and short-term profit maximisation. The risk of failure can be reduced by choosing to produce a range of goods and services so that if revenue from any of them contracts it represents only a small part of the whole. A policy of diversification can be equated broadly to an insurance contract, and there is a price to be paid in both cases. In the case of insurance the price is in the form of a premium, and in the case of diversification it is the cost of choosing less profitable but more diversified activities. It is also possible, indeed likely, that the expertise of top management will fall short of encompassing all the diverse skills and detailed knowledge called for in such a wide range of undertakings.

The managing director, like the conductor wielding a baton on his rostrum, has the often unenviable task of orchestrating the diverse activities into a purposeful concerto.

G. Correct a report

You are the Personal Assistant to Richard Grieves, the Sales Manager at Fenton Floyd Ltd. He has been asked for a brief report on sales for the last quarter by Robert Davidson, the Managing Director. The report was drafted and sent down to the typing pool but it has emerged with a number of mistakes in it. Richard has asked you to go through it correcting any errors you find. 'There are at least ten obvious errors,' he says, 'and there may be more.'

```
To    Richard Greves,                    From   Robert Davidson,
      Sales manager                             Managing director

              Sales for the last quarter of 199-
for the first time in six years we have fallen short of our quarterly
sales target (by approximately 3%) and while this was a dissapointment
to the whole of our team there are some simple explanations for the poor
results. I understand you have already been given a detailed breakdown of
the sales figures.
```
Overseas Division
```
The recent falls in the value of the US dollar have had an adverce effect
on our sales in that part of the world. We find ourselves in an extremely
competetive market, with a number of domestic companys already undercut-
ting our prices. We have until now managed to retain our 10% share of the
market, but the further decline of the dollar has put new pressure on us.
```
New Products Division
```
This is the other area which has produced dissappointing results. The ex-
planation here is, as you will know, that the Head of the Division re-
cently suffered a heart attack and will not be returning to work. His re-
placement, Michael Graeme, had to be brought in from outside the company.
While I am sure he will soon bring about a recovery, there has been a
temporary downturn in sales in this division.
```
Action being taken
```
every member of my team has been made aware of the seriousness of the
situation and I am glad to say that from the projections in front of me
it looks as if our total sales are once again beginning to rise. please
let me know if you reqire any further details.


Richard Grieves
```

13: The board of directors

H. Meanings

The following memorandum was recently circulated to members of staff at Grenadier Products. You are asked to explain the meaning of the highlighted words and phrases.

Grenadier Products   **MEMORANDUM**

To All Office and Sales Staff   From Julie Bright, Office Manager
date

The directors have **expressed concern** that the telephone account for Grenadier Products has increased by 12½% over the past twelve months. The total bill for the year has amounted to approximately £37,800 or over £150 for each **working day**. To get this figure into perspective, the telephone charges could be **equated** to the salaries of two fairly senior members of staff for a whole year. I fully appreciate that in a **marketing orientated company** such as ours a variety of contacts need to be made with customers and it would be foolhardy for telephone conversations to be abruptly terminated just because some **arbitrary time limit** has expired. However, the importance of the telephone to our business should not deter us from attempting to reduce the costs to a reasonable level.

With the full approval of the directors I am now introducing the following **guidelines** which are to be followed by all members of staff from now on:

i) Before you make a 'phone call you are expected to **plan out roughly** what you are going to say. Have any files which may be necessary close to hand.

ii) If you are unable to reach the person you require do not hang on while they are **on the line to someone else**.

iii) Take advantage of any cheaper rates which are offered in **off-peak hours**.

iv) Bear in mind that our customers also have to pay expensive 'phone bills. Doubtless they will also appreciate any reasonable attempt you make to deal with their enquiries quickly, **smoothly** and pleasantly.

v) Personal calls are not allowed except in emergency. The normal arrangement will be to ask your **immediate superior** for permission before making a non-business call. This rule is not intended to be applied harshly but any misuse of the telephone service puts **greater pressure for economies** on the rest of us.

vi) When staff are using the 'phone from now on they should be particularly concerned to be **cost-conscious**. If everyone plays their part more drastic measures can be avoided.

vii) Nothing which is written here can be used as an excuse for **curtness and inefficiency** in dealing with our clients/customers without whom this business would cease to exist, as would our jobs.

While these rules come into force **immediately, the debate is by no means over**. I would welcome ideas from any member of staff who can suggest further ways in which we can solve these (or any other) problems. Two ideas which have already been **floated** are:

a) that a spell of telephone training should be included in the normal **induction programme**.

b) that a small but **thought-provoking** label (see below) should be fixed to each telephone receiver in the company.

13: The board of directors

I. Apostrophes

The following discussion took place at Beauty Unlimited between Terry Cotwood (Production Director), Helen Laleham (Chief Engineer), Sally Forster (Personnel Director) and Tom Burnett (Chief Timekeeper). The Production Director has brought them together to discuss a problem. His secretary has brought them in some coffee to start the proceedings. That is good psychology. It gives them a chance to socialise before they get down to business.

TERRY: *(to Helen)* Well thats great Helen. I hope the mortgage goes through alright. You'll feel a toff living up at the Common... (he taps on his desk)... Can I have your attention?... Thank you... I think youve got an idea of what I want to discuss with you this morning. Its this business of absenteeism. Toms got the figures for us.

TOM: Ive handed out copies to everyone. Id like you to look at the second page in particular. Its quite obvious where the main problems lie. The lipstick production lines the one that gives us most trouble.

SALLY: Theyre always the problem. Youve got to understand how boring it is. The operations are repeated over and over again. Weve tried all sorts of things to make it a bit more bearable but its still one of the factorys worst jobs.

TERRY: Id like to see some rotation of the jobs. Havent we tried that Sally?

SALLY: It didnt work when we tried it a few years ago but Im quite prepared to try it again.

TERRY: Thats good. Well leave that problem in Sallys hands and move over to Helens problem.

TOM: By its very nature its the exact opposite of Sallys problem.

TERRY: By its very nature?

HELEN: The explanations simple enough, Terry. The engineers jobs are quite demanding in comparison with most jobs here. Our young engineers dont think theyre getting enough pay. Theyre leaving as soon as theyve got another job lined up. Those who are left are overworked. Thats whats keeping my people away from work. They cant keep up the pace.

Your task

You are asked to go through this passage of recorded speech putting in the various apostrophes which have been omitted.

J. Complete the sentences

Complete the following sentences using your own words.
1. A non-executive director may ...
2. Although the directors only meet ...
3. The directors are primarily ...
4. Long-term plans are necessary because ...
5. A personnel director ...
6. A financial director ...
7. The managing director in a manufacturing company ...

8. The lines of communication in a large company ...
9. The shareholders will expect the directors to ...
10. The directors are elected ...
11. When the directors choose their senior executives ...
12. When the directors vote in the boardroom ...

K. Vocabulary*

shareholders	dividends	strategic	tactical	expertise
eminent	frequently	obligations	remuneration	delegation
curtness	co-ordinate	diversify	objectives	take-over
integrity	executive	enterprise	administration	conflicting
majority	arbitrary	initiate	compliance	generalist

Match the words listed above with the dictionary definitions which follow.

1. To avoid the situation where all the eggs are in one basket.
2. Someone in a position of authority.
3. An undertaking with a view to profit.
4. The quality of being reliable and straightforward.
5. Brevity to the point of rudeness.
6. Payments made to those who own the equity of a company.
7. To bring together effectively.
8. The decision which chooses the direction in which a company is going.
9. The part of a business concerned with day-to-day problems.
10. Opposing or warring.
11. Meeting with the set requirements.
12. Someone who is able to contribute to a business in a variety of its departments.
13. Having a reputation in a particular branch of business, such as law.
14. The sort of decision which is not based on facts.
15. The opposite of rights.
16. Targets or goals.
17. To commence or start.
18. More than half, for example, of votes cast.
19. Part proprietors of a company. Those who collectively own the equity.
20. Specialised skill or knowledge.
21. A description for salary, usually reserved for more senior officers.
22. The act of giving authority to one's subordinates, while retaining the responsibility for the outcome.
23. The situation when a majority of a company's voting shares are acquired by outsiders.
24. Occurring often.
25. The decision which concerns using the resources which have been allocated to the best possible effect.

14: Business decisions

A. Comprehension

When we talk about making decisions in business we tend to think of the major decisions which are made from time to time, such as the decision to go ahead with the Eurotunnel Project, or the decision to appoint a new chairman for the National Coal Board. The fact is that a multitude of decisions are being made in business every day. Certainly there are major decisions in process as the boards of directors and chief executives in large public companies decide to enter new markets, spend millions on new plant and machinery or advertising campaigns, and buy new buildings or make take-over bids against their most threatening competitors. Yet, for every one of these monumental decisions there are a hundred thousand decisions made by more ordinary mortals.

In fact, man is a decision-making animal. He is continuously making decisions every moment of his life. Many of us wake in the morning to the sound of an alarm clock. Here is our first decision of the day. Should we turn off the alarm and go back to sleep? Or should we turn off the alarm and get up'? There is even a possible compromise. We can turn off the alarm and stay half awake for another few minutes.

We come down to breakfast and face another decision. Do we have toast or cereals? One or two slices? And what about something to drink? Fruit juice or tea? Coffee? Black or white?

Breakfast over we move on to the next bout of decision-making. What shall we wear today? The black shoes or the brown? Shall we take a raincoat or an umbrella? Shall we go by bus or tube? The decisions we are obliged to make are endless, and interestingly, all the decisions we make, to the extent that we are logical in our approach, are dealt with in precisely the same way.

We are confronted with a problem. We then look for the alternative solutions to the problem, weigh up the advantages and disadvantages of each and select the one which gives us most pleasure and least pain. In business terms we are looking for the options which allow us either to achieve our objectives at the lowest possible cost, or allow us to emerge with the greatest profit.

Take the case of the Eurotunnel. As Britain is now a member of the European Community, her trade with Europe is growing. Unlike the other members of the Community we are an island, separated by an inconvenient expanse of water. Do we build a bridge? Or a tunnel? What would be the advantages of a bridge? And the disadvantages? What sorts of tunnels are available? What would be the benefits of a road tunnel as compared to a train tunnel? How much would each of the alternatives cost? And how much would they cost to maintain? How much traffic could they take? How much revenue could they be expected to earn? And who would provide the funds? These were the questions which needed to be answered by the French and British governments and their respective entrepreneurs before any decisions could be made.

These are, of course, monumental decisions, but the basic principle is the same: the advantages and disadvantages of the various possible alternatives are weighed up and an option is chosen. That is how all our decisions are made.

Your tasks

a) Consider three careers which might be available to you. Make a short list of the potential merits and demerits of each and then decide (and indicate) which of the careers you would prefer.

14: Business decisions

b) Make a list of the likely merits and demerits of the Eurotunnel and then decide (and indicate) whether you think Britain will benefit from this venture.

c) Consider where you will take your next holiday. Make a short list of the options and write under each the merits and demerits of each of the proposals. In the light of your analysis where do you think you will be taking your next holiday?

B. Fill in the blanks*

Rewrite this passage filling in the blanks from the list of words below.

Decision-making

The problems confronting a manager are likely to be ...... and varied and it is not suggested they can always be ...... by reference to a rigid formula, but an analytical and ...... approach is certainly to be commended. Whether the decision ...... to personnel, finance or marketing, the ...... of the process are the same.

First, the ...... must be defined. Where it is ...... it may be necessary to break it down into parts. All the relevant facts should be ...... and the various aspects of the situation brought together. Then the full ...... of alternatives (or options) should be considered. A choice will have to be made between the alternatives and this weighing up the pros and cons of each of the alternatives, before deciding on what ...... to be the best solution in the given circumstances. What is best in the ......may not be so appropriate in the long-term – and vice versa.

In a business ...... the decisions will be made in terms of a ...... evaluation. The best alternative will either be the option which gives the greatest profitability, or the one which allows a given goal to be achieved with the ...... expenditure.

At this ...... the decision is still in the mind and it now requires implementation. Subordinates need to be told what is ...... of them and their ...... need to be monitored to make sure they are ...... with the instructions.

Subordinates are often given the ...... to participate in the ...... phases of the routine. They can ...... information and usefully discuss a situation with their manager. However, the ...... between the alternatives is the manager's prerogative, since he ...... responsible for the outcome.

minimum	context	required	involves
mechanics	problem	complex	appears
mixed	tackled	objective	relates
assembled	range	short-term	opportunity
monetary	actions	complying	early
choice	provide	remains	point

A second task

Complete the diagram below by placing the appropriate words in the five different boxes.

Determine the problem   *Obtain feedback*   *Implement the decision*
       Modify if necessary   *Decide what to do*

14: Business decisions

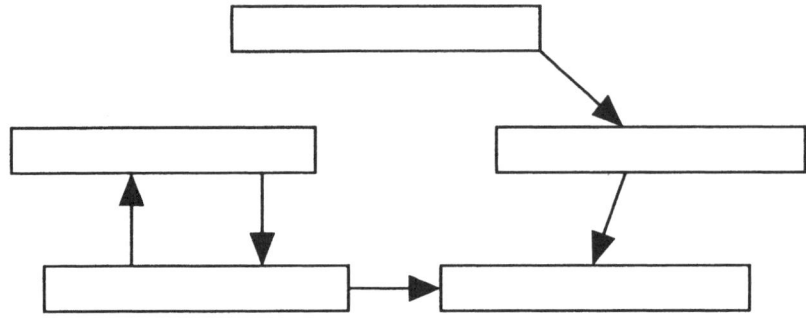

C. Case study

Juniper Ltd

Juniper is a medium-sized company based in Norwich producing a variety of natural health foods in three separate factories around the town. The Personnel Director, Ben Walton, has recently seen some statistics on the subject of lateness and absenteeism among his workforce and they have displeased him. A summary of the figures for the last two years is shown here.

Juniper Ltd – Absenteeism and Lateness Last Year				(Previous year's figures in brackets)	
Site	Workforce*	Days lost through†			
		Absenteeism		Lateness	
Belton	600	(600)	13,000	(10,000)	18,000	(15,000)
High Fenn	600	(500)	12,000	(11,000)	18,000	(11,000)
Greensward	300	(600)	3,000	(11,000)	3,000	(13,000)
*Rounded to the nearest hundred †Rounded to the nearest thousand					

He has asked you as his newly appointed Personal Assistant to write him a brief but formal report (maximum 200 words) setting out your interpretation of these figures. He is considering the possibility of introducing flexible working hours at Juniper and would like to know what you see as the merits and demerits of this proposal. He would also like to know whether you have any other ideas on how the problems of absenteeism and lateness might be tackled.

You may include diagrams in your report if you wish.

D. Verbs and adjectives*

Add an appropriate verb or adjective from the list below to each of the following sentences where indicated.

a) If subordinates are .... in the decision-making process they will show .... interest in their work.

b) The .... work can all too easily become a battle to .... with piles of paperwork before the time runs out.

c) Like a good car driver the .... manager looks as far ahead as he can so as to spot hazards and then .... them.

d) The whole business organisation, from the board of directors down to the .... pool, is a network of teams each trying to .... its own goals.

e) Each team in the business will .... its target more easily and effectively if everyone is pulling in the .... direction.

f) Before you decide on a course of action it is wise to .... the .... consequences.

g) Most firms are aware of the need to .... good public relations.

h) When a .... plan is being .... it is necessary to bring into account its effect on the environment.

Verbs: *achieve consider maintain avoid deal reach evaluated involved*

Adjectives: *same day's astute typing greater likely development*

'I've made the decision!!! I'll have my coffee without milk this morning!'

E. Join the halves*

On the left of the page are the first halves of sentences. On the right are the second halves of the sentences, though not in the same order. Pair the halves and then write your own list of the completed sentences.

i) When you are building a team to take your company on to bigger and better things

ii) First you make your decision, based on facts wherever possible,

iii) The basic question is not are we doing better than last year

iv) Innovation should always be customer-driven

v) A decision will usually have to be carried out by subordinates

vi) A golden rule is to be objective

a) and your company's performance will suffer.

b) but are we doing better than our competitors.

c) so a manager would be wise to take their views into account.

d) when a new work flow been introduced.

e) you have to be certain you are choosing the right people.

f) and then you put the ideas into practice.

14: Business decisions

vii) The personnel manager may face a difficult task
viii) You need to know what models are available
ix) Make a wrong appointment to a key post
x) An office manager would benefit from an early feedback
xi) Typing pool supervisors should know which members of their staffs are working well
xii) A variety of data usually needs to be analysed

g) and that means finding what the customers need.
h) before a decision can be made rationally.
i) so they can be recommended for pay increases and/or promotions.
j) and so a manager must avoid being swayed by emotions.
k) before you can make up your mind which word processor to buy.
l) when a number of first-class candidates are short-listed for a job.

F. Summarising

Give the following passage an appropriate title and summarise it in about 100 words.

So you fancy yourself as a manager? You are not alone in having that ambition. What does it mean to be a manager? I suppose the first thought that comes to mind is that a manager gives orders and tells other people what to do. That is partly true. But it is not quite as simple as that. In fact, managers have to take orders as much as anyone else. The term 'executive' actually implies executing orders – orders perhaps not under their power to influence.

Every business has to decide where it is going. What it is trying to achieve. Words like objectives and targets are used in management theory. Whether these targets are related to items such as sales or budgets, they are broken down into sub-targets as they go further down the organisational hierarchy. The managers at the various levels in the structure are given these targets or objectives to achieve. Sometimes they are given considerable freedom to achieve the targets in the way they see best. Sometimes their independence is limited, perhaps very limited.

Subject to these constraints a manager has certain clear-cut functions. First, he has to plan – to look ahead – to anticipate. When you drive a car you look as far ahead as you can to see what hazards lie ahead. If you see some children playing in the road ahead you start to slow down, check your breaks are working and generally watch for trouble. What would you think of a driver who kept his eyes on the road – six feet in front of his bonnet? A manager who is able to anticipate problems has more chance of coping with them.

Another function of managers is to control. We have already seen that managers are expected to achieve targets of some sort or another. The manager has to keep these targets clearly in mind when he is involved in the decision-making process. Progress towards the targets needs to be monitored and any deviations corrected. It is a bit like the captain of a liner sailing across the Atlantic to New York. Every now and again he will check to see whether or not the ship is on course. If it is beginning to drift to port or starboard he has to bring it back onto course. That is what we mean by control.

Managers are expected to get results of one sort or another, in one way or another, but they get their results through people. The manager of the England football team never kicks a ball in an international football match, but he is expected to get the best out of his team. Everyone in the team is expected to co-operate to get the ball in the back of

14: Business decisions

the opposing team's net. All have to be persuaded to pull together – in the same direction. In management terminology this aspect of a manager's work is called co-ordination.

G. Opposites and synonyms*

Complete the following table.

part of speech	word	synonym	opposite
noun	inquest		
verb	manage		
adjective	accidental		
noun	co-operation		
verb	propose		
noun	purpose		
verb	control		
adjective	dynamic		
adverb	rationally		
noun	subordinate		
verb	object		
verb	persuade		
verb	inform		
adjective	strict		
adverb	appreciatively		
adjective	supportive		
verb	anticipate		
adjective	sensitive		
verb	monitor		
verb	confer		
noun	information		

H. Meanings

First read the passage below. Then explain the meanings of the words and phrases which have been highlighted.

In order to be successful a firm has to identify **unsatisfied needs** within society and then proceed to satisfy them. Some would say businesses **create needs** by various forms of advertising, in order to satisfy them subsequently. Examples of this are the **frivolous demand** for chocolate Easter eggs and greetings cards and flowers for Mothers' Day.

The main difficulty facing businesses, however, is that **their markets** are constantly changing. Consider the firms which were making gas mantles in the early years of the twentieth century. **Their future looked assured.** London and all other western cities

14: Business decisions

were lit by gaslight. Then came the switch to electricity and gas mantles had become **museum pieces** almost overnight. There was a similar situation with the textile called rayon. Up to **the middle of the twentieth century** it was the fashion for western ladies to **don** rayon stockings. Then nylon was developed and the market for rayon stockings completely disappeared. At the present time we are seeing typewriters **giving way** to electric typewriters – giving way to word processors –and we wonder what is **the next in line**. Likewise accounting machines gave way to mainframe computers which are now being **revolutionised by the microchip**. Markets and technologies are forever changing and the successful business is the one which can **keep abreast** of the changes.

The moral for the modern firm is to be forward looking, anticipating and projecting trends, **forestalling problems by foreseeing them**. Questions need to be constantly **posed.** What are we producing now? What should we be producing next? What changes need to be made? **What are our competitors up to** – at home and overseas? What is happening to the markets for our goods? Should we be **diversifying our products**? Where do they stand in their **life cycles**? What resources (including **human resources**) do we need to carry out our plans and how are we going to obtain these resources? To survive in business we need to be **eternally vigilant**.

I. Write a report

You are the Personnel Assistant to Sally Forster, Personnel Director at Beauty Unlimited. It has been suggested that the company set up a suggestion scheme whereby employees are encouraged to put forward their ideas for improving any aspect of the work. Mrs Forster has indicated that she would be prepared to ask the directors for a contribution of up to £10,000 in the first twelve months of the scheme and she is now asking you to write a brief but formal report (up to 200 words) indicating the likely value of the scheme to the company. She is envisaging setting up a special committee to vet any proposals put forward but admits she has an open mind on the subject at present. She is hoping you will come through with some ideas.

There are approximately 500 workers employed at the factory. Most of them are women under the age of 30. The company uses mass production techniques to produce a range of beauty aids from hair dyes to cleansing creams.

J. Complete the sentences

Complete the following sentences using your own words.
1. Businesses will flourish ...
2. An aspiring manager should learn ...
3. Businesses are often affected by situations ...
4. By anticipating problems ...
5. The decision-making process ...
6. If we can minimise our costs ...
7. The good manager is one who ...
8. The most valuable subordinate is the one who ...
9. When a business is faced with falling sales it can either ...
10. If only one member of staff can be promoted ...
11. If a member of staff is consistently late ...

K. Vocabulary*

evaluation	feasibility	flexible	frivolous	criteria
ineffective	projection	redundancy	bureaucracy	options
emphasis	competitive	co-operative	discretions	autocratic
supportive	analytic	deviation	permissible	complex
hazardous	subordinate	implement	anticipation	remedial

Match the words listed above with the dictionary definitions which follow.

1. Capable of adaptation to changing situations.
2. This type of manager tends to make decisions without referring to those affected by them.
3. An objective and rational approach.
4. A weighing up of the pros and cons in a given situation.
5. A situation where an employee is no longer required by the employer.
6. The type of management which is both caring and helpful.
7. Risky, as when sailing in uncharted waters.
8. A description of a problem with many aspects to be brought into account.
9. A look forward in an attempt to spot future threats or opportunities.
10. To put a decision into effect.
11. Someone who is below another in the organisational hierarchy.
12. The alternatives available to one in the decision-making process.
13. Certain delegated powers given by a manager to his staff.
14. Stress laid on or importance attached to a particular aspect of a problem.
15. The type of action which is intended to solve a problem.
16. Something which is allowed.
17. Light-hearted and of no great consequence.
18. Factors to be brought into account when deciding on a course of action.
19. A study which helps to determine whether a particular course of action is possible or not.
20. The treatment of data so as to determine what is likely to happen in the future.
21. The type of person who is prepared to work with others in order to reach a mutually desired target.
22. An organisation which is governed by the strict application of unbending rules.
23. A movement away from the chosen path.
24. Describing a solution which does not produce the desired result.
25. The type of person or organisation that likes to be in front.

L. Discussion topic

There are a number of benefits for managers when they allow their subordinates to participate in the decision-making process. Two heads are better than one, even if the manager has more experience than his subordinates. Of course it is by no means certain that the manager will have a better idea than his subordinate. Today's subordinate is tomorrow's manager.

14: Business decisions

One of the functions of management is to motivate, and one of the ways to motivate subordinates is to feed their egos. It charges their motivation batteries when their manager asks them what *they* think, or what course of action they would recommend. It helps to develop self-confidence which is so vital to someone who is new to the game of business.

Along the same lines, participation can be seen as a training device. Few people are born with a genius for decision-making. Most of us need our talents cultivating. But it is not just a question of managers nurturing the talents of their subordinates. The managers are judged by their ability to comply with targets set, and they can only achieve their targets with the aid of their subordinates. The last thing a wise manager wants is a poorly trained team.

Finally, in a democratic society, people expect to be consulted with regard to matters which will affect them. The workplace is no exception. Many societies now enjoy a reasonable degree of political democracy and are moving towards the next stage in the process – industrial democracy – including supervisory boards of directors, works councils and various types of co-ownership. The only questions remaining, in fact, are 'how far?' and 'how fast?'.

Your views

1. What do you see as the merits and demerits of allowing subordinates to participate in the decision-making process?
2. To what extent to you think employees should have a say in the running of a business?
3. Do you think there should be workers/directors on the boards of limited companies?
4. Do you think employers should operate a 'full disclosure policy' so far as their employees are concerned? What are the dangers?
5. How far do you think industrial democracy can, and should, be introduced?
6. Which groups in society benefit if a business succeeds, and which groups lose if it fails?

15: Information technology

A. Comprehension

The microchip revolution is having a huge impact on modern business. While the advent of completely automated (robotised) production systems is producing legions of unemployed workers, people at work are most likely to come into contact with microelectronics through the medium of 'information technology'.

Information technology (IT) covers a wide range of operations based on a combination of computing and telecommunications techniques. It includes the compilation of information in the form of data banks and the material, which may be textual, numeric, pictorial or even vocal can be processed and stored until retrieval is required.

In the past, information management involved massive dependence on paper, but today tiny electronic pulses are stored on floppy disks. Although modern disks have an incredible capacity, newer and even more compact devices are being developed.

The earliest forms of computers were so-called mainframe computers, programmed electronic machines capable of processing almost limitless amounts of routine data and making complex calculations repetitively, speedily and accurately.

Microelectronics involves the design, application and production of very small electronic devices containing many miniaturised components. Microcomputers are obviously much smaller in size than the mainframe computers. They are also cheaper and more flexible in operation. A substantial range of software programs are on offer to perform many of the key office functions such as accounting, stock control and word processing.

The other branch of information technology is telecommunications, which covers the transmission of information by electronic cables (telephone and telegraph) or radio waves. Fibre optics (very fine strands of glass) transmitting high speed pulses of light are replacing the old-fashioned, conventional copper cables and allow many thousands more telephone calls to be made. Using microwave transmissions, static space satellites are also revolutionising international communication.

Perhaps the example of the new concepts with which we are most familiar is the infra-red system which we use to operate our television sets by remote control.

Questions

1. What benefits as an individual do you expect from the increasing use of computers in our society?
2. What do you see as the major problem arising from the increasing use of computers? For example, do you think they depersonalise work? What dangers do you see with respect to possible computer frauds? Do you see any military implications?
3. Do you think the microchip revolution has created unemployment? If so, what do you see as the answer to the problem? Shorter working weeks? Work sharing? Earlier retirement?
4. How do you think satellite communications can be useful to:
   a) multinational corporations
   b) companies providing information on world events for newspapers and television news and entertainment?

15: Information technology

B. EFTPOS

Cashless shopping, or electronic funds transfer at point of sale (EFTPOS), will soon become the commonest form of retail trade. There are already 63,000 establishments with 132,000 terminals in France, and the other major European countries are not far behind.

It works like this: a customer goes into a shop to buy goods, and when it comes to payment, he or she draws a plastic card through an electronic terminal and then enters a code number known only to him or her. Details of the transaction and the code are then sent by a telecommunications network to a central computer which checks that the card is neither 'out of order' nor stolen. Funds are then transferred electronically from the customer's bank account to the shopkeeper's.

Your task

There are obviously advantages and disadvantages in this new method of payment and you are invited to complete the tables shown here.

For   *Against*

From the customer's point of view:

For	Against
1. **Time saved at checkouts**	1.
2.	2.
3.	3.

From the retailer's point of view:

For	Against
1.	1.
2.	2.
3.	3.

From a bank's point of view:

For	Against
1.	1.
2.	2.
3.	3.

C. Multiple choice*

The following sentences relate to various aspects of information technology (IT). There are words missing from each statement. Tick the box which follows the appropriate word.

1. The future development of world-wide integrated networks for funds transmission ...... difficult questions of security both for the network itself and the customer using it.

    A. raise ☐
    B. raises ☐
    C. raised ☐

2. The ...... in digital technology are providing a boost for the reprographics industry, enabling companies to produce higher quality business forms and documents rapidly on desktop publishing systems.

    A. advances ☐
    B. research ☐
    C. researches ☐

172

15: Information technology

3. The processor, memory and electronic controls for the periphery equipment for a microcomputer are ...... put together on a printed circuit board.
   - A. seldom
   - B. usually
   - C. always

4. The trend in software is towards integrated systems where a number of different products from a software ...... are designed to work in a single system.
   - A. purchaser
   - B. user
   - C. manufacurer

5. When data needs to be saved for an ...... period of time it is stored on magnetic tapes or magnetic disks.
   - A. extended
   - B. short
   - C. long

6. Sorting is the ...... of data into a pre-determined sequence to assist further processing, and the most common sorting sequences are numerical and alphabetical.
   - A. collection
   - B. arrangement
   - C. disposal

7. Data verification procedures are a method of trying to ...... the integrity of data.
   - A. eliminate
   - B. preserve
   - C. restore

8. A local area network (LAN) is a system of interconnecting microcomputers over a small geographical area, ... within a few hundred metres.
   - A. typically
   - B. occasionally
   - C. specifically

9. Wide area networks (WANs) operate on a wide geographical scale and, since they send data over telecommunications links, they need modems which ...... digital form data into wave form.
   - A. modify
   - B. convert
   - C. define

15: Information technology

10. A timesharing system is a multi-user/multi-access system in which many users have ...... access to the computer for their own data processing requirements.
    A. immediate ☐
    B. continuous ☐
    C. simultaneous ☐

11. A real time system is one in which data is received and processed and results are transmitted ...... enough for the data to be capable of influencing the sources of data (for example, air traffic control, airline bookings and process control).
    A. accurately ☐
    B. rapidly ☐
    C. slowly ☐

12. Batch processing means processing a group of similar routine transactions in one processing operation at the same time, but the processing does not begin until they have all been ...... in a transactions file.
    A. collected ☐
    B. distributed ☐
    C. analysed ☐

D. The smart card

The so-called smart card is an ordinary plastic credit card with an embedded microprocessor plus a computer memory chip. It can be used as an identity card, a passport, for access to medical records and even for paying for telephone calls, train and bus fares and satellite television programmes.

Although in its infancy in the UK there are currently 17,000,000 such cards in use in French and French banks are expecting all their customers to own one. Outside Europe, perhaps not surprisingly, it is Japan which is showing most interest in the concept.

In Britain, the Barclays and Midland banking groups are conducting pilot schemes. The Midland scheme is centred on Loughborough University and smart cards are being used in three applications:

i) Being charged (like a battery) with money, they can be used for purchases at shops and bars on campus. They can also be used by students paying for photocopying. The card can be recharged at an automatic telling machine.

ii) They can be used as a debit card. As the goods are purchased, the cost is transferred directly from the student's account into that of the shopkeeper. With the aid of a personal identity number (PIN), details of all transactions stored in the memory can be viewed at any terminal.

iii) Finally, of value to the students at Loughborough, but with obvious commercial applications, information can be accessed from a variety of publishing sources.

There are two major advantages from the bank's point of view. First, smart cards cut down on paperwork. Second, they improve the effectiveness of controls over bad debts and frauds. Customers and retailers may still need to be convinced of the advantages of smart cards, but the implications are incredible.

In terms of signature verification, it is possible to check the shape of letters, speed at which the signature is written and the amount of pressure on the pen. The variables are then converted into algorithms which are fed into the card's memory store.

15: Information technology

Even more exciting is the possible integration into biometric systems. Unique shapes of eye retinas or fingerprints can be stored digitally on the card and matched with the owners when required.

At this point of time the expense of the smart card is prohibitive, but, as with all technological innovations, the price to the consumers is likely to fall as the initial development costs are recovered.

Your task

Having read the above passage you are invited to complete the following sentences:

a) The Midland Bank is ...
b) The smart card has been introduced in France and ...
c) Students at Loughborough are able to ...
d) With smart cards travellers could ...
e) The banks feel that bad debts could be reduced because ...
f) By using fingerprints ...
g) By charging the cards at an automatic telling machine ...
h) One of the problems with smart cards is ...

E. Fill in the blanks*

At least one word has been omitted from each of these sentences. Fill in the blanks from the list of words below:

programs	graphics	binary	utility	code
software	integrated	backing	operating	orbits
optic	terminals	retrieval	library	microwave
manipulation	translators	lightpen	satellites	computers

1. Fibre .... cables allow data to be transmitted as pulses of light along thin strands of glass about the thickness of human hair.
2. Data communications over very long distances can make use of communication .... which are placed in fixed .... above the earth.
3. Data can be communicated over long distances and over water by using .... radio links.
4. A .... terminal is specially designed to display pictures, maps, graphs and diagrams, and has a .... attached to allow the user to 'draw' on the screen.
5. A mainframe computer and its .... are situated a long distance apart.
6. The numbers used in computers are called .... numbers.
7. .... are sets of instructions telling the computer what operations have to be carried out and in what order they should be done.
8. Database programs are for information .... and word processor programs are for text ....
9. A collection of applications programs kept in a .... store is known as a program ....
10. .... packages have a number of programs combined in one package so that the same data can be shared by them all.

15: Information technology

11. The .... system consists of a group of programs designed to manage and co-ordinate all the hardware and .... of a computer system as efficiently as possible.

12. .... programs are small systems programs which perform one simple task.

13. Language .... convert programs written in various computer languages into machine .... and include assemblers, compilers and interpreters.

14. .... understand commands expressed in the form 0 and 1.

F. Synonyms and opposites*

Find synonyms for the words in *italics* and words with the opposite meaning for the words highlighted.

In his presidential *address* to the Chartered Institute of Bankers, Sir John Quinton said information technology was at the heart of banking. 'Whether as corporations or as individuals,' he said, 'we **ignore** the implications of IT at our *peril*. The *impact* of IT upon banking is so *radical* that it will be a *key* determinant of success or failure in the industry; a key determinant of whether 'banks' as a **recognisable** grouping continue to exist, and a key determinant of the *differentiation* between competitors in financial services.'

If information is seen as a resource, it follows that it can be managed. We can *attempt* to produce it in the **most** cost-effective manner, determining how it should be processed, stored, *retrieved* and disposed of. The implication is that businesses – not only banks – should be **prepared** to develop an information *strategy*.

To relate *information* to the management function it has to *contribute* to the achievement of some organisational *objective*. The relationship between the information and the attainment of the objective needs to be clearly shown, and the relationship has to be **capable** of being tested empirically. If we see information as a **resource**, it also follows that we have to be *selective*. As Sir John Quinton also said, 'it really comes back to the basic **question** that all companies need to ask themselves – what *business*, or should I say, businesses, are we in?' Having **answered** that question we can decide what information we need, how it is to be obtained, and how it is to be *treated*.

G. Linking statements with purposes*

Link each statement in the first column with a purpose in second column.

i) Application programs are designed for general use

ii) Custom programs are written for the user

iii) A program library is often kept in backing store

iv) A word processor justifies each line of text

v) A high resolution monitor is used

vi) A graphics terminal includes a lightpen

vii) A computer is often leased rather than bought

a) to produce detailed graphics.

b) to provide easy access to a range of programs.

c) so the user can 'draw' on the screen.

d) to prepare, test and document computer programs.

e) so they can be used in many different situations.

f) as an economy measure.

g) to distinguish diverse values or features.

viii) The functions of programmers are   h) to suit a particular situation.
ix) The keyboard of a computer is used   i) to input data.
x) Dual-density characters are introduced   j) to form a straight edge.

H. Vocabulary*

core	cursor	track	robot
spreadsheet	off-line	on-line	matrix
floppy	byte	bugs	access
flowcharts	algorithm	digital	decoder
chip	punched	user	screen

Match the words listed above with the definitions which follow:
1. A printer which uses pins to print a pattern of dots on paper.
2. Very light, flexible, plastic diskettes usually used with microcomputers.
3. The channels of a magnetic tape on which information is recorded.
4. Another word for program errors.
5. A sequence of steps or instructions used to solve a problem, as in a program.
6. This is the individual operating the computer.
7. When the computer system operates independently of the central processing unit.
8. A small metal ring, part of the computer memory, which can be magnetized and demagnetized.
9. A group of eight binary digits considered as a single unit. In other words, eight bits make one of these.
10. This type of computer works by counting, and data is represented by combinations of discrete electronic pulses.
11. This is the display unit on which the data and/or graphics appear.
12. This type of card is used to input information or to receive the outputted result.
13. To retrieve information which is on tape or disk.
14. A piece of silicon on which several layers of an integrated circuit have been etched.
15. This takes the coded instruction and breaks it down into the individual commands which allow it to be carried out.
16. An arrow or similar marker to show where the next character will go if you enter data.
17. These are diagrams used to sort out the procedural steps in a program and as an aid to program construction.
18. A machine which replicates human thinking and behaviour patterns.
19. When the computer system is connected to the central processing unit.
20. A package used extensively in financial planning, budgeting, forecasting and other financial modelling.

I. Discussion topic

Most of the world's hardware manufacturers are either in the United States of America or Japan. Is this because the Americans and the Japanese have innate skills which the rest

15: Information technology

of us do not possess? Perhaps that is the explanation, but it is far more likely to be the result of economies of scale. American manufacturers are catering for a domestic market of over 220,000,000 while the Japanese domestic market tops 120,000,000.

If you accept that both these domestic markets tend to be 'captive', with the Japanese market particularly difficult to enter, one reason why individual companies can afford to spend large sums on research without overpricing their product becomes clear.

If a Japanese company produces 100,000 units and spends (the equivalent of) £10 million on research, the price at which it sells its units has to be increased by £100 to cover the research costs. However, if a smaller British company produces 10,000 units and spends £10 million on research, it will have to increase the price of its units by £1,000 to cover its costs. Is it any surprise to find the Americans and the Japanese, with their large, and rich, domestic populations dominating world markets in technological products?

By contrast the present European computer scene is dominated mainly by software and services, but this is not such a disadvantage as it seems. As users look more and more for systems that work the way their business requires, the role of the software element is becoming more important. At the same time, in cost terms alone, software is becoming the major part of IT investment as hardware costs tumble. Why should hardware costs tumble? The manufacturers of technological products always aim to recover development costs as quickly as possible. After that, as competition begins to bite, prices become more competitive.

Perhaps there is another explanation. It could be that the scope for further development in the IT industry lies in the field of software rather than hardware, at this point in time anyway.

Europe, with a population larger than that of the USA but with an IT market only half its size, offers more potential for growth, but is not by any stretch of the imagination a single market, nor is it likely to be so for many decades. The 12 national markets that make up the European Community are separated by differences in culture, language and hardware environments. The European software and services market is likely to be dominated by four or five indigenous heavyweights coming from France, Italy and Britain, but since the unified Germany has a domestic market which is likely to extend deeper and deeper into Eastern Europe, its progress is likely to prove most significant.

One of the big question marks will be whether, as a result of mergers in the IT industry in the new Europe, the Europeans are able to challenge the Americans and the Japanese in the hardware market. An encouraging factor could be the inevitable linkage between hardware and software. The formation of large, pan-European user companies will open up fresh markets for pan-European suppliers, for both hardware and integrated software.

Your views

1. How do you see the European Community affecting and being affected by developments in IT?

2. Which European countries/companies do you see benefiting most from the enlarged markets?

3. What do you think users are looking for when they buy new IT systems? Compatibility with the existing equipment? The size and stability of the vending corporation? The user-friendliness of the system? The cost? The estimated working life – or conversely, the obsolescence date?

4. How do you think developments in IT are affecting, and will affect
   a) your future career, and   b) the world of business generally?

5. Do you think IT tends to help women gain equal treatment with men, or the reverse? Justify your opinion.

16: Stocks, shares and take-overs

A. Comprehension*

'Before a business can function two ingredients are essential: people and money. Without either, no business could take off.

For the limited company, funds are initially provided by the shareholders. Ordinary stocks (or shares) are commonly described as 'equities', indicating that the holders are entitled to what is left of the assets and profits, after certain claims have been met.

The stock is broken down into units of, say 50p each, which is then described as the nominal value. This is the value used for the calculation of dividends. So, if a dividend of 10 per cent is paid on a 50p stock unit, the dividend will amount to 10 per cent of 50p, i.e. 5p per unit.

The dividends on ordinary stock will be related to the profits made by the company. Thus, if the profits are good the ordinary stockholder can expect to receive an attractive dividend. However, before the dividend is paid the directors of the company may wish to recommend part of the profits being ploughed back into the business.

The fact that dividends normally vary in line with profits gives the person who holds ordinary stock some possible protection against the falling value of money – another description for inflation.

This hedge against inflation operates in the following manner. In the case of a typical manufacturing company, where there is a rise in the cost of raw materials and wages, the company can usually compensate for this by raising the price of its finished goods. In this way its profits can be increased, wholly or partially, in line with the general rate of inflation.

Ordinary stocks normally, but not invariably, carry voting power. Some stock units are even issued which give more than one vote per stock unit, but multiple voting stock, as it is called, is not common. Some investors are willing to accept non-voting ordinary stock (usually designated 'A' stock) on the grounds that they do not wish to exercise voting power in any case. However, when there is a take-over in the offing, the voting stocks will become more valuable and, for this reason, the market price of the voting stocks would be expected to stand at a premium in relation to the price of the non-voting stocks.

Whoever owns more than 50% of the voting stock is sure of controlling the elections to the board of directors. Yet many boards own much less than this proportion of voting stock between them. They are still able to select their own replacements for any directors who die or retire, since other groups of shareholders will be disorganised and unaware of the issues and personalities involved.

The existing board of directors in a large public limited company (PLC) are likely to remain in effective control so long as the company's performance satisfies the majority of the voting shareholders. But if the company falters there could be a stockholders' revolt leading to the replacement of the existing board – or at least elements of it.

Your task

Now complete each of the following sentences with one of the words listed below.

    a)   Ordinary stocks are usually described as ....

    b)   If the company's .... rise the ordinary stockholders can expect a good ....

16: Stocks, shares and take-overs

c) If shares do not carry voting power they are unlikely to increase in value as a result of a .... bid.

d) If a company's profits fall drastically the .... might change the board of .... at the next Annual General Meeting (AGM).

e) Ordinary stocks can be expected to provide a useful .... against inflation.

f) A company's board of directors is likely to retain .... of the company so long as they make reasonable profits.

The missing words:

shareholders	equities	hedge	dividend
directors	control	profits	take-over

'You know that fellow Heatherington-Smythe you sacked last month? He's using his redundancy pay for a take-over bid.'

B. Fill in the blanks*

Fill in the following passage using words from the list below.

The Football Business

In Britain the football clubs in the national leagues are run by limited companies. The .... decisions are therefore made by the board of directors, and the directors are .... by the shareholders as in any other company.

Some clubs are successful and make .... profits. Most have perennial cash flow problems. Having discovered a talented player, they are obliged to offer him to the highest .... in order to meet their debts.

If the football business is generally so ...., why are there so many highly successful business tycoons prepared to 'bale them out'?

Before we answer that question we should look at the .... of the club's assets. There are usually at least a couple of acres of potentially valuable building land. Often the shares can be .... cheaply because the club, languishing in the lower divisions, never makes a profit.

16: Stocks, shares and take-overs

Is it any .... then that there are sometimes builders and developers who are prepared to buy the apparently .... shares? If the club succeeds, the shares go up in value. If the club fails, the company is .... up and the major shareholder has some valuable land to develop. It could be .... as a win-win situation.

This can be such an .... proposition that the entrepreneur, in addition to buying shares, might be .... to lend substantial sums to the club – no doubt taking a .... on the land as security.

In the circumstances it is difficult to know whether an offer of financial help is coming from a genuinely .... fan of the club or someone who has an eye for a bargain. A wolf sometimes wears sheep's clothing!

substantial	prepared	mortgage	elected
devoted	attractive	major	bidder
worthless	wound	acquired	nature
unprofitable	surprise	described	

C. The Guinness affair*

One of the most **intriguing** legal cases in the UK in recent years related to the Guinness take-over of Distillers. Guinness, one of the largest breweries in Europe, had decided to bid for Distillers, another giant brewery.

The Board of Directors of Guinness were offering a mixture of cash and their own shares to the shareholders of Distillers. This is a common **ploy** in taking over large and successful companies, because it reduces the financial **burden** for the bidders.

In the Guinness affair, however, a new and disturbing **element** was introduced. In order to raise the market value of the shares which were being offered, an **artificial** demand was created by a group of wealthy **backers** who bought large amounts of Guinness shares **prior to** the take-over bid. The **perpetrators** were taken to court, fined substantially, and sentenced to long **terms** of imprisonment.

Why inflict such punishments? The main reason was that the Distillers shareholders were fraudulently **misled** as to the real value of the shares they were being offered. The question remains how many similar incidents have gone **undetected**.

The Guinness affair is one which will be debated in Stock Exchange circles for many years to come, proving as it does how difficult it is to **regulate** take-over bids effectively.

Your first task

Each of the words highlighted in the passage above has a synonym in the list of words below. You are invited to match them.

before	discussed	supporters	control
interesting	unreal	wrongdoers	misinformed
increase	cost	undiscovered	technique
factor	periods		

Your second task

Explain in your own words what happened in the Guinness affair.

16: Stocks, shares and take-overs

D. Discussion topic

Since quoted shares are freely transferable, they can be acquired by anyone who is prepared to pay the market price for them. However, there are certain rules to be observed in the UK. One is that you may bid up to 29.9% of a company's shares before making a full bid, but after that you must make a full offer for all the remaining shares, at the highest price you have paid for the shares so far.

Another basic rule is that shareholders must be treated equally, and when an offer is announced, the share transactions must be reported by all parties to the City Take-over Panel, the Stock Exchange, and the financial press. It will be interesting to see how take-over rules are harmonised in future in the European Community.

If the ground rules for take-overs are negotiable, the reasons for take-overs are likely to remain the same everywhere in the world. Acquiring a majority of the voting shares in a company gives one the power to appoint directors and thereby control the policies of that company. For what purpose?

i) To buy shares at a bargain price. If shares are good value it seems logical to buy as many as possible. This could lead to asset-stripping where the break-up value of the company is higher than the price of the shares.

ii) To enjoy economies of scale as a result of the enlarged operations. If unit costs can be reduced, pricing policies can be more flexible and profits increased.

iii) To eliminate competition. For example, newspapers X and Y may be in competition with each other. X finds that Y is eroding its market share. With the financial backing of its bankers X takes over Y. It then has two basic options. It can either close down Y or segment the market so that for example X goes for upmarket readers, leaving the downmarket for Y. Or X can go for family readers, leaving Y to go for sports and politics, and so on.

iv) To secure future supplies at a reasonable price. Thus, a company owning a chain of supermarkets may take over a factory processing a variety of foods. This is called backward integration.

v) To ensure markets for the goods or services of the parent company. This might be where a company making shoes, takes over one owning a chain of shoe shops. This is called forward integration.

vi) To benefit from a policy of diversification, a company becoming involved in a wide variety of activities.

vii) To rescue an ailing company, in which case the impetus for the take-over might come from the company which is seeking to be taken over. Management buy-outs might be included in this category.

How can a company combat a suspected take-over bid? One way is to avoid a situation here shareholders are unaware of the true value of their shares. Accountants and auditors are expected to be prudent, but a policy of prudence can lead to low dividends. Low dividends can lead to low share prices, and that is the ideal setting for a take-over.

Your views

1. Do you think take-overs can be justified in economic terms? How would you feel about a foreign company taking over one of your country's banks or insurance companies?
2. Why do think shareholders need to be protected from take-over predators?
3. Do you think take-overs are likely to be more or less common in the European Community? Why? Which sorts of companies are most likely to be involved in take-overs in the new Europe?
4. What problems are likely to be faced in multinational European companies?

5. What sorts of take-overs do you think a) a hotel group and b) a motor manufacturing company might seek?

E. Reply to a letter

Matthew Freeman, a chartered accountant, has received the following letter from one of his clients. You are asked to draft a reply for his signature. Mrs Wiseman's husband, Thomas, died last year, and she is carrying on their small tobacconist and confectionery business.

The Candy Box The Esplanade, Brighton, Sussex BN5 9JT   Telephone 0504 454545

Date:

Mr M Freeman ACCA
37 Marlborough Chambers
Cornhill
Brighton
Sussex BN4 7PQ

Dear Mr Freeman,

A few days ago I received notification from the bank that 2000 ordinary stock units in Sentinel Security Systems had been transferred into my name. The stocks originally belonged to my husband, Thomas. I was thinking of selling them, but my daughter tells me there is likely to be a take-over bid for the company within the next couple of months. She thinks I should hold on to the stock for the time being.

I do not know anything about stocks and shares; Thomas always handled that aspect of our finances. Will I lose the stocks if the company is taken over? What do you think I should do?

Yours sincerely,

Alice Wiseman

Alice Wiseman

F. Rights issues

One of the most popular methods for a public company to acquire funds is through a rights issue. The existing stockholders are sent a provisional allotment letter (see example on page 185) which offers them the new shares on favourable terms. A rights issue would operate like this. Delta PLC has the following structure:

> 5,000,000 ordinary shares of £1 each fully paid
>
> (currently quoted on the Stock Exchange at 220p each)

The directors wish to raise funds to the extent of £1,500,000 in order to modernise the plant. They therefore send a provisional allotment letter to their shareholder offering one new ordinary share at 150p for every five shares held.

From the company's point of view, because the shares are offered at a favourable price, the company can be sure of receiving the funds they require. If they have been too generous with the terms, it is only the existing equity owners who will benefit. It is an inexpensive and effective method of raising additional funds which is likely to prove acceptable to the shareholders, so long as proportionately large sums are not required.

From the shareholder's point of view consider the case of Mark Johnson, who was holding 1,000 ordinary shares in Delta. He would have been invited to take up 200 of the new ordinary shares at a price of 200 x 150p, i.e. £300.00. If he wishes to acquire all the new shares to which he is entitled, all he needs to do is to send a cheque for this sum to the company registrar, together with the allotment letter.

16: Stocks, shares and take-overs

If he does not want to take any of the new shares he may sign the form of renunciation and give the allotment letter to his broker who will then sell the rights on his behalf.

How much can Mark expect to receive from any rights he sells? The stock market has assessed Delta as being worth £11m, i.e. 5,000,000 x £2.20. With the new inflow of cash from the rights issue, the amended valuation of Delta would be £12.5m. Divided between 5,000,000 old and 1,000,000 new shares (6,000,000 in total) the value of the shares – after the rights issue – would be

$$\frac{£12,500,000}{6,000,000} = \text{approximately } £2.08$$

So, if shares costing £1.50 each are worth £2.08, the value of the rights to each new share (called the premium) will be around 58p. In practice, the premium may exceed 58p where the injection of cash is expected to improve the efficiency of the company. You will recall that Delta wanted the cash to modernise their plant.

If Mark sells all his rights, he will receive a cheque from the broker (having sold the rights on the stock exchange) for 200 x 58p = £116.00.

Your task

Beta PLC has the following capital structure: 10,000,000 ordinary shares of £1 each.

The shares are selling on the Stock Exchange £4.00 each.

The company is now making a one for ten rights issue at a price of £3.00 each.

a) How many new shares would you expect to be offered if you are presently holding 5,000 of the Beta ordinary shares?

b) How much would you have to pay the company for your new shares?

c) How much would Beta raise from the rights issue?

d) How would you be informed about the rights issue?

e) What is attractive in such a rights issue from the company's point of view?

f) What are the merits and demerits of the rights issue from the shareholder's point of view?

g) With regard to the Beta rights issue, what would you expect the premium to be on the rights?

h) How much would you get for your rights to new shares if you sold them instead of taking them up?

Delta plc

Floor 5 Winston House, Bloomsbury, London WC2 Telephone: 071 700 1000 Fax: 071 700 2000

Page One

PROVISIONAL ALLOTMENT LETTER

Holding of Ordinary Shares of £1 each in the name of Mark Johnson	1000
Number of New Shares of £1 each provisionally allotted	200
Amount payable at £1.50 per share	£300

Dear Mr Johnson,

The Directors have provisionally allotted to you the number of new Ordinary Shares of £1 each set out above. The Shares have been allotted to the holders of existing Ordinary Shares on the basis of one New Ordinary Share for every five Ordinary Shares previously held.

If you wish to take up the Ordinary Shares provisionally allotted to you, you must send an appropriate remittance for the amount shown above to this address.

If payment is not made by 15 January 199- this provisional allotment will be deemed to have been declined and will lapse.

By Order of the Board of Directors

R G Blakeney

Page Two

FORM OF RENUNCIATION

To the Directors of Delta plc:

I/We hereby renounce my/our right to the Shares comprised in the Allotment Letter in favour of the person named in the Registration Application Form. .... YES/NO

Signature of person(s) named on Page One: ....

All Joint Holders must sign: ....

....

In the case of a company its Common Seal must be affixed: ....

Page Three

REGISTRATION APPLICATION FORM

This form is only to be completed where there has been a renunciation.

It is used to identify the purchaser(s) so that Delta plc can record the change of ownership of the shares.

First Name(s) .... Title (Mr, Mrs, Ms, Miss) ....

Surname ....

Address ....

....

.... Postcode ....

16: Stocks, shares and take-overs

G. Summarising

Give the following passage a title and summarise it in about 100 words.

> A maxim which should be followed by all investors is 'buy at the bottom and sell at the top'. Prices of all stocks fluctuate from time to time, and the art of speculation is to buy securities at the best time. It is not as easy as it sounds for two reasons. First, it is as difficult to know when share prices have finished falling as it is to know when they have reached their peak. Second, the maxim assumes that the speculator is in a position to take the necessary action. For example, funds may not be available for a purchase at the vital moment.
>
> The Stock Exchange is a highly sensitive market and stock prices fluctuate in response to a wide variety of pressures. Speculators should always be looking to the future and attempting to anticipate events. For example, businesses are interdependent to a large extent and will be affected by the general economic climate. Orders for ships lead to orders for steel which in turn leads to money in the pocket of shipbuilders and steelworkers to buy television sets and carpets. Conversely, the closing of a motor assembly plant causes a fall in the sale of beer which increases the number of redundancies, this time in the breweries.
>
> Speculators pay attention when the Chancellor of the Exchequer introduces his Budget. This is the time when tax rates are changed, future government spending patterns are declared and the effect of the changes on their securities can be gauged.
>
> The government also promotes its policies through the Bank of England, perhaps using the government broker to conduct open market operations. Government stocks are sold when the government wants to reduce the supply of money. This will pressurise the banking system to raise interest rates with the effect of reducing inflation. The government broker buying government stocks will have the opposite effect, lowering interest rates and reducing unemployment.
>
> All these things will affect the price of shares on the Stock Exchange, as will the fact that some political parties are seen as more sympathetic to business interests. Prices will be particularly sensitive at the time of parliamentary elections.

H. True or false*

If you think the statements are true, tick the column headed true. If you think they are not true, tick the column headed false.

		True	False
1.	The Stock Exchange does not provide companies with funds; it is a market place for the purchase and sale of stocks and shares.	☐	☐
2.	The purpose of a take-over bid may be to eliminate competition.	☐	☐
3.	The directors may recommend that part of the profits are ploughed back into the business.	☐	☐
4.	Non-voting shares will be of no interest to a take-over bidder.	☐	☐
5.	Ordinary shares carry one vote each at the company's general meetings.	☐	☐
6.	If shares are quoted on the Stock Exchange they will fetch a lower price.	☐	☐

16: Stocks, shares and take-overs

7. When a company is taken over, the existing board of directors will be unaffected. ☐ ☐

8. If you won 1,000 ordinary stock units of £1 each in ICI and a dividend of 10p per unit is declared, you will receive £100, less tax. ☐ ☐

9. If directors pay low dividends to the shareholders over a period of time, take-over bidders will be discouraged. ☐ ☐

10. An inexpensive way for a company to raise funds is by a rights issue to its own shareholders. ☐ ☐

I. Multiple choice*

Tick the box following the phrase which **best** completes each sentence.

1. If you own shares in a pharmaceutical company selling a wide variety of medicines, you will be pleased to hear
   A. that the government is reducing its expenditure on the National Health Service. ☐
   B. that the birth rate is falling. ☐
   C. rumours that the company is to be taken over by an even larger German competitor. ☐

2. If you decide to sell shares it is best to sell them when
   A. prices have reached a record low. ☐
   B. prices look as if they will not be going any higher. ☐
   C. Other people are also rushing to sell. ☐

3. If you own shares in a life assurance company with subsidiaries in the USA, it will be bad news to hear that
   A. the value of the dollar is falling in the foreign exchanges. ☐
   B. that a new drug has been found to cure cancer. ☐
   C. that the government is planning to spend more on the National Health Service. ☐

4. You have bought shares in a commercial bank in the expectation that the price of its shares will rise soon and you will be able to sell the shares at a profit. When the accounts for the year are produced you will be pleased to hear that it has
   A. increased its dividend. ☐
   B. increased its provision for bad debts. ☐
   C. reduced its costs. ☐

16: Stocks, shares and take-overs

5. Prices of shares on the International Stock Exchange in London would be most likely to rise if
   A. the rate of tax on profits (corporation tax) was to increase by 2p in the £.
   B. interest rates fell by 1%.
   C. there was political unrest in the Middle East.

6. The price of equities in a UK group which owns a number of hotels in Eastern Europe would increase if there was
   A. an enlargement of the European Community.
   B. a break-up of the European Community.
   C. a substantial increase in the price of oil.

7. A speculator on the Stock Exchange buys some British Petroleum ordinaries. Which of the following items of news would be most welcome to him?
   A. The government increases the petrol tax.
   B. The government places restrictions on the import of foreign cars.
   C. Income tax is reduced by 2p in the £.

8. One of the companies represented in your portfolio of securities has sent you notice of a general meeting at which it is proposed to elect three new directors to the board, none of whom is known to you. Which of the following is the most logical reason for staying away from the meeting?
   A. The company have sent you a proxy which will allow you to vote without attending the meeting.
   B. Your stake in the shares is too small to justify the expense of the journey.
   C. The new directors would have no effect on your stake in the company.

J. Case study

Unit trusts

Even if you think a particular company has a bright future, it is unwise to invest the whole of your surplus funds in one venture. The proverb tells us not to put all our eggs in one basket, and the investment experts advise us to diversify, which means the same thing. It may be easy for a wealthy investor to diversify, but what about someone who only has, say, £3,000 to invest? One way in which the smaller investor can diversify is by buying units in a unit trust.

A unit trust buys large blocks of specified stocks which are then broken down into sub-units and offered to the public. The sub-units can be bought and sold through the company which manages the fund. Bid and offered prices will be quoted. The bid price is the price at which the company will buy back the securities from the sub-unit holders. The offered price is the price at which the managers are offering the securities to the public. The bid price will obviously be below the offered price on any particular day.

There are a great variety of unit trusts (or 'funds' as they are also called) offered to investors in the United Kingdom, from those specialising in Japanese industrial shares to those concentrating on gold-mining equities. It may help to convey an impression of the various types of unit trusts available to the investor if we study a selection of of those on offer by one of the Big Four, National Westminster. They include the following funds on their list:

16: Stocks, shares and take-overs

Title	Aim	Special features
Capital Trust	to produce a high level of capital	Income earned by the trust is not distributed but held and applied to the purchase of further securities.
Growth Investment Unit Trust	to provide overall growth of both capital and income through investment in a wide range of high-class equities both in the UK and overseas.	Invested in over 132 high-class securities with over one-fifth in North America.
Income Trust	to provide an increasing income together with a measure of capital growth.	Portfolio weighted towards income rather than capital growth but about one-tenth of the portfolio is in banks and insurance.
Financial Trust	to produce long-term capital growth by investing in an international spread of financial shares.	Nearly half the portfolio is taken up in UK banking and insurance equities. Approximately one-quarter of the securities are overseas mainly in North America.
Universal Fund	to provide capital growth from world-wide investment.	The bulk of the portfolio is in USA securities.

Your task

During the course of the morning Gordon Davis, the Deputy Manager of the Hightown branch, discusses the possibility of investment in unit trusts with four different customers:

Ms Elizabeth Hart is 68 years old. She inherited her flat from her parents, but is finding it difficult to live on her old age pension. She has been left a legacy of £5,000 in the will of a friend who has recently died, and is considering investing part of the legacy in a unit trust.

Sarah Parry is a 52 year-old architect who is financially self-sufficient, but wants to boost her income on retirement in eight years' time. She has £20,000 to invest, but has no knowledge of the stock markets.

Peter Webb is the proprietor of a small engineering works producing specialised farming equipment. He already has a portfolio of UK securities, mainly in banks and insurance, with a current market value of £50,000.

Andrew Carter wishes to make a gift of £3,000 to his ten-year-old grandson. He is thinking of investing the money in a unit trust for him.

Consider which of the unit trusts listed here Gordon Davis would be most likely to recommend to each of these customers on the evidence available.

16: Stocks, shares and take-overs

K. Vocabulary*

tax	capital	auditor	replaced
voting	broker	majority	asset-stripping
premium	equities	dividend	supplies
inflation	report	Guinness	annually
securities	risk	quotation	satisfactory

Match the words listed above with the definitions which follow:

1. You can expect to receive these annually providing your company is making good profits.
2. Another name for ordinary shares.
3. One of the factors which will determine the price of the shares is the degree of ....
4. The member of the Stock Exchange who will arrange purchases or sales of stocks on your behalf.
5. This happens when a company is taken over and sold off in parts.
6. This is the difference between the value of the new shares and their cost in a rights issue, assuming the difference is positive.
7. Only these shares are likely to be purchased by a take-over bidder.
8. In order to take over the control of a company you need to acquire a ...... of the voting shares.
9. A take-over bid may have as its objective the securing of these.
10. One way of hedging against this is to buy growth equities.
11. If a company is taken over its directors may be ....
12. Appointed by the shareholders at an Annual General Meeting (AGM) to verify its accounts during the coming year.
13. This affair was the result of directors artificially raising the price of shares on the Stock Exchange go avoid a take-over.
14. Long-term investors are usually looking for ...... growth in their portfolios.
15. The chairperson of a company will produce this for the shareholders at the AGM.
16. Deducted from the dividend before being paid over to the shareholder.
17. The company's accounts have to be produced ...... for the shareholders.
18. The board of directors can expect to stay in power, so long as the company's results are ....
19. Another name for stocks and shares.
20. When shares have a ...... on the Stock Exchange they can be sold more easily and at a higher price.

17: Money and banking

A. Comprehension

John Davies is a coal miner in South Wales and is saving up for his summer holidays. He is hoping to take his family to Spain again in the summer. He collects his pay on Friday and every Saturday morning his wife, Jane, deposits £20 with the Building Society which has a **branch office** in their town. The Building Society in turn have an account with Barclays Bank and transfer their **surplus cash** to the bank from time to time.

David Miller is the Quality Control Manager in a motor assembly plant in Coventry. His salary is paid monthly and the firm credit his **cheque account** at the local Barclays branch. David spends most of his salary during the month but maintains an average balance of £1,000 so the Bank do not make an administration charge for the cheques he **draws.**

The bank looks after the money of many customers like David and John. However, just having enormous funds at their disposal does not give them profit. They have to put these funds to work. That brings us to British Petroleum. This company is drilling for oil in the Irish Sea. It looks promising but they are in need of funds to purchase another oil rig. They turn to Barclays for help and the bank give them a loan for £1,000,000. They only lend the money to the oil company for a fixed time, say two years, and at the end of that time the loan will have to be repaid. In the meantime the oil company will have to pay interest on the loan.

Of course banking is a risky business. Loans like these are usually repaid, but sometimes the borrower **defaults** and then the bank loses its money. Customers like David Miller will still expect to be paid cash when they **present their cheques over the counter**, and that is why bank managers grant loans warily. On the one hand, they want to grant loans because the interest they earn gives them their profits, but they also have to make sure they have enough funds available to meet the claims of their depositors. Banks are always having to choose between profitability and liquidity.

Perhaps John will not be happy to know his money is being used to provide us with more oil. He is a coal miner and if more oil is available the demand for coal will go down. However, we all stand to be richer if the drilling is successful.

At the head of our banking system is the Bank of England. In the same way that our surplus cash ends up with the commercial banks like Barclays, National Westminster, Midland and Lloyds (now joined by the Trustee Savings Bank), their surplus cash is held at the Bank of England. Each of these banks has an account with the Bank of England, which is also known as the Central Bank. The Bank of England is the banker's bank. It is also the Government's Bank and holds all the surpluses of the various government departments. From time to time the government and the commercial banks will need funds from the Central Bank and the rate of interest they are charged will **influence** interest rates in the rest of the economy.

Your tasks
- a) Explain the meanings of the highlighted words or phrases.
- b) Why do banks have to choose between liquidity and profitability
- c) Why might John not be happy to know his money is being used to drill for oil in the Irish Sea?
- d) Who are likely to benefit if British Petroleum find oil in the Irish Sea?
- e) Summarize the role of the banks in about 30 words.

17: Money and banking

f) Complete the diagram below by placing the appropriate words in the four different boxes.

How the bank helps to create prosperity

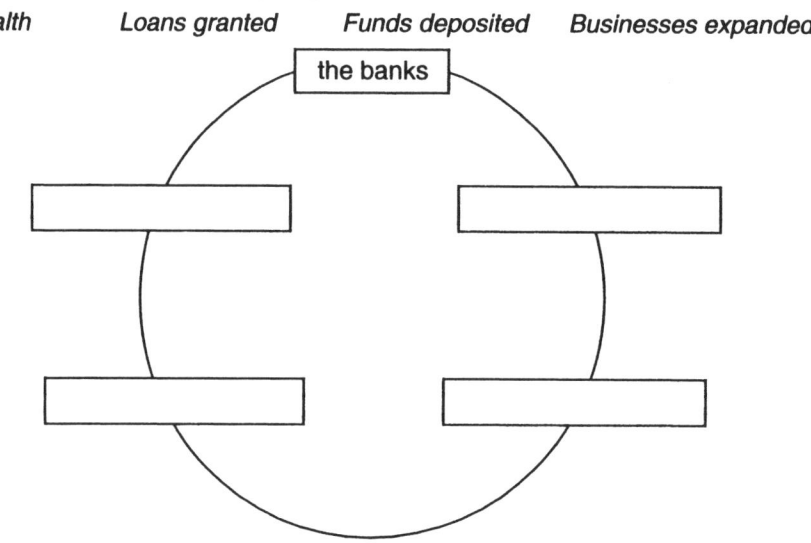

More wealth   Loans granted   Funds deposited   Businesses expanded

B. Fill in the blanks*

Rewrite the passage filling in the blanks from the list of words below.

Most customers of a bank have current (or cheque) accounts. Interest is not paid on these accounts but withdrawals can be made by cheque. The other type of bank account is the deposit or savings account. Interest is paid on these accounts but notice of .... is required.

Banks lend .... money to their customers in two ways. They grant loans or overdrafts. Loans are for a fixed sum and .... has to paid on the whole .... borrowed. Another name for a loan is an advance. In .... to loans to businesses, banks also .... personal loans. By contrast, by means of an overdraft it is possible for cheques to be drawn in .... of the sum standing to the customer's .... in the current account. Interest is .... paid only on the actual amount overdrawn.

If customers wish to buy items such as new cars or double glazing for their houses they may .... the bank manager for a loan or overdraft. Providing they have .... their accounts satisfactorily in the past and the amounts involved are in keeping with their .... the manager will normally oblige.

me	withdrawal	excess	approach
amount	interest	addition	grant
credit	conducted	surplus	then

C. Interpretation of diagrams

Look at the following pie-charts showing the breakdown of a typical Bank Balance Sheet and answer the following questions in the form of a sentence.

17: Money and banking

For example:
- Q. What happens to the bulk of a commercial bank's funds?
- A. The bulk of a commercial bank's funds are lent to customers.

The balance sheet of a typical commercial bank

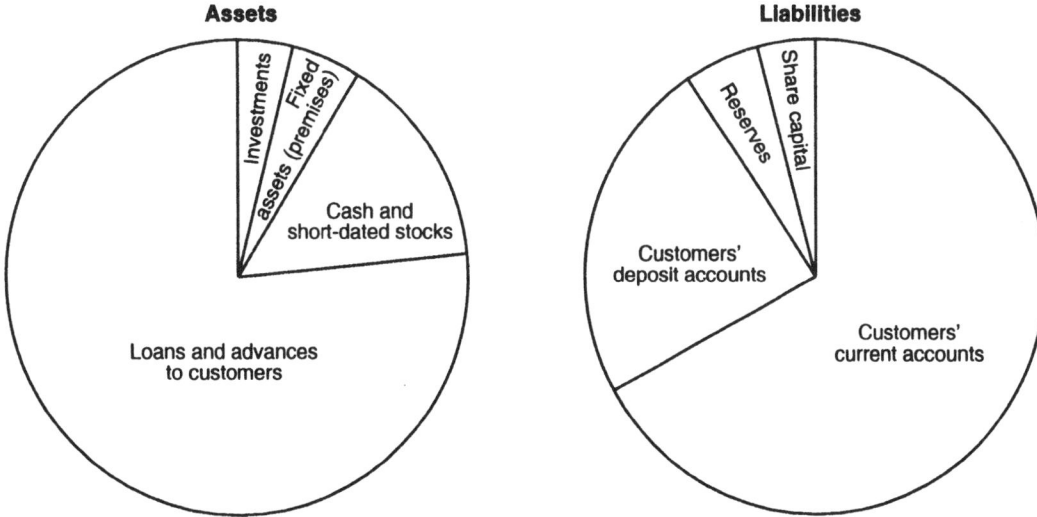

1. Are current accounts or deposit accounts more popular?
2. About what proportion of the bank's funds are lent to customers?
3. About what proportion of the bank's liabilities are represented by customers' accounts?
4. Why is the item 'Cash and short-dated stocks' critically important from the bank's point of view?
5. Why is the same item of critical importance from a customer's point of view?
6. Do the assets of a commercial bank tend to be liquid or frozen?

D. Complete the table*

verb	adjective	noun
to guarantee	guaranteed	guarantor
to apply		
	authorised	
		overdraft
to alter		
	requisite	
		implication
to specify		
	abbreviated	
		indorsement
to secure		

193

17: Money and banking

	confidential	
		cancellation
to modify		
	prescribed	
		beneficiary
to economise		
	remedial	
		legality
to accumulate		
	completed	
		negotiation
to confirm		
	fabricated	
		negligence
to agree		
	definitive	
		enforcement

'I'm sorry Mr Merridrew, I can't take your rabbit as security for a loan.'

E. Write a letter

A customer may have regular payments to make such as a monthly insurance premium or an annual subscription to a sports club. In this case the bank can be given a single instruction to make these payments. An example of a standing order is shown below:

17: Money and banking

```
                                              The Willows
                                       Glenbarrow Crescent
                                                 Porchester
                                          Wiltshire SW9 8PQ

                                              15th May 199-
The Manager
Barclays Bank PLC
High Street
Porchester SW2 1WR

Dear Sir,

Please pay to National Westminster, Station Road, Porchester on account
of the Porchester Lawn Tennis Club (a/c number 634/541) the sum of £50 on
the 1st May next and the same amount on the same date each year until
further notice.

Yours sincerely

David Miller

David Miller
```

Your task

Play the part of David Miller and write a letter for him to his bank manager. You have been informed by the tennis club that the subscription rate was increased to £60 last year and another £10 is now due.

F. Summarising

Read the following passage carefully. Then give it a title and summarise it in about 150 words.

> Banks are as likely as any other business to suffer the consequences of an economic recession. Their business customers will suffer from falling sales and losses which will reflect in a surge of bad debts as business loans fail to be repaid. Their private customers are unlikely to fare better. For them the problem becomes redundancy and meeting the normal household bills.
>
> The problem is compounded because banking is becoming increasingly international. The banks' customers are not confined to these shores. They are spread across the world. Even the resources of a giant banking group like Midland or National Westminster are not enough to finance oil exploration or the development of satellite communication systems and this explains the growth of banking consortia. Banks from all the developed countries of the world join forces to supply the capital required for some of the most ambitious (and risky) projects. Unless these international ventures are successful the banks are faced with the problem of collecting debts from customers in countries which are often politically unstable. As if this were not enough, the banks in the UK are also confronted with foreign banks which are beginning to look covetously towards our domestic market for financial services.
>
> Another problem for the banks is the increasing competition between our various financial institutions. At one time there was a clear-cut distinction between the banks and the building societies. The building societies collected savings from ordinary members of the public and lent that money to people who wanted to buy their own homes. In the past banks were not interested in such long term loans, but in recent years they have shifted their ground. They are now increasingly prepared to grant loans to house purchasers, and in response the building societies are offering cheque

17: Money and banking

facilities to their own depositors. The result is that the dividing line between banks and building societies is becoming blurred as the competition warms up. The public at large are the beneficiaries.

Technology provides both opportunities and threats to the banking community. Credit cards have made it easier for the public to buy goods and services and in doing so to run up debts which, when converted into formal borrowings, are very profitable from the banks' point of view. Similarly, the cash dispensing units which give customers greater access to their funds are likely to be popular, particularly among 'downmarket' customers. However, cash dispensing units are cheaper than cashiers and, while this may increase the profitability of banks, it is also putting pressure on the Staff Departments to review their recruitment policies.

The major clearing banks report that half the cash withdrawn from branches is taken out of cash dispensing machines – dumb bankers as they are called. Ten years ago, for every National Westminster transaction through a cash dispenser, 15 were conducted over the counter. Now the two systems are level-pegging. The banks and building societies are both affected, but hope they will be able to use the staff freed to sell and service more sophisticated products such as insurance, unit trusts and private pension plans.

G. Documentation

Here are two common documents associated with banking:

A cheque

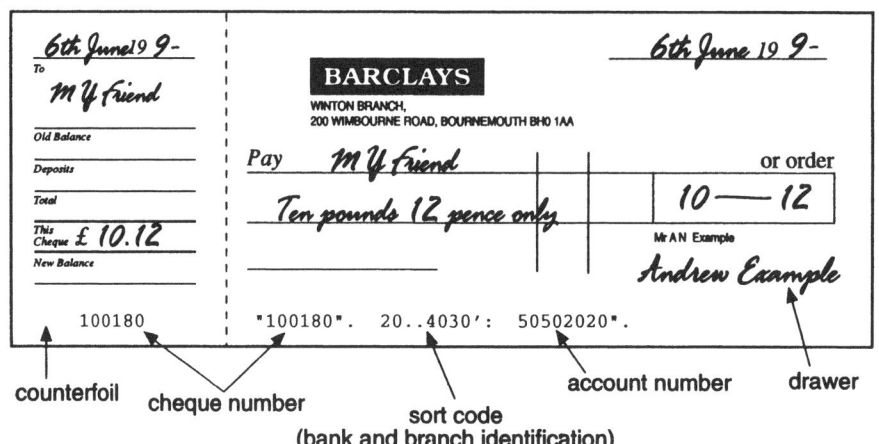

A paying-in slip

17: Money and banking

Your task

Write concise answers to the following questions:

1. What is the purpose of a cheque?
2. What happens to a cheque when you have passed it over to someone in payment?
3. What would be the danger in leaving around signed but otherwise blank cheques?
4. What would be the effect of your negligence if you lost your cheque book but did not tell the bank?
5. What would happen if you made out a cheque for more than the credit balance on your account, not having made an application for an overdraft?
6. How would you deal with an alteration of the amount on a cheque?
7. What is the purpose of a paying-in slip?
8. What would you expect to happen to a paying-in slip after it had been presented to the cashier?
9. Why is it important to keep a copy of the slip stamped by the cashier?
10. What might happen if someone else's account was credited in error?
11. Bearing in mind the bank's duty for confidentiality, why do you think they might hesitate to tell you over the telephone the balance standing on your account? What confirmations might they require?
12. What action would you prescribe for a friend who wants to cancel one of his cheques?

H. Missing words

There are a number of missing words in the following passage. You are asked to find appropriate words to complete the text.

> Every day, each banking branch receives from its head office all the cheques which have been drawn on that branch and paid in for the .... of accounts at other banks and branches. The staff now have to ensure that each cheque is .... drawn and that they have the .... to debit the customer's account. They have to .... that the customer has not countermanded (stopped payment) of the cheque, that the customer has .... funds in his account to meet the cheque or that .... facilities have been arranged, and that the signature is in order. A cheque may be returned unpaid for a variety of reasons. Perhaps the cheque is ...., or alterations made to the cheque have not been initialled. Another reason for non-payment is that the value of the cheque given in words is different from that stated in the figures. The payee will be most upset if the cheque is returned because the .... has insufficient funds. The cheque is then .... as dishonoured.

I. Multiple choice*

Choose the word which best completes each sentence.

1. Building ...... lend money to people who want to buy houses, taking a mortgage of the property deeds until the loan is repaid.

    A   companies ☐
    B. associations ☐
    C. societies ☐

17: Money and banking

2. A bank will sometimes give you a loan if someone is prepared to stand as your guarantor, agreeing to ...... the loan if you fail to do so.
   A. resurrect
   B. repay
   C. resign

3. Persons are described as ...... when they cannot meet their liabilities.
   A. bankrupt
   B. affluent
   C. dishonest

4. Before you ...... a cheque for more than you have on your account you must apply for an overdraft.
   A. withdraw
   B. withhold
   C. draw

5. You will be deemed negligent if you do not ...... the bank when you have lost your cheque book.
   A. inform
   B. instruct
   C. indemnify

6. The Bank of England is a ...... bank and acts as banker for the government and the other banks.
   A. data
   B. central
   C. local

7. When the payee signs on the back of a cheque it is described as an indorsement and can then be ...... to another person.
   A. debited
   B. charged
   C. transferred

8. If you wish to ...... a large sum from your bank the branch manager may require authorisation from his Head Office.
   A. receive
   B. convey
   C. borrow

9. The banker is expected to treat any information he has in regard to his customer's ...... affairs as confidential.
   A. private ☐
   B. domestic ☐
   C. financial ☐

10. A customer who ...... his overdraft limit will have to pay additional bank charges as well as interest on the excess.
    A. uses ☐
    B. exceeds ☐
    C. loses ☐

J. Explanations

Explain carefully the meanings of the highlighted phrases in these sentences.

1. The customer must exercise reasonable care when giving written instructions, so that the bank is not misled or **forgery facilitated**.
2. The bank's **duty to repay** can be overridden on a countermand of payment by the customer.
3. When a bank receives notice of a petition to wind up a limited company it will **freeze the company's** account.
4. It is a well established practice that bankers will reply to enquiries concerning the **financial status** of their customers.
5. The commercial banks issue travellers cheques which can be cashed at banks all over the world, providing the person tendering the cheque can provide a **matching signature** to that which appears on the cheque.
6. Access and Barclaycard, the two main **credit cards** used in Great Britain, allow the holders to pay for goods or services without cash passing across the counter.
7. A bank will not usually allow a customer to draw cash against **uncleared cheques**.

K. Vocabulary*

security	bankrupt	payee	application
authorisation	drawer	credit	overdraft
mortgagor	bankruptcy	guarantor	liquidity
indorsement	counterfoil	negligent	central
building	excess	principal	confidentiality

Match the meanings shown below to the words above.

1. A signature by the payee on the back of a cheque making it transferable.
2. Complementary part of a bank cheque recording particulars of the payee and the amount paid.
3. Something deposited or pledged as a guarantee that a loan will be repaid.
4. The amount by which an overdraft is above the agreed limit.
5. The capital sum invested as opposed to the interest earned on it.
6. One of the main duties owed by a banker to his customer.
7. This society helps people to own their own property.

17: Money and banking

8. A situation where assets can be easily converted into cash.
9. The person to whom a cheque is addressed.
10. The person who answers for the due fulfilment of a contract.
11. The right given by a senior official for a subordinate to act.
12. The person who deposits the deeds of his property as security for a loan.
13. The side of your bank account on which an entry is made when you pay in.
14. An act which was carried out without proper care and attention.
15. The person who signs a cheque authorising the banker to debit his account with the sum in question.
16. A formal request for a loan or overdraft.
17. Someone who is unable to pay his debts.
18. An inability to meet one's commitments may lead to this.
19. A form of short-term borrowing from a bank.
20. The Bank of England is this sort of bank.

L. Pairs of words

The pairs of words on this list are often confused.

access	(noun) means of reaching e.g. It is difficult to gain access to the bank's vaults.
excess	(noun) too much of e.g. The debit balance on the current account was in excess of the overdraft limit.
affect	(verb) to influence or change e.g. The customer's record will affect the outcome of his application for a loan.
effect	(noun) the resultant change e.g. If the bank had called for Henry's loan to be repaid the effect on his business would have been disastrous.
stationery	(noun) writing paper and envelopes e.g. The Securities Clerk, noting that the stationery had run out, ordered some more from Head Office.
stationary	(adjective) not moving e.g. The bank's security van was stationary when the robbers struck.
principal	(noun) chief/capital sum (adjective) main/leading e.g. The principal cause of the firm's failure was a lack of working capital.
principle	(noun) one of a set of beliefs e.g. With regard to loans, banks work on the principle that the borrower must stand to lose as well as the lender.

Your task

Write eight sentences of your own, each of which includes a different one of these words.

M. Exchange rates*

What would be the effect of the following events on the exchange rate of US dollars in relation to pesetas? Tick the appropriate column.

	Pesetas would fall in value	Pesetas would rise in value	Pesetas would be unchanged
1. Congress approves substantial cuts in the US defence budget.	☐	☐	☐
2. The Deutschbank takes over a major Spanish bank.	☐	☐	☐
3. The US Congress approves a massive package of economic aid to Russia and the newly emerging democracies in Eastern Europe.	☐	☐	☐
4. Researchers in the United States warn that the ozone gap has made sunbathing dangerous. It has been positively linked to a deadly form of skin cancer.	☐	☐	☐
5. Spanish car workers have won a 15% increase in pay.	☐	☐	☐
6. The monthly rate of inflation in Spain has increased faster than in any other major industrialised country over the past six months.	☐	☐	☐
7. A mammoth US-owned oil tanker, insured with Lloyd's of London, has split apart and sunk off the Costa del Sol.	☐	☐	☐
8. The Spanish Finance Minister has announced a record budgetary deficit.	☐	☐	☐
9. The US Federal Government raises a tariff on the import of European wines.	☐	☐	☐
10. The US Senate and House of Representatives are rocked by a wave of political scandals.	☐	☐	☐

N. Questions and answers

Read the following questions and then cover them and try to repeat them, one at a time, as accurately as possible.

Questions asked by a bank manager to a customer/client seeking a loan or overdraft

1. How much do you need? *or* How much are you looking for? *or* What sort of figure are we talking about? *or (more formally)* How much do you want to borrow?
2. Why do you need the loan? *or* What do you have in mind?
3. How are you going to pay back the loan? We'd like to see you making regular reductions.
4. What security can you offer? Have you any freehold or leasehold property? We'd prefer it to be uncharged/without a mortgage. We'd like to hold the deeds at the bank.
5. As it's a loan to a company we'll need to ask the directors to sign personal guarantees.
6. Can you let me see a copy of the latest accounts - the profit and loss account and the balance sheet?
7. I'm sorry to tell you your application for a loan has been rejected.

17: Money and banking

8. I'm pleased to tell you your application for an overdraft has been granted. We've put a limit of £2,500 on the account for a period of three months. Is that enough? the rate of interest will be 3% above the base rate.
9. I notice you haven't made any reductions on your loan account for the past few months. If you don't do something about it within the next three days I shall have to call in your loan. What's the explanation for the delay?
10. There are various forms to sign. Would you mind signing here... and here... Thank you.

Queries from a customer

1. Would you let me know the balance on my account please?
2. Would you kindly send me my statement of account?
3. I haven't received my statement of account this month. It usually comes on the 13th. Will you look into it for me please?
4. I'd like to open a cheque account please. What do I have to do?
5. I'd like it to be in the joint names of myself and my wife. Do we both have to sign?
6. I'd like to transfer £5,000 from my current account to a new deposit account. What's the rate of interest now? How much notice do you need for withdrawals?
7. I'd like to speak to the manager please – about a loan. Do I have to make an appointment?
8. The company will be short of funds for a few months. Can I have an overdraft please?
9. I put my card into the cash dispensing machine but it was rejected. Can you tell me what happened?
10. Unfortunately a cheque has gone astray in the post and I'd like to stop payment. Can you check that it hasn't already been paid?
11. I'm going on holiday and I need some Swiss francs. What is the latest rate of exchange? How much commission do you charge?
12. Can you tell me the minimum balance I have to keep in my account to void paying charges?

Questions and answers

1. Q. I want to change some English money into French francs. Can you help me?
   A. Certainly, sir. The exchange rate today is 1.53 francs to the pound. How much do you want to exchange?
2. Q. I'd like to transfer some money to my account in London please.
   A. You have an account here, madam? How urgent is it? Would you like us to send it by mail transfer?
3. Q. Can you tell me whether my account has been credited with the dividend for my $3^1/_2$% War Loan? It was due on the 1st.
   A. I'll check it for you sir ... Yes, your account was credited with £108.75 from the Bank of England on the 3rd.
4. Q. How long does it take for a cheque to clear? I paid the cheque into the account on Friday.
   A. Unless it's a local cheque it will take a full five working days to clear. That means we should be able to treat it as paid by this time next week.

18: Insurance

A. Comprehension

Life assurance has existed, in one form or another, for thousands of years. When Roman soldiers were paid, part of their earnings went into a fund on their behalf. If they were killed in battle then this money was given to their families. Or, if they were retired from the army, they were given this money to help them start a new career.

In the days when pirates used to attack ships at sea, many sea captains used to club together by putting money into a fund. Then when one of these captains was unlucky enough to get captured, money from the fund was used to pay his ransom and so allow him to be released as soon as possible.

Gradually, over the centuries, the basic principles of life assurance were growing.

One very important idea or principle that began to develop was that – if life assurance was to work well – a **fund** of money was needed. People who wanted to have assurance would have to join a club or society and pay money regularly into the society's fund each year.

In this way, the fund would gradually grow, and if one of the society's members did die there should be enough in the fund to be able to pay out the amount assured. The problem that remained was this: **how much should each person put into the fund?**

This important question was solved by a mathematics teacher who worked in London two hundred years ago. He was James Dodson. He realised that the amount each person should pay into the fund rested on the principle of probability. That is – how probable or likely was it that the person might die?

Using his mathematics, James Dodson calculated the probability of death for each individual who wanted life assurance. Today, we say that we are working out a person's **life expectancy** – how long the person can expect or hope to live.

Much will depend on the age of the person, how healthy he or she is, and how risky the job he or she does. James Dodson realised that the more likely a person was to die, the fewer years he or she would be expected to pay into the fund and, therefore, the more he or she should pay each year. With this information, James Dodson could calculate mathematically the fixed amount that the person should pay each year, in order to be assured that an agreed sum of money would be given to his or her family when he or she died. This fixed amount of money is known as a level premium – because it remains at the same level for as long as he or she keeps up the policy.

So, in 1762, the first scientifically calculated life assurance began – although, sadly, James Dodson himself died before his scheme started working properly.

18: Insurance

The level premium (policy starts at age 30)

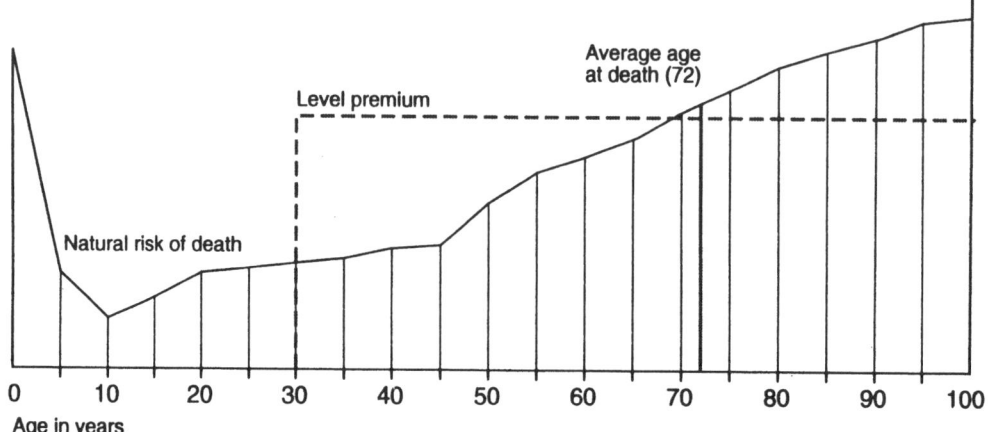

By courtesy of the Association of British Insurers

Your task

Having read the above passage answer these questions in your own words.

a) What are some of the practical problems the Romans must have encountered in running their life assurance scheme?

b) How do you think the scheme run by the sea captains would have worked?

c) What contribution did James Dodson make to the world of insurance?

d) In what ways do you think people's occupations affect the premiums they pay?

e) Explain how level premiums work.

f) According to the graph, at what age is the death rate lowest?

g) How would you explain the fact that the natural risk of death rises continuously throughout adult life?

h) What does the perpendicular line tell us about ourselves?

B. Fill in the blanks*

Rewrite the passage filling in the blanks from the list of words below.

The whole business of insurance is based on the .... of pooling risks. Insurance risks are those which are calculable. For example, the insurance company's .... (or statisticians) know that the average .... of life for a male in the United Kingdom is 75. So, if a man aged 65 wants to take out life cover – assuming he is normally healthy – he can expect to survive for another ten years, and at that time the insurance company will .... to pay out on the policy. They will set their .... accordingly. The .... the man, the less he is likely to die in a given period, and the lower the premiums charged.

The main service offered by insurance to businesses is to .... many of the .... they would otherwise have to carry. However, the businessman still has to .... the risk that the goods or services he is offering will not find a ready market, that the costs he incurs will .... the revenue he obtains from his sales (so that he makes a loss), and that his customers fail to pay him the money they owe. These are the so-called uninsurable risks. Goods in transit, claims from third parties for .... they have suffered, loss of property through fire, loss of stocks

204

18: Insurance

through .... and theft, all these items can be covered through insurance policies.

premiums	bear	actuaries	expectation
burdens	expect	younger	remove
principle	exceed	injuries	pilferage

C. Case study

Coldstream Insurance PLC

This is a newly formed insurance company – a subsidiary of one of the major banks. It started operations just over two years ago, concentrating on three particular branches of insurance. The bar charts shown here indicate the main cash inflows and outflows over its first two years.

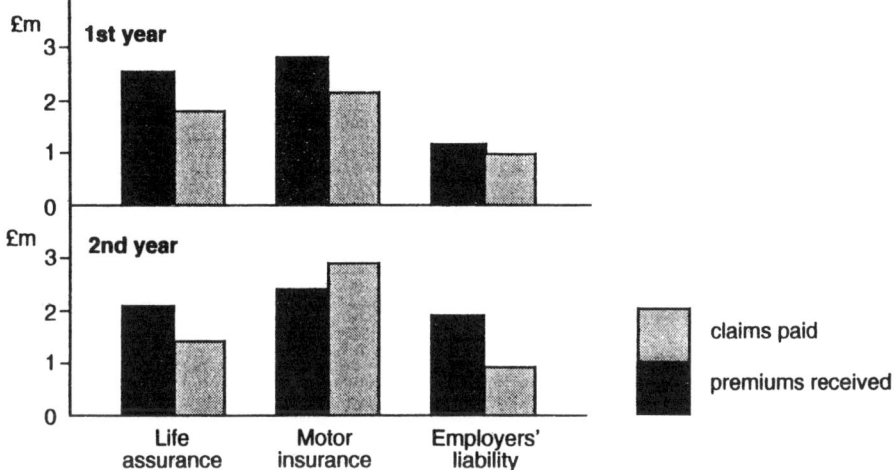

As a trainee supervisor you have been asked to draft a brief report (up to 150 words) to Ms Jennifer Smith, Senior Training Officer explaining how the company's different branches of insurance have fared in their first two years on the evidence of the diagrams.

D. Complete the table*

verb	adjective	noun
to insure	insurable	insurance
to indemnify		
	calculable	
		expectation
to diversify		
	proposed	
		adjuster
to invest		
	comprehensive	
		maturity
to renew		

205

18: Insurance

	different	
		dependant
to retire		
	successful	
		conversion
to satisfy		
	specific	
		protection
to concentrate		
	specialised	
		consideration
to speculate		
	expired	
to continue		
	investigative	
		consolidation
to classify		

E. Reply to a letter

You are employed by Coldstream Insurance and have received the following letter from a potential client. Draft a suitable reply.

```
                                                    13 High Reach
                                                    llchester BL19 5VX
The Manager, Coldstream Insurance PLC               Date:
Boddington House
llchester BL1 1EE

Dear Sir or Madam,

I have received a life proposal form from your office with a request that
I complete the document as soon as possible and return it to you. After
reading through the document I find the questions about my private life
to be impertinent. For instance, you ask:

1.   What is my occupation? What has that got to do with my application
for a life policy? Does it matter whether I am a milkman or a lorry
driver?

2.   Am I likely to live or work abroad? How can I answer that question?
Yes, if I get the right opportunity I will go abroad. Would your reply be
any different?

3.   Do I smoke? If so, how many a day? What is my daily consumption of
alcohol? What is my height? And my weight?

Frankly I find all this probing into my private life grossly offensive.
All I want is a £1,000 policy on my life. Do you really need to ask all
those silly questions?

Yours faithfully

William Rivers

William Rivers
```

18: Insurance

Motor insurance: 'M'lud, my client says he was going no faster than 30 miles per hour when he overtook the defendant's Porsche!'

F. Summarising

Read the following passage carefully. Then give it a title and summarise it in about 100 words.

There are two parties to an insurance contract, the insurer (usually an insurance company) and the insured (the person whose life or property is being covered against loss). Complete honesty is essential if the insurance contract is going to be enforced against the insurer. If the insurer has held back any information which would affect the willingness of the insurer to accept the risk, then the insurer may escape from liability when a claim is made under the policy. Utmost good faith is one of the principles of insurance. Suppose, for example, that Michael insures his business premises for £100,000 with Coldstream Insurance. In the proposal form he was asked whether any inflammable materials were stored on the premises. He said 'no'. As a result of a fire which later gutted the premises it was discovered that a ground floor storeroom was used to store drums of petrol. Because he failed to disclose this on his proposal form, Coldstream Insurance may avoid the claim.

Another fundamental rule is that there must be insurable interest. This means that any person taking out an insurance policy must be in a position to suffer a direct loss if the event insured against happens. So if Michael wants to insure his house against fire damage he can do so, but if I want to insure his house, since I would lose nothing if it burned down, I cannot do so. If it were otherwise, there would be a danger that unscrupulous people would insure strangers' houses, burn them down, then claim the insurance. It would be a charter for arsonists.

Another axiom of insurance is indemnity. The effect of this principle is that you cannot expect to make a profit out of the insurance contract. Consider first the case where Michael takes out a policy to cover his house against fire. The premium is £2.50 per £1,000 of cover. He reckons his house is worth £100,000 so he takes out cover for that amount, paying £250 premium per annum. Subsequently there is a fire and the house burns to the ground. An architect is consulted and it is estimated that it will cost

18: Insurance

£150,000 to reconstruct the house as it was before the fire. The insurance company will only contribute £100,000 to the cost of rebuilding.

The question of indemnity does not apply to life assurance of course, because no-one can say how much a human life is worth. If a life is insured for £100,000 that is how much will be paid out on the death of the insured.

G. Join the halves*

On the left of the page are the first halves of sentences. On the right are the second halves of the sentences, though not in the same order. Pair the halves and then write your own list of the completed sentences.

i) Days of grace refer to the limited period after termination

ii) Lloyd's of London are the great marine insurers

iii) For an insurance claim to be valid there must be a financial loss

iv) Whole life assurance means that the sum assured is

v) With endowment assurance you are able to save for the future while

vi) A proposer is a person who has completed a proposal form and is

vii) Before an insurance claim can be met there must be a financial loss and

viii) Aviation insurance is

ix) Employers' Liability policies cover the employer's responsibility for

x) A fidelity guarantee policy is aimed at

xi) The crime rate will be of particular interest to companies

xii) Insurance brokers play a useful role in

a) having developed from an eighteenth-century coffee-house in the heart of the City.

b) offering cover against theft and burglary.

c) enabling their clients to find the cheapest and most effective cover.

d) during which non-payment of the premium is accepted

e) the insured must complete a claim form.

f) payable only when death occurs.

g) waiting for it to be accepted by the insurance company.

h) providing safe working conditions for his employees.

i) becoming increasingly important as air traffic and freight grows.

j) resulting from a peril covered by the contract.

k) protecting employers against the potential dishonesty of employees.

l) insuring your life at the same time.

H. Missing words

There are a number of missing words in the following passage. You are asked to find appropriate words to complete the text.

A married man with a wife and children is well advised to insure his .... so that, if her were to die, his family would be .... and provided for. This is especially important if he has debts, such as a mortgage or a .... loan.

A life assurance policy can also prove to be an excellent way of saving for the future. The endowment policy .... that if you live until the policy comes to an end you will receive back all the .... you have paid, together with interest, in one lump sum. This can be a .... nest-egg for later life.

Many people use this form of saving to prepare for the time when they retire. Retirement almost invariably brings with it a .... in income, and the lump sum paid over by the insurance company can be used to invest in stocks and shares or a building society to boost one's .... of living. The lump sum could also be used to pay an annuity, which is the same as having an .... pension for the rest of your life.

I. Multiple choice*

Choose the word which best completes each sentence.

1. Life expectancy is the length of time a person is ...... to live for.
   A. going
   B. likely
   C. bound

2. The life fund is a pool of money into which all the premiums are paid and from which all ...... are eventually paid out.
   A. loans
   B. savings
   C. benefits

3. The greater the risk or the chance of it happening, the ...... will be the premium needed to cover it.
   A. higher
   B. lower
   C. cheaper

4. The ...... date is the date in the future when the policy comes to an end.
   A. fixed
   B. official
   C. maturity

5. Insurance makes trading easier by ...... a variety of risks.
   A. eliminating
   B. describing
   C. ensuring

6. Risks must be ...... before they can be insurable.
   A. understood
   B. unexpected
   C. calculable

18: Insurance

7. It can be ...... with reasonable accuracy how many houses in Britain will be destroyed by fire next year.
   A. predicted ☐
   B. indicated ☐
   C. emphasized ☐

8. A £100 excess clause in a motor policy indicates that the ...... will have to pay the first £100 of any loss incurred.
   A. insurer ☐
   B. insured ☐
   C. underwriter ☐

9. When a householder is calculating the value of his house for ...... insurance purposes, he or she should deduct the value of the land.
   A. life ☐
   B. marine ☐
   C. fire ☐

10. A company dealing with motor insurance would be ...... by a long bout of very cold weather.
    A. unaffected ☐
    B. dismayed ☐
    C. delighted ☐

J. Explanations

Explain carefully the meanings of the highlighted phrases in these sentences.

1. In dealing with an insurance company the insured is presumed to have acted in **utmost good faith**.
2. A cover-note is a document giving **temporary cover** while the formal policy is being prepared.
3. When you insure your house against burglary it may not be burgled but, if it is, **you will be indemnified**.
4. The premium paid for life assurance is based on the assured's **expectation of life**.
5. The life offices (or life assurance companies) pay out benefits to policy holders or **their dependants**.
6. The life fund is a great **pool of money** from which the payments (or benefits as they are called) are eventually paid out.
7. The first step in an insurance contract is usually the completion of a **proposal form** by the person seeking cover.
8. An underwriter needs to know the **material facts** in order to calculate the extent of the risk and the amount of the premium.

K. Vocabulary*

lapse	annuity	actuary	renewal
confirmation	excess	cover-note	premium
underwriter	indemnity	claim	broker
adjuster	comprehensive	syndicate	insured
insurer	cancellation	catastrophe	fidelity

Match the meanings shown below to the words in the table above.

1. Something which would cause an insurance company substantial losses.
2. What a policy does when the premium is not paid.
3. The policy is due for this when the period of insurance runs out.
4. An acknowledgement that a policy is in force.
5. Like a pension it provides for a sum of money to be paid at regular intervals to the policy holder.
6. The type of insurance policy which protects an employee against the dishonesty of his employees.
7. Someone who advises and arranges policies that are offered by many different companies.
8. A group of underwriters at Lloyd's of London.
9. The extent of a loss to be borne by the insured.
10. The type of policy which offers cover against a variety of risks.
11. A document giving temporary cover while the formal policy is being prepared.
12. The person who has an insurance policy – also called the policy holder.
13. The organisation which provides insurance cover.
14. The person who applies the mathematical doctrine of probabilities to insurance problems.
15. The principle that anyone who suffers a loss should be fully compensated for the loss incurred.
16. The act of terminating a policy because it is no longer required.
17. What needs to be made when a loss is incurred.
18. The payment made to the insurance company when the proposal is accepted.
19. The person who assesses the loss after a claim has been made.
20. Another name for the insurer.

18: Insurance

L. Proposal form

Here is a specimen life proposal form. You are asked to complete it as if you are personally taking out a with profits endowment with Stockminster for a term of ten years. The sum to be assured is £5,000.

Stockminster Assurance Society Limited
44 High Street Stockminster SR1 1AA Tel: 0022 3334444

LIFE PROPOSAL FORM

You must answer the following questions to the best of your knowledge and belief. Failure to do so may result in part or all of the benefits due under any policy issued as a result of this proposal being cancelled. If you are in any doubt about the relevance of certain facts you should disclose them. Each question should be answered fully in your own handwriting.

1. Name (in full) .... Marital status ....
   Address ....
   ....
   Occupation .... Age next brithday ....
   Born at .... on the .... day of .... 1 ....

2. Type of policy .... With or Without Profits .... Sum to be assured £ ....
   (a) Payable at death only .... (b) Payable at end of given term of years or previous death
   State terms of years ....
   Premiums to be payable annually or monthly? .... Number of years payable ....

3. Has any previous proposal on your life been made to this Society? .... Policy No ....
   Has any proposal on your life been declined, postponed, withdrawn, or accepted on special terms by this or any other Company? ....
   ....
   It is important that the name of the Company, the date and full particulars be given in every case.

4. Are you ever likely to: If YES please give details:
   (a) fly other than as a fare paying passenger?   ....
   (b) be engaged in a hazardous occupation or activity? ....
   (c) live or work abroad?   ....

5. Names and addresses of all Doctors you have consulted within the last five year with dates and reasons for consultation:

Name and address of Doctor	Reason for consultation	Date

6. Please state: Height .... ft .... in   Weight (in indoor clothes .... st .... lb
7. Have you smoked cigarettes in the last 12 months? .... If YES, how many per day? ....
8. Do you consume alcohol? .... Average daily consumption ....
9. Are you now in thoroughly sound health? ....

DECLARATION

I hereby declare that the above statements are true and complete, and I agree that these statements, together with the statements to be made to the Medical Examiner if a medical examination should be required, shall be the basis of the contract between me and the Society. I consent to the Society seeking medical information from any doctor who at any time has attended me, and making inquiries of any Life Assurance Company to which I have at any time made a proposal for life assurance, and I authorise the giving of such information.

Date .... Signature of Proposer ....

By courtesy of the Association of British Insurers

M. Lloyd's of London*

Find opposites for the words highlighted in the following passage and synonyms for the words in *italics*.

Lloyd's is a unique insurance market. Almost anything can be insured, from fleets of ships and aircraft to supertankers and jumbo jets. While these risks are derived from the marine insurance for which Lloyd's is **famous**, risks of every conceivable description can be covered. Lloyd's underwriters deal with burglary cover, loss of profits through fire, and motor insurance, etc. One in six private motorists in Britain is **covered** by Lloyd's policies.

Lloyd's underwriters also have a reputation for insuring the more unusual risks such as *injury* to a concert pianist's hands or a winetaster's palate.

Lloyd's is not a company. It has no shareholders and there is no corporate liability for risks insured there. The underwriters, operating in syndicates, **accept** insurance risks for their personal profit or loss. They are liable to the full extent of their *private* fortunes to meet their insurance *commitments*.

Lloyd's underwriters do not have contact with members of the public. Business is taken to them by *accredited* insurance brokers who negotiate the best possible terms for their clients. The brokers may choose to place the business with one or other of the syndicates, or with an outside insurance company.

When Lloyd's brokers receive requests for insurance cover, they make out 'slips' – folded sheets of paper setting out the risks to be covered. They then *approach* one of the underwriters expert in the particular type of cover. The premium rate is then negotiated and, if the broker thinks the rate might be **better**, a second underwriter will be approached.

An underwriter who accepts the contract signs the slip thereby taking a *proportion* of the risk for the syndicate. Having established the premium rate for the risk, and armed with this 'lead', the broker will now approach other syndicates to get their **acceptance** for the remaining portion of the business. As each underwriter accepts the business on behalf of a syndicate the slip is signed, indicating the percentage of the risk the syndicate is *prepared* to cover.

The relationship between broker and underwriter is based on good faith, and the underwriter knows that the broker will have disclosed all the material facts honestly and fairly. In return the underwriter will assume liability for claims as soon as the signature has been added.

The history of Lloyd's goes back to the late seventeenth century. Edward Lloyd encouraged ships' captains and merchants to meet in his coffee house, and out of their conversations arrangements were made to insure their ships and cargoes.

Your task

Complete each of the following sentences with one of the words listed below:

a) Once a Lloyd's underwriter has added a .... signature to the 'slip' the contract is bound to be honoured.

b) The relationship between the .... and the underwriter is based on good faith.

c) Both ships and .... can be insured at Lloyd's.

d) The underwriter accepts the .... on behalf of the syndicate.

18: Insurance

e) Each syndicate will accept an agreed .... of the risk.
f) The brokers will try to get .... for their clients at the lowest possible premiums.
g) The .... of motorists in Britain are covered by a Lloyd's insurance policy.
h) There is no limit to the extent of the underwriters' liability to meet their .... under the policy.

The missing words:

| cargoes | major | proportion | broker |
| cover | commitment | risk | signature |

N. Telephone conversation

Julie Shaw is an insurance executive in the fire insurance department of Coldstream Insurance PLC. She is presently dealing with a 'phone call from Harry Cartwright, a Dorset farmer whose outbuildings were damaged by fire last night. His barn was gutted and two of his three wooden cowsheds were badly damaged.

JULIE: Fire department.

HARRY: I'd like to speak to someone about a fire I had last night at my farm.

JULIE: Do you have a policy with Coldstream?

HARRY: I do. That's why I'm 'phoning you now.

JULIE: Alright, sir. Could you give me the number of the policy?

HARRY: It's FM 768543 B88.

JULIE: Can you give me a moment while I look up your records on the computer … Are you Mr Cartwright … Harold Cartwright at Crane Farm, Swyre's Head?

HARRY: That's right.

JULIE: You say you've had a fire. Can you tell me what happened?

HARRY: Well, we woke up in the night to find the barn blazing. We managed to get the cattle out of the cowsheds, then the fire spread.

JULIE; This policy doesn't cover the livestock.

HARRY: I realise that.

JULIE: Do you have the policy in front of you?

HARRY: Yes.

JULIE: Can you refer to Schedule One?

HARRY: Yes, yes, I'm looking at it.

JULIE: Can you confirm that the items we're referring to are the outbuildings numbered one to four?

HARRY: That's right. Only we managed to save the cowshed… number three on the schedule.

JULIE: No damage?

HARRY: Well, it's badly scorched.

JULIE: Do you know how the fire started Mr Cartwright?

HARRY:	Not really. It's an open barn and with this warm dry weather, it can get very hot. It could have been internal combustion. But we've had a fire-raiser in the area. Old Joe Connell lost a couple of haystacks last month ... and that was deliberate.
JULIE:	If there's any question of arson, the police will have to be notified.
HARRY:	I realise that ... but there's no way I can tell.
JULIE:	Alright. I'll send you a claim form right away. Incidentally, I'm Julie Shaw. If you have any difficulties in completing the claim form let me know.
HARRY:	Thanks for your help. Goodbye.
JULIE:	Goodbye Mr Cartwright.

Your task

Julie Shaw is required to make a brief note (in the form of a memorandum) of any telephone calls she deals with. Play the role of Julie and make out the memorandum for her.

O. Correspondence

Following on from the previous telephone conversation (see Exercise N), Julie Shaw has now sent a brief letter to the policy holder together with an accompanying claim. You are asked to complete the claim form from the following information:

Crane Farm consists of a farmhouse and four outbuildings, all of which are covered by Coldstream Insurance PLC Policy No. FM 768543 B88. The premium of £4,000, due on 1st January last was paid on that date and the amount of cover is £300,000 for the buildings and £50,000 for farm equipment and machinery. The sole owner of the farm is Harold Cartwright.

Harry's wife woke him in the early hours of Friday last because of sounds of distress coming from the cowsheds. When they looked through the window they saw the barn on fire. Even as they watched the blaze was spreading to the cowsheds and they rushed downstairs with their son and daughter to see what could be done.

While Harry's wife and daughter led the dairy cattle to safety, he and his son concentrated on putting out the fire in two of the cowsheds.

Two young calves were unfortunately killed before they could be helped. The roof of one of the cowsheds was totally destroyed, while the walls of both buildings were badly damaged. They gave up any attempt to save the barn which was razed to the ground before the fire engines arrived.

In one of the cowsheds, a milking machine, which cost £1,200 when it was purchased eighteen months ago, was severely damaged.

18: Insurance

Coldstream Insurance plc   Goldhawk House, Vale Road, London NW6 5JT

Telephone 071 242 2000 Fax 071 242 3000

```
Date:
Mr H Cartwright
Crane Farm
Swyre's Head
Dorset BH12 5HA

Dear Mr Cartwright
```

Fire Policy FM768643 B88

```
In response to your telephone call this afternoon I am enclosing a claim
form for you to complete. As soon as you return the form I will arrange
for a loss adjuster to visit the farm to evaluate the losses you have in-
curred and discuss the scope of cover afforded under the terms of your
policy.

Yours sincerely,
```

Julie Shaw

Ms Julie Shaw

Coldstream Insurance plc   Goldhawk House, Vale Road, London NW6 5JT

CLAIM FORM

First name(s).. Surname...

Address...

.... Postcode..

Policy Number ....

Type of Insurance ....

Please describe fully the events giving rise to the claim:

Please advise the steps you have taken to mitigate the losses:

Please give a complete list of assets lost or damaged as a result of these events:

Description	Date of purchase	Original cost (£s)	Estimated cost of replacement* (£s)	Estimated extent of damage (£s)

*Please submit two competitive estimates for each asset.

Signature of policy holder: Telephone:

....   Home..............................   Work...........................

19: Exporting

A. Comprehension

Exports are of two main kinds, goods and services, the former being known as visible items and the second as invisibles. Over a period of time the total value of exports should balance with the total value of imports. To the extent that exports exceed imports we are said to have a favourable balance of payments. To the extent that imports exceed exports the balance of payments is said to be unfavourable or adverse.

Napoleon once called the British 'a nation of shopkeepers'. That was intended as an insult, but had he called us a nation of traders it could not have been disputed. In Britain we buy and sell more per head of population than the people of any other country. Our island is too small to grow enough food for our people and so we need to earn enough from our exports to sustain our population.

One complication of the export trade is that each country has its own independent currency system; and another is that many countries impose customs duties or other restrictions on imports.

The would-be exporter is faced with a number of problems. First there is the need to find a customer for his goods. The actual operation of selling is made more difficult because of language barriers and cultural differences. There are also additional transport problems because of the greater distances involved and often unfamiliar territories. When the manufacturer turns from selling at home to selling overseas, his problems are magnified. This is particularly true in terms of finance.

The first financial problem facing the exporter is the time taken to deliver his goods. There could be a long delay while his merchandise is in transit between London and, say, Karachi. He has incurred the costs of production, but when is he going to be paid? The second problem is even more serious. How sure can he be that he is going to be paid at all? And even when he receives payment his troubles may not be over. If he is paid for his goods in a currency other than sterling, he has to convert that currency into sterling, and what if the other currency has fallen in value since the contract was made? These are the perennial problems for the exporter.

Fortunately for our exporters, and for our economy generally, help is available both from the government and the banks. From the government side, the Export Credits Guarantee Department offers British exporters, in return for a fee, insurance against bad debts incurred as a result of sales to foreign buyers. The Export Intelligence Department also helps by providing them with useful advice and information. The most straightforward method of financing the operations is for the exporter to borrow the necessary funds from his bank. This way he can ship his goods abroad and draw on his bank for the funds needed to carry on production while he is awaiting the proceeds. But of course the borrowings from the bank will lower his profit margins.

Another method of financing international trade is by documentary credit. A document known as a bill of exchange (which is similar to a cheque but payable at a future date rather than immediately) is drawn by the importer in favour of the exporter and, although the bill of exchange is not yet due, the exporter can get it discounted (or encashed) immediately at his bank. While it is a very convenient method of payment for overseas trade, once again it serves to reduce the profit margin for the exporter.

Your task

Having read the above passage answer these questions in your own words.

19: Exporting

a) Why are exports vital to Britain's wellbeing?
b) What is meant by an adverse balance of payments?
c) What are invisible exports?
d) What problems are posed to exporters by language barriers and cultural differences?
e) How does the government help British exporters?
f) How do the banks help British exporters?
g) Why are the exporters profit margins likely to be lower for overseas sales?
h) What do you think will happen to our balance of payments when the oil in the North Sea dries up?

B. Fill in the blanks*

Rewrite the passage filling in the blanks from the list of words below.

Each country has its own .... and, since exchange rates are continuously changing, the exporter is constantly faced with an .... of uncertainty. The danger is that the rate of exchange will change between the date of the .... and the date of payment. Consider, for example, the case of the London dress manufacturer who contracts to sell $150,000 worth of dresses to a New York store. The rate of exchange is $1.50 to the £ so the manufacturer hopes to receive £100,000 on .... of the transaction. As the dresses cost him £80,000 he hopes to make a profit of £20,000. However, before the dollars are paid over the exchange .... changes. The dollar has fallen in value so that there are now $2.00 to the £. The .... is that the manufacturer will only receive £75,000 for his dresses and what should have been a profitable .... has turned into a loss. This was an extreme example, but rates of exchange can .... rapidly, particularly when there is no international .... to fix the rates for a particular currency. The banks can help the exporter to overcome this .... by providing forward exchange cover. In the case of the British dress manufacturer he would agree to sell the $US to the bank at the prevailing rate (less a discount) when the deal was made. It would then be the bank which suffered the loss if and when the dollars fell in value, but they would make a profit if the dollars .... in value, and of course they always .... to the extent of the discount they charge.

rate	element	transaction	contract
agreement	problem	rose	benefit
completion	fluctuate	result	currency

'And on what basis are you expecting a 10% increase in sales next year Mr Snow?'
'Global warming Ms Fanshawe, global warming ...'

C. Interpretation of data

Study the following information and then answer the questions below.

	Items per 1000 inhabitants			
	Television receivers	Telephones	Passenger vehicles	Doctors
United Kingdom	339	535	322	0.6
West Germany	412	634	454	2.4
France	305	605	364	2.1
Italy	246	457	350	3.5
Japan	263	556	227	1.3
USA	668	763	495	2.3

Questions (answer on the evidence available)

1. Which country has most passenger vehicles per 1000 inhabitants?
2. Which country has least passenger vehicles per 1000 inhabitants?
3. In what rank order do the countries stand in terms of television receivers?
4. Which of these countries is the richest?
5. Which of these people appear to be looked after best? What other explanation could there be?
6. How would you describe the position of the Britons compared to the West Germans?
7. What do you think might be the difference between 'passenger vehicles' and 'motor cars'?
8. Why do you think such information as shown here might be misleading?

19: Exporting

D. Verbs, adjectives and adverbs*

Add an appropriate verb, adjective or adverb from the list below to each of the following sentences where indicated.

a) The UK has .... had a surplus of trade in goods and a deficit in primary products.

b) The .... period is .... much longer in the .... trade and exporters to do not have the same degree of control over the goods they sell once they are .... to their destination.

c) UK exporters face .... competition in an increasingly tough world market and can also .... protectionism, ... quotas, and .... unrest in many countries.

d) Profitable trade overseas depends .... on the right market or markets to ....

e) Although rules of trading .... from country to country, ... rules of conduct have been .... for the countries of the European Community.

f) Export documents are .... necessary for the movement of goods, for .... the customer, for receiving payment for the goods .... , and to .... various government regulations.

g) Much of the more tedious work .... involved in filling out .... documents is now being done .... and more .... by computers.

Verbs:	selecting	formulated	invoicing	shipped	encounter	satisfy
	enter	vary				
Adjectives:	general	manufactured	delivered	fierce	political	transportation
	import	export	vital			
Adverbs:	inevitably	historically	normally	largely	vitally	systematically
	increasingly					

E. Case study

C & K Pharmaceutical Supplies PLC

One of the explanations for the world's population explosion during the last hundred years has undoubtedly been the increasing availability and effectiveness of medicines. That, in turn, accounts for the growth of the modern pharmaceutics industry.

For C & K the story starts in 1902 when Kurt Krageloh left his native Bavaria to set up as an apothecary in the City of London. As well as selling his various medications and potions to the City gentlemen he began to provide them in bulk for others of his profession in the outlying districts. By the outbreak of war in 1914 he had switched completely to wholesale operations. It was then that the business faced its first major crisis, since a large part of its medical supplies came from Germany. Fortunately for Kurt his sister had married an American surgeon and when she heard of his predicament she was able to put him in touch with a New York merchant, Sam Cordle, who was able to bridge the gap in the supplies of vital medicines.

Subsequently, Sam Cordle visited England and, after lengthy discussions with Kurt, they agreed to set up a new company, Universal Medicines Ltd, in which Sam held the controlling interest. The objective of the new company was to act as the European distributing agent for the products of Cordle's firm in New York. Universal Medicines expanded steadily through the 1920s and 1930s, even after the death of the founders. In 1969 it changed its name to C & K Pharmaceutical Supplies and went public. Soon after that Sam's eldest son, Jim, bought out the interests of the Krageloh family and the company now functions as a wholly owned subsidiary of the Cordle Group.

Questions (to be answered in writing)

a) How might a war damage any company which conducts business overseas?

b) How did Kurt's sister come to his rescue in the C & K story?

c) What problems would you expect to emerge when a company like Cordle's, tries to exercise control over British (and European) subsidiaries?

d) Do you think a government should encourage or discourage overseas investments such as these?

e) How would you expect the operations of C & K to affect the UK balance of payments?

f) How do you view the contention that British companies should avoid trading with overseas companies as far as possible?

F. Summarising

Read the following passage carefully. Then give it a title and summarise it in about 100 words.

When a British marketing manager turns his attention to overseas markets one of the problems could be seen as communication in an unfamiliar environment. If we are attempting to penetrate an international market we first have to receive an accurate picture of that market. What is its nature and extent? How does it differ from our more familiar home market? The further afield we look, the more difficult it becomes to get an accurate picture. In brief, our market research becomes more difficult and less trustworthy.

In order to trade profitably overseas we have to select the right market or markets to enter. There is a temptation to try and sell in as many markets as possible, but that temptation should be resisted. By concentrating our resources on a few carefully selected areas, we can maximise total profit on sales rather than spread investment too thinly. Some information can be assembled without us moving from our desks. Our banks can help us with information on general economic and trading conditions, the sort of competition we might expect, and even the marketing methods which are most likely to succeed.

When we have identified our market, we will have to visit the country or countries concerned. We will have to make contact with potential customers whose very language is strange to us. Of course we have in our favour the fact that English is the international language, and certainly the language of commerce. Yet, in some ways, it is the overseas buyers who have the advantage. They know our language almost as well as theirs. Our handicap is that we know only our own language as we go about our task of persuading them to buy our products.

No doubt this is why British exporters are generally advised to avoid direct selling in a new export market. The best way to gain a foothold is through a local agent or distributor. Once again our bank can help in finding an agent in the overseas territory who is both reputable and effective.

19: Exporting

G. Write a report

You are employed in the Exports Department of the Mediterranean Trading Corporation and your Manager, Denise Appleton, has asked you for a brief report (no more than 200 words) on the data shown in the accompanying pie-charts. She wants to know what these diagrams show with regard to Britain's trading patterns.

Analysis of visible trade last year by commodity

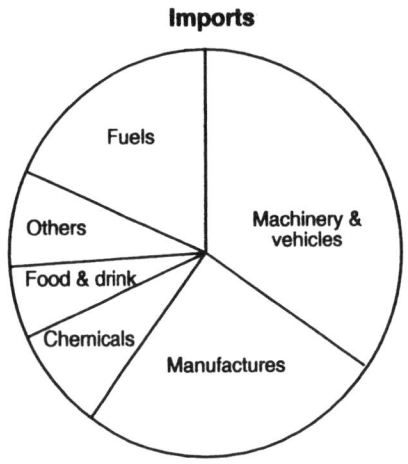

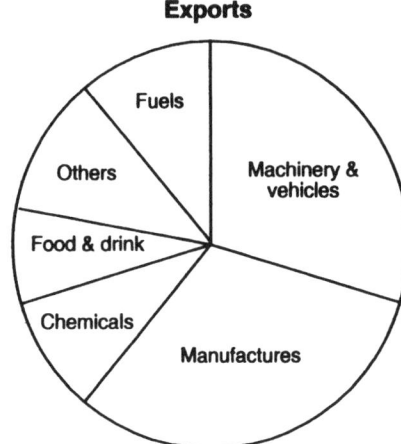

Analysis of visible trade last year by area

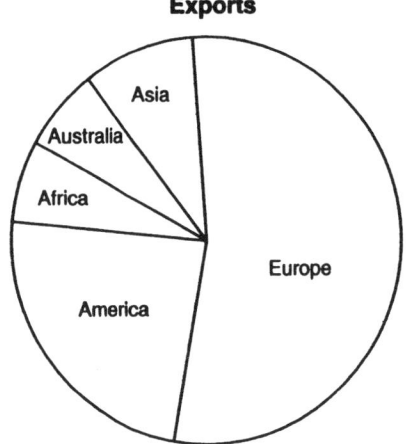

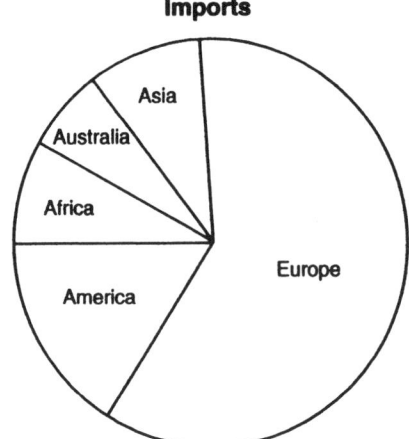

19: Exporting

H. An organisation chart

Here is a part of the organisation chart for the Mediterranean Trading Corporation setting out the lines of communication and control.

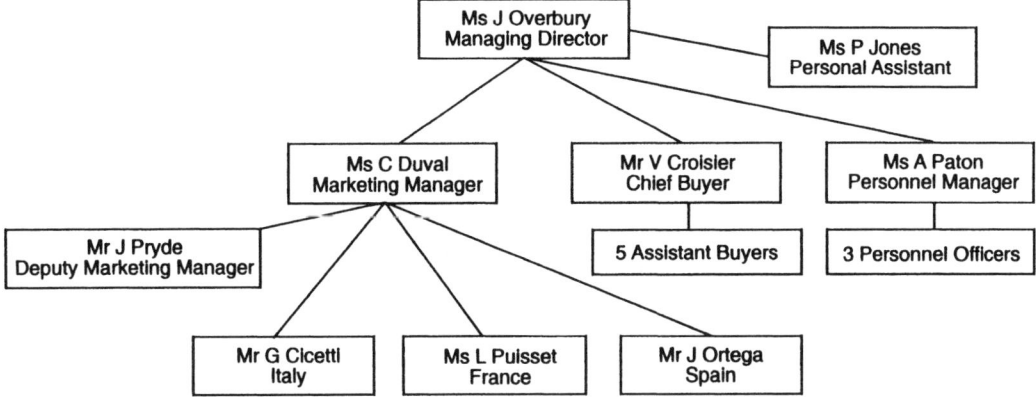

Questions

1. If the Managing Director called a meeting of his immediate subordinates, who would you expect to attend?
2. To whom does Mr Paton report?
3. From whom would Miss Jones receive instructions?
4. Through whom should Mr Pryde approach Ms Overbury?
5. What sorts of discussions would you expect to take place between Mr Duval and Mr Croisier?
6. In what circumstances would you expect Miss Jones and Ms Duval to discuss business matters?
7. Which of the named executives would you expect to deal with a letter of complaint from a department store in Rome?
8. What duties would you expect Mr Pryde to have in this set-up?

I. Write a memo

Barry Turner is General Manager at Contratex Fashions. He is discussing with Erica Khan, the Exports Manager, a trip she is making to South America. You are present at the meeting, as his Personal Assistant, together with Pamela Sharp, the Marketing Manager. Mr Turner has asked you to let him have a short memo containing the essentials of the discussion.

BARRY: I'm glad you're making this trip Erica. I think you've got to see for yourself what the possibilities are. I'm going to give you a fixed budget. I haven't worked it out yet, but it will be enough to help you to test out at least a couple of the most likely markets. I'll want you to give me a detailed itinerary, so I know where to contact you at any time. I think that's only common sense.

PAMELA: You did say Erica should try and contact as many customers as possible before she goes. I've got a list of contacts – with addresses and 'phone numbers.

ERICA: That's useful.

19: Exporting

BARRY: You'll have to work out some attractive packages for them.

ERICA: I'm working on various ideas. The trouble is some of the fabrics are terribly expensive and I'm not going to be able to offer them anything cheap. I'll come back to you on that when I've had a chance to go through Pam's list.

PAMELA: Take plenty of samples.

ERICA: I'm going to.

BARRY: I suggest you concentrate on the big stores in Buenos Aires and Rio. I think that's where we can do big business.

ERICA: That's my intention. Oh by the way, you were going to put me in touch with a modelling agency out there.

BARRY: Hasn't Pam given you the details yet?

PAMELA: I'm still waiting to hear from Sylvia Parnell.

BARRY: Chase her up Pam. We need the best models we can get. And don't forget to organise the ECGD cover. I'd hate to see Erica going to all this trouble for nothing.

A second task

Erica has obtained the following details from British Airways for her flight to Rio de Janeiro. They will also arrange the hotel accommodation for her during her stay.

Prices per person in £s one way first class – including all airport taxes			
Nights in resort	Daily departures on or between:		
	6 Jan – 9 Mar	10 Mar – 1 Sept	2 Sept – 5 Jan
7	13.95	18.95	14.50
14	16.25	21.95	16.80
Flight times from Heathrow: 21.50 Wednesday and Friday			
Flight time 10 hours (Rio time 3 hours ahead of ours)			

Write a brief memorandum from Erica to Barry Turner telling him she intends to fly out on Friday 16th May for 14 days. Give him as much information as possible about price and general arrangements at this stage.

J. Join the halves*

On the left of the page are the first halves of sentences. On the right are the second halves of the sentences, though not in the same order. Pair the halves and then write your own list of the completed sentences.

i) An exporting company can arrange the dispatch of its products

ii) Some governments require a signed and certified invoice

iii) The bill of lading is a receipt for goods shipped and is the document of title

iv) Fluctuations in exchange rates are an added hazard for exporters

a) to goods in transit.

b) risk for up to 90% of any loss from insolvency of an overseas buyer.

c) while goods are in transit.

d) through the services of a freight forwarding agent.

19: Exporting

v) Under the basic ECGD policy exporters are insured against
vi) With the growth of trade with Europe 'roll-on roll-off' road transport is
vii) A documentary letter of credit transmitted through the bank
viii) Until bill of exchange is paid or accepted by an overseas buyer
ix) The buyer's government might impose restrictions
x) The terms of the contract should make it clear who pays the insurance

e) bearing details as to the value and origin of the goods.
h) becoming the main method of transit for exported goods.
i) becomes the means by which the exporter obtains payment.
j) the goods cannot be released.

K. Vocabulary*

customs	tariffs	quota	shipper	documentary
agent	subsidiary	consignment	procedures	dumping
irrevocable	bond	accepted	licence	invisible
intermediary	surcharge	devaluation	maturity	multinationals
franc	lira	peseta	guilder	convert

1. A written instrument issued by a bank or insurance company guaranteeing that the exporter will comply with the terms of the contract.
2. What an exporter has to do with foreign currencies before he can pay his workers.
3. A legal permit to do something.
4. What a bill of exchange has to be before it is of value.
5. Companies operating in a number of different countries.
6. Exports which earn valuable foreign currency but are intangible.
7. Duties charged on imports.
8. The unit of currency in Spain.
9. The sort of credit which ensures that an exporter receives payment.
10. An additional tax on imports to reduce a balance of payments deficit.
11. The unit of currency in Italy.
12. The person either importing or exporting goods.
13. A downward change in the rate of exchange.
14. Someone who can help you to find markets in a foreign country.
15. The maximum amount of a commodity which can be imported during a given period.
16. The unit of currency in the Netherlands.
17. An alternative name for a middleman, broker or agent.
18. A shipment of goods.
19. An exporter might set up one of these in a foreign country.
20. The methods of conducting business. Vital to understand in exporting.
21. Cannot be revoked.

19: Exporting

22. Either the authorities responsible for the collection of duties on imports – or peoples' habits.
23. The date when a bill of exchange becomes payable.
24. The unit of currency in France.
25. The act of selling goods at a very low price in an overseas market.

L. Correspondence

Riba produce a range of kitchen furniture in their factory and have recently started exporting their products to the UK. They are using the services of a number of independent agents on a regional basis. They recently exhibited at a furniture exhibition in Zurich and one of the visitors subsequently telephoned to express interest in their products. The following letters were sent in response to this call.

Riba GmbH

Kirchstrasse 176, 7597 Blumenfeld, Deutschland Telephone: 04.03.21.58 Fax: 04.30.22.67

Date:

Ref: AG/PT/345

Mr John Whitbread
Chief Buyer
Henway Furniture Co Ltd
17/27 Stoke Road, Leek
Staffordshire ST23 AG9

Dear Mr Whitbread

Thank you for your recent telephone call. I understand you are interested in our Schwarzwald range of kitchen furniture and I am asking our Midlands agent, Mr Philip Truelove, to call on you during the coming week. I am sure he will be able to show you some samples of the high quality work we produce in our new factory.

Our Schwarzwald kitchen furniture is now selling in sixteen different countries and we have an international reputation for our craftsmanship which we boast is second to none. The furniture has been skilfully designed to combine ergonomic perfection with aesthetic excellence. While the price of the units necessarily reflect the quality of the product I am sure you will find a ready market for the furniture among your more discerning customers.

I am sure Mr Truelove will be able to give you all the information and help you require in displaying units in your store, but please do not hesitate to let me know if you encounter any difficulties. We do employ a team of expert fitters who are available to deal with the more tricky problems.

Yours sincerely

Ursula Schneider

Ursula Schneider
Marketing Director

19: Exporting

Riba GmbH

Kirchstrasse 176, 7597 Blumenfeld, Deutschland   Telephone: 04.03.21.58   Fax: 04.30.22.67

Date:
Ref: AG/PT/345

Mr Philip Truelove
Woburn House
Upper Road
Beaverstock
Staffordshire ST3 TR3
England

Dear Philip

We have received an enquiry from John Whitbread, Chief Buyer at Henway's Furniture Co. Ltd, 17/20 Stoke Road, Leek. He is particularly interested in the Scharzwald range. I have written to him today indicating you will be calling on him during the coming week. I hope this is possible. I have not specified any particularly day or time. His telephone number is (0358) 613.

We have had no previous contact with this company but it sounds promising. According to our telephone conversation they are one of the biggest suppliers of kitchen furniture in the West Midlands.

Let us know if you require any backup and please let us know how you get on with Mr Whitbread. Mr Whitbread apparently saw our displays at the recent Furniture Exhibition in Zurich. Perhaps we should exhibit in England? I understand there is an annual Ideal Home Exhibition in London. Would it be possible to book a stand there?

We were sorry to learn that the business with Stafford Enterprises did not materialise. The excuse that our prices were uncompetitive seems feeble bearing in mind the high quality of our product, but I am sure you emphasised the quality aspect in your negotiations. It would be interesting to know who they have decided to buy from and in what way, if any, we are 'falling short' of our competitors in anything other than price. Do you have any information on this?

Best regards

Ursula Schneider

Ursula Schneider

PS I hope the package of catalogues arrived safely. They cost 1600DM per thousand to produce but we hope they will help you to boost your sales. We would very much like to know what you think of them.

Questions

1. Explain in your own words the story conveyed by these two letters.
2. How does the tone of the two letters differ? Why the difference?
3. What are the advantages and dangers in using an agent like Truelove?
4. How would it be possible for Riba to check on the effectiveness of their agents?
5. What are the merits and demerits of displaying products such as these at for example the Ideal Home Exhibition?
6. How would Riba be able to get a meaningful feedback from the consumers who actually use their product, bearing in mind that agents like Truelove sell the kitchen furniture to retailers like Henways who sell it to the public (the consumers). How would you suggest dealing with this problem?
7. Do you have any criticisms of either of these letters? Try rewriting the letters in your own words.

19: Exporting

M. Telephone conversation

Antonio Carlos Gomez is a director of a company in Malaga which exports Spanish and Moroccan wines. He is telephoning one of his clients in London, Barton and Read, who blend and bottle wines from all over Europe and sell them mainly to hotels and restaurants in the capital.

RECEPTIONIST:	Barton and Read.
ANTONIO:	This is Antonio Carlos Gomez, I'm 'phoning from Malaga. I'd like to speak to Paul Read please.
RECEPTIONIST:	One moment Senor Gomez… You're through…
PAUL:	Good morning, Antonio. What can I do for you?
ANTONIO:	Good morning, Paul. I'm wondering whether you received the samples I sent a couple of weeks ago.
PAUL:	They arrived safely, thank you Antonio.
ANTONIO:	Have you had a chance to taste the new sherry?
PAUL:	It was superb!
ANTONIO:	I thought you'd like it.
PAUL:	But I did notice there'd been a big increase in the price.
ANTONIO:	I'm afraid that's inevitable. It was a poor harvest so the supply's very limited. Let's hope it's a different story this year.
PAUL:	I'll drink to that! Oh, by the way I also tried some of your new light table wines. I've got a feeling they'll go down well with our more discriminating restaurateurs.
ANTONIO:	That's good news, Paul. I certainly hope so. I'm getting a bit worried though because the stocks are getting low on some of the better wines. I'd hate to let you down.
PAUL:	OK Antonio. I do understand. I'm making out the order for you now. I promise I'll fax it within the next few days.
ANTONIO:	That's fine. I look forward to hearing from you.
PAUL:	Thanks for calling, Antonio.
ANTONIO:	It's nice to have a few words with you. I hope you come to the Costa del Sol again before too long.
PAUL:	I'll probably be coming over some time next month.
ANTONIO:	I look forward to that. Goodbye for now, Paul.
PAUL:	Goodbye, Antonio.

Questions
1. Why did Antonio telephone Paul?
2. Was the outcome satisfactory from Antonio's point of view?
3. Why do you think Antonio told the receptionist he was 'phoning from Spain?
4. Why did Antonio send Paul samples of the new wines? How could it be seen as a form of market research?
5. What was the explanation for the increase in the price of the sherry?
6. What might happen if Paul delays sending his order?

N. Useful phrases

Negotiating

What price are you quoting? Is that the lowest price you can offer?

Can you quote in sterling/francs/lira?

I'm sorry but that price is too high. I'll have to think about it.

It's a bit more than I expected to pay.

I've got a supplier in Korea who's offering a better product at a much lower price.

My customers expect a higher quality than this.

It's a very difficult market. There isn't much demand for these.

I'm prepared to offer 600,000 pesetas a crate. No more.

Is that price Ex Works or FRC (free carrier)?

That quotation is CIP (freight or carriage and insurance paid).

I assume that price includes the cost of insurance and freight (CIF)?

Alright, I'll accept that.

When can you deliver? I must have them by the 13th.

What discounts are you offering?

What method of payment are you proposing?

Is there after-sales service? Who would I refer to if there were any complaints? What about spares?

That sounds reasonable. I'll confirm the order by telex tomorrow.

Could I ask you to confirm the order in writing?

Will there be any problems with customs?

Can I leave you to deal with the documentation?

Will you fax me the details?

Arranging meetings

I shall be in Frankfurt/Birmingham next week. Can I call on you?

Could we meet? Where would you suggest?

Could we get together to discuss that?

When would it be convenient? I could fly out on Friday.

I'll confirm the arrangements by telex.

When will you be arriving? Would you like me to arrange accommodation for you? Will you be on your own?

Would you mind if I brought my Production Manager with me?

How many will there be in your party?

Would you like me to arrange transport?

Would you like me to arrange hotel bookings?

I'll leave you to make the arrangements.

I don't know how to get there. Can you give me some directions? A map would be useful.

Perhaps we could have lunch together?

Do you have any preference?

19: Exporting

Let's make it, say, Tuesday at 10.30. Does that suit you?

Selling

Would you like me to call again when it's more convenient?

We have some new lines I think you'll be interested in.

I'll send you a copy of our latest brochure/catalogue.

I'll arrange for our representative to call on you; he'll be in Hamburg early next month.

What did you think of the samples we sent?

Shall I take an order now? How many will you be needing?

If I take an order now I can get you a special 15% discount.

We're running out of stocks.

What is it you're looking for? *or* What do you have in mind?

Who's your present supplier?

The quality's exceptional. They're excellent value.

If you order before the end of the month, I can give you a special price.

They're on sale or return. We supply customers all over the world.

I've been working for the company for six years and I've never had a complaint, but in any case there's a twelve month guarantee.

We're one of the biggest firms in the industry.

You won't find better quality anywhere. Our reputation's second to none.

Your task

Using as many of the above phrases as possible, create a telephone conversation between Daniel Betschart in Hamburg and Antonio Carlos Gomex in Malaga, using the previous exercise as a model. Daniel is the Purchasing Manager for a large supermarket group in Germany.

O. Discussion topic

When our sales are falling in domestic markets we will be tempted to look towards other countries. But studious market research is called for before we commit our resources to such a course of action.

We need to study the different features of the new market, discover the age structure of the population, find out the national income per head, determine existing patterns of expenditure, and identify the nature of the competition. We also need to be aware of the local laws and customs.

If, after investigation, we decide the situation is favourable we can expect various benefits from the extension of our markets. One of these benefits is related to the increase in the level of production. It seems reasonable to assume we would need to provide more goods if we are servicing a new market.

Production on a larger scale should help us to achieve economies, bearing in mind that a proportion of our costs will remain fixed. Our unit costs should move downward and this in turn should give us an opportunity to review our pricing policies. In facing the challenge of a new and untried market, penetration pricing may well be the order of the day, though this may be viewed as 'dumping' in some quarters.

Selling in a foreign market is seldom easy. A lack of detailed knowledge of the market is one handicap. An inability to understand the language or the culture would be another.

19: Exporting

We may get help from our government since exports are vital to the national economy. The government will certainly provide us with useful information and may even offer financial support in one form or another.

Among the other risks we face are fluctuating exchange rates and political and economic uncertainties. For example, if the importer pays us for his purchases in US dollars which have fallen in value since the contract was made, we could end up by making a loss however successful we might otherwise have been.

However, we could deal with this problem by entering into forward exchange contracts. The effect of this type of contract is that we can fix the rate of exchange now for foreign currency we are to receive at a future date. There would be similar result if a change of government in the importer's country brought with it a policy of import restrictions, through a system of quotas or punitive tariffs.

Many questions still need to be answered. What is our budget for advertising? Should we employ agents? Or set up a subsidiary? Who can we trust? How can we retain control over the operations?

Your first task

Complete each of the following sentences with one of the words listed below.

a) Exporting becomes .... when the importer's country is politically unstable.

b) As our scale of production increases our .... costs should fall.

c) If we can .... our unit costs we can reduce our prices.

d) We can .... foreign markets if we can sell our products cheaply.

e) International trade will be discouraged when exchange rates ....

f) We can .... entry to a foreign market wither by employing an agent or setting up a subsidiary.

g) If we .... an agent we have to trust him to maximise our sales.

The missing words:

| penetrate | gain | fluctuate | lower |
| employ | unattractive | unit | |

Your second task

Consider the following statements critically:

1. 'Free trade should be encouraged throughout the world, but dumping should be prohibited.'

2. 'When governments help their exporters by giving them financial aid of any sort, they are really playing a variation on the game of protectionism.'

P. Bankers and exporters

Although Elite Racers PLC is a public company, it only has a few hundred shareholders, and its shares are not quoted on the Stock Exchange. This makes is very dependent on the financial support of its bankers. Elite Racers have concentrated production on a small range of high quality racing cycles. Until recently the bulk of their sales were in the UK, Germany and Scandinavia, but last year they sponsored a group of riders in the Tour de France and one of them came first in one of the mountain climbs. The favourable publicity has produced customers from all over the world and Christopher Chesterton, the Financial Director, is running into a new set of problems. It is proving difficult now to collect pay-

19: Exporting

ments from some of the newer and more distant customers, and sometimes they are paid in foreign currencies which have gone down in value since the contract was agreed. He has asked for help from the company's own bankers and a factoring company which has been recommended to him. He has received the following letters in reply.

Factoring International Tavistock House, Leadenhall Street, London EC3 1NN

Telephone 081 325 3253

Date:

Mr Christopher Chesterton
Elite Racers PLC
Overton Works
Cranmoor Road
Wheatley
Sheffield S27 5YQ

Dear Mr Chesterton,

Our reference ENQ JHW

I am writing in response to your letter of the [date] enquiring about the facilities we offer to companies like yours in the export business. We are one of the largest factoring companies in the world and can certainly offer you the benefit of our long and wide experience. Through our factoring service we can eliminate the risk that you will not be paid for the goods you sell overseas.

To achieve this outcome we take over complete management of your export sales ledgers. It would not be logical for us to accept only the most difficult collections. Indeed it is because we take over the whole portfolio of our clients' overseas debts that we are able to quote such competitive rates for commission.

One of the benefits of us taking over like this is that your staff are relieved from the routine duties of sending out reminders to slow-payers, and dealing with bad debts generally. Another is that we are normally prepared to advance up to 80% of the invoiced amount which means you are paid earlier than you would normally expect.

Another service we offer is forfeiting. This enables you to provide your buyers with up to 100% finance on credit terms and tailor repayment programmes without risk to you. It is simple, finance can be arranged quickly, and the documentation is minimal.

I need to meet you to explain the full range of our services and hope to be in the Sheffield area on Wednesday and Thursday of next week. Could we arrange a meeting during that time? I would be available from midday on Wednesday to six o'clock on Thursday.

I look forward to hearing from you.

Yours sincerely,

Alistair Thornton

Alistair Thornton
Executive Assistant

19: Exporting

Barchester Bank plc
Foreign Department
Stanton House, Central Parade, Sheffield S1 3BY
Tel 0742 396541 (ext 13) Fax 0742 667345

Date:

Mr Christopher Chesterton
Elite Racers PLC
Overton Works
Cranmoor Road
Wheatley
Sheffield S27 5YQ

Dear Mr Chesterton,

In reply to your letter of [date]. I am pleased to give some basic information on how the bank can help you to eliminate the risk of losses arising from adverse fluctuations in the currency exchange rates. The best advice might be to ensure that all your contracts call for payment in sterling, but this only passes over the exposure to your customer who might be entitled to expect some compensation in the form of a lower quotation.

What the bank offers you is a forward deal by means of which the bank agrees to exchange the foreign currency for you, at a rate determined now. According to market expectations agreed will be either above or below the 'spot' (or current rate of exchange).

One of the big advantages you would find from the use of these forward deals is that you would be able to calculate costs and quote prices with confidence. We can offer you forward exchange contracts in 35 different currencies and quote you forward rates for delivery up to three years ahead, or even longer in some cases.

We have a whole range of other services we can offer and I would certainly like to explain them to you in such detail as you require. Would you like to come to my office? Or would it be easier if I came to the Overton Works?

I look forward to hearing from you.

Yours sincerely,

Julia Squires

Julia Squires
Assistant Manager

Your first task

After studying the letters you are asked to complete the following table. Use key words and phrases to convey your understanding of the situation. Remember you are looking at the situation from Elite Racers' point of view.

Factoring

Merits: i)
         ii)

Demerits: i)
          ii)

19: Exporting

Forward deals

Merits:
- i)
- ii)

Demerits:
- i)
- ii)

Your second task

Explain, in about 200 words, ways in which banks might help exporters to overcome some of their problems.

20: Government and business

A. Comprehension

To what extent should a government interfere in the economic system? There are two extremes in the spectrum. On the one hand a government can intervene minimally, allowing the forces of demand and supply and the price mechanism to determine what goods and services are to be produced. This is called a laissez-faire (or leave it alone) policy. The argument runs that people will vote with their money for the sorts of things they want. If they want to read a particular newspaper, they will buy it, and the newspaper will stay in business. If they do not like the newspaper, they will not buy it, and the newspaper will go out of business. The same applies to television sets and motor cars, holidays in Spain and Chinese take-aways.

At the other end of the spectrum is the centrally planned economy in which the government makes all the major decisions such as what is going to be produced, who is going to produce it, where it is going to be produced, and who is going to benefit from it when it is produced.

Most governments operate somewhere between these two extremes. In capitalist countries governments tend to let the business world get on with the job of catering for the needs of the people. If they make profits, and we hope they do, we will tax these profits and use the proceeds to support the Welfare State (which offers free education, subsidized health care and pensions) and defend ourselves against external aggression. There is, however, general agreement that some economic activities should be controlled by the state, which explains our nationalised industries.

In Britain governments tend to concentrate their interest on controlling inflation, minimizing unemployment and encouraging economic growth. It is often the case that a policy which would be good for us in the short run would be against our interests in the long run. The point might be made in connection with a government's policy towards energy. In the short run we might benefit from a rapid disposal of our North Sea oil and gas supplies, but what happens when these supplies run out? Should the government intervene in these circumstances, or allow the multinational oil companies to make the crucial decisions?

Another problem facing a government in modern Britain is dealing with regional development. Inevitably, at the present time, as Britain draws closer to Europe economically, the south east of the country is prospering while the north goes into relative decline. Should the government let this happen or should it try to reverse the flow of people and jobs to the south east. It is not an easy decision for a government to make because it seems wrong to let parts of the country decline while others prosper.

Whatever decisions are made by a government they are bound to affect the business community. If taxes are increased on beer, the brewers' profits will go down and jobs will be lost. If interest rates are lowered, businesses will borrow more from the banks, jobs will be created, but prices might rise and that means inflation. Whatever action a government takes it will have repercussions on the business community, which is why the captains of industry are so watchful and wary of their political masters.

Your task

Having read the above passage answer these questions in your own words.

    a)   What is meant by laissez-faire? To what extent do you think it is possible for a government to 'let things happen'?

20: Government and business

b) What do you see as the benefits and disadvantages of a centrally planned economy?

c) How do you think the problem of unemployment should be dealt with?

d) Do you think that people should go to where the jobs are, or that jobs should be taken to the people?

e) Would you generally prefer to see the government more active or less active? What sort of actions, if any, would you like to see them taking?

B. Fill in the blanks*

Rewrite the passage filling in the blanks from the list of words below.

One of the problems faced in a society aiming to produce an equitable distribution of national wealth is that those who are wealthy find it comparatively easy to increase their .... further, while those who are poor are caught in what might be described as a .... trap. Since there are more poor people than rich people in our society, and since we live in a .... where every adult has a vote (rich or poor), it is not surprising that our governments produce a .... of taxation which generally directs wealth away from the rich to the poor. The actual rates of taxation are liable to change every year when the Chancellor of the Exchequer .... his budget proposals to Parliament. Among other things the taxes .... are used to distribute to the less fortunate members of our society in the form of unemployment .... and old age pensions etc.

Direct taxes are those levied on the taxpayer such as income tax, which is charged through the system known as PAYE (Pay As You Earn). Companies pay Corporation Tax which is .... on their profits. Indirect taxes, by contrast, are charged when goods or services are procured, so that you pay more. In this sense indirect taxes could be said to .... saving. This type of tax .... the tax on cigarettes and alcohol as well as VAT (Value Added Tax) which has to be paid on most goods .... .The ultimate problem with taxation is the need to ensure that taxation is not so punitive that it demotivates the wage .... and the profit-makers, thereby 'killing the goose that lays the golden egg'.

assessed	collected	includes	system
poverty	presents	democracy	earners
prosperity	benefits	encourage	purchased

C. Interpretation of data

After studying the following diagram answer the following questions.

Government income and expenditure (%)

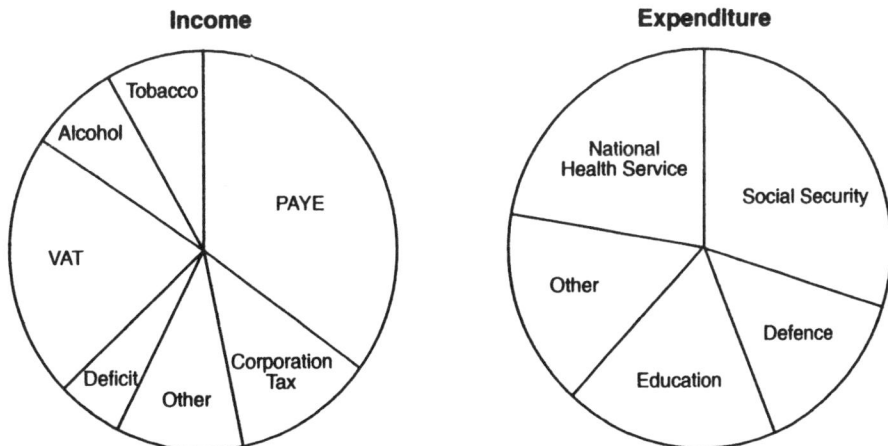

1. Which two items of taxation bring in about half of the government's revenue?
2. Which are the three largest items of government expenditure?
3. What could be some of the effects of increasing the rate for corporation tax?
4. What would be the effect of companies making more profits?
5. How do you expect the declining school population to affect future Chancellors' budgets?
6. What effect on national spending patterns would you expect from lower death rates?
7. How do you account for the deficit shown on the income side of the equation?

D. Complete the table*

word	synonym	opposite
deficit (noun)	lack	surplus
equitable (adjective)		
mobile (adjective)		
public (adjective)		
adequately (adverb)		
fluctuating (adjective)		
confirm (verb)		
reveal (verb)		
depreciation (noun)		
collectively (adverb)		
gather (verb)		
random (adjective)		
popular (adjective)		

20: Government and business

distinguish (verb)		
declining (adjective)		
purposeful (adjective)		
decisively (adverb)		
co-operative (adjective)		
rashly (adverb)		
autocratically (adverb)		

E. Missing words

A number of words have been omitted from the following passage. You are asked to find appropriate words to complete the text. When you have done this, rewrite the passage including these words.

In the western democracies emphasis is laid on the freedom of the individual, both as a consumer and the owner of resources. As a .... he expresses his choice of goods through the price he is willing to pay for them. As the owner of a factor of production (his own labour), he seeks to obtain as large a .... as possible. If he wants more of the good than is being .... at the current price, he will 'bid up' the price. As a result, resources are attracted to that .... industry and supply expands. On the other hand, if consumers do not want a particular good or service, its price falls, ... make a loss, and resources leave the industry. There is no .... of labour; people are free to work wherever they choose. The role of government is simply to correct any .... which might develop in the system. However, western governments do not settle for a passive role. Rather they take it upon themselves to redistribute .... income, succour the sick and the underprivileged, generate national wealth and provide for national defence. To achieve these ends they are .... to raise taxes from the populace and in doing this they are almost bound to become ....

F. Summarising

Read the following passage carefully. Then give it a title and summarise it in about 100 words.

The world faces an energy crisis in the not-too-distant future. For the time being there are plentiful supplies of oil, but this situation will not last. Oil supplies are finite, and what happens when the world's reserves arc exhausted? In Britain we are comparatively fortunate. We have North Sea oil and gas, and they will give us self-sufficiency for another couple of decades. We also have substantial reserves of coal. According to some estimates our coal reserves could last for another sixty years. That should give us a breathing-space at least until alternative forms of energy are developed. There is a world-wide search for new sources of energy.

The government of Saudi Arabia has been making encouraging progress in the development of solar energy. Plants they have built in the desert are turning the rays of the sun into what can only be described as permanent sources of energy. So successful have the experiments been that when they eventually run out of oil – as run out of oil they must – they will be switching to an even more durable form of energy.

20: Government and business

Not only has the government of Saudi Arabia been working hard to develop solar energy. They have also been working hard to convert the desert to rich agricultural land. Impossible? By no means! Beneath the Arabian Desert lies an enormous water basin. The problem is to bring up those water supplies from the bowels of the earth. How to do it? Sink wells deep into the earth, seeking water this time instead of oil. As the water is drawn from the earth it is sprayed over the crops of wheat and vegetables and of course they flourish in such an environment.

Perhaps it is unrealistic to expect all governments to play such a positive role in the development of their economy and the long term wellbeing of their people, but they do set the standards by which other governments can be judged.

G. Cause and effect

Your first task

Listed below are a number of companies. These are followed by brief details of possible government actions. Consider in each case whether the government's action would be beneficial or otherwise to the company in question.

1. The company is an insurance company specialising in motor insurance. Possible government actions:
   a) A relaxation of the drinking and driving laws.
   b) The introduction of a lower speed limit on motorways.
   c) A substantial reduction in National Health Service expenditure.

2. The company manufactures cigarettes.
   a) An extensive television publicity campaign encouraging young people to stop smoking.
   b) A slight increase in the tax on cigarettes.
   c) A substantial increase in the tax on beer.

3. The company operates coach tours to the continent.
   a) A substantial increase in the tax on petrol.
   b) A new law limiting the number of passengers who can be carried in coaches.
   c) A lowering of the retirement age to 55.

4. The company is in the business of life assurance.
   a) A substantial increase in pay for nurses.
   b) A substantial increase in the tax on cigarettes.
   c) The abolition of prescription charges for all medicines.

Your second task

Play the role of a Personal Assistant to David Rothwell, Marketing Manager for Crufties Pet Foods. He is going to meet a local MP next week. The MP is a Junior Minister and Mr Rothwell has asked you for a brief memorandum setting out your ideas on what government actions might benefit the company. Your boss has made it clear he does not expect to change government policy but would just like to have considered all the angles before he meets the Minister.

H. Explanations

Explain carefully the meanings of the highlighted phrases in these sentences:

20: Government and business

i) Since goods and services in the economy as a whole are limited, the government has to **cut its coat according to the cloth**.

ii) The arguments against a political union (or federation of states) in the European Community centre on the **loss of sovereignty** of the British Parliament.

iii) One of the most serious problems which any government has to face is **a downturn in the world economy**.

iv) One way of judging the effectiveness of a particular government is to note the success it is having in stimulating the **growth of the national income**.

v) No government can afford to disregard the interests of its people caught in the **poverty trap**.

vi) If a government is able to lower interest rates, businesses will no doubt respond by undertaking projects which were **hitherto unattractive**.

vii) Where an economy is adapting to changing conditions, there will always be some persons unemployed as they switch jobs or as **seasonal or casual work** comes to an end.

viii) In order to protect its exporters a government will do its best to **stabilize the exchange rates**.

I. Write a letter

The following advertisement appeared in the Times newspaper yesterday. Write a letter applying for the job.

> ### Superb opportunity for travel!
> for lively-minded person interested in medical work in developing countries. Government-sponsored scheme. Enthusiasm essential. Write a short letter (no more than 100 words) explaining why we should interview you. The work will involve meetings with medical teams though no medical knowledge is required at this stage.
>
> **Ms Sarah Barnes, Personnel Recruitment Agency**
> **Benham House, Christchurch, Hants CH1 1AA**

J. Complete the sentences

Complete the following sentences using your own words.

1. The economic recession ...
2. When there is a high level of unemployment ...
3. A government should never ...
4. The Chancellor of the Exchequer ...
5. To stop industrial pollution we need to ...
6. The problem with the National Health Service is ...
7. The Eurotunnel ...
8. If interest rates were raised ...
9. By raising the school leaving age ...
10. Since people are tending to live longer ...
11. Most industrial disputes ...
12. If people pay less tax ...

20: Government and business

K. Vocabulary*

subsidy	stability	privatisation	inflation
corporation	budget	deficit	sterling
minister	Treasury	redistribution	nationalisation
census	bullion	legislation	recession
recovery	boom	depression	conciliation

Match the words listed above with the dictionary definitions which follow.

1. A period of heavy unemployment and economic stagnation. There are many bankruptcies and businesspeople have no confidence in the future.
2. A temporary downturn in economic activity, but it may be sustained.
3. Laws made by governments to change the rules by which the country is controlled.
4. Gold bars each weighing 400oz. May be held as part of the country's gold reserves.
5. The use of taxation to reduce the inequality of income.
6. The type of tax paid by companies. Based on their profits.
7. When this is happening prices are rising.
8. A member of the government with departmental responsibilities.
9. A period when economic activity is at a high level. Production expands. Prices and wages rise. Unemployment declines.
10. The means by which a government takes over control of an industry such as the railways or coal.
11. To take a count of something, such as population, production or distribution. A government device to monitor economic developments.
12. When nationalised industries are being returned to shareholders.
13. One of a government's principal aims both in terms of currency and employment.
14. A payment by the State to producers in order to reduce prices.
15. The attempt to bring the two sides together in an industrial dispute which is damaging the national economy.
16. A time when businessmen are beginning to regain confidence. Order books are beginning to fill up and more jobs are being created.
17. The currency for the UK.
18. The budgetary situation when the Chancellor of the Exchequer raises less in taxes than he spends.
19. The government department concerned primarily with finance.
20. The national income and expenditure plans.

L. Discussion topic

Homeostasis and the balance of payments

In Britain the monthly balance of trade (and payments) has become a major test of the effectiveness of the government's economic policy. The figures are given on all the television news programmes, and are analysed by the morning newspapers. A surplus brings a sigh of relief from the government. A deficit is a signal for the opposition parties to get 'hot under the collar' and tell us just where the government is going wrong. The provocative suggestion here, though, is that we may all be a little over-sensitive to the short-term fluctuations in the balance of trade (and payments).

20: Government and business

In mathematics we learn that when we add to, or subtract from, one side of the equation we have to add an equal amount to the other side, if we are to maintain an equilibrium.

In law we learn that while citizens acquire valuable rights in a democratic society, they also incur obligations.

In our accounting studies we are taught the principle of double entry. If we buy an asset we must debit the asset account, but we must counter with a credit in the cash book, or the personal account of the vendor.

When we make these observations are we identifying a universal phenomenon? Fascinatingly, in the natural sciences we learn of an inherent tendency towards equilibrium in physiological processes. We call this homeostasis. So perhaps when we are dealing with economic models we should not be surprised to find that by changing one of the inputs we are almost certainly providing a stimulus for a movement in the opposite direction. For example:

i) According to the eighteenth-century economist Thomas Malthus, since the world has limited resources, a rise in the world's population will eventually bring about a fall in the world's standard of living, reducing the population to the predestined level.

ii) Economies of scale produce lower unit costs – and larger business units. But excessive numbers of employees become more difficult to manage in an impersonal organisation. Industrial relations and productivity suffer. Operating units then have to be reduced to a manageable size.

iii) In trade cycle theory, the excessive activity (or over-heating) of the economy we call a boom is followed by recession, recession by depression, depression by recovery, recovery by boom. We come back to where we started.

iv) The operation of the price mechanism is such that the equilibrium price acts as a magnet ensuring that, however far the market strays, it is always drawn back towards the equilibrium.

So, what happens when an unfavourable balance of payments develops? From the examples given above we would expect some sort of corrective mechanism to develop. Consider, when Greek importers buy goods from Britain, they create a demand for sterling and the balance of trade between the two countries will be in Britain's favour. In a free market, the price of sterling will rise against drachma. Holidays in Greece will become comparatively cheap for the British. The result? If there are no artificial barriers imposed, a reversal of the previous tendencies. According to this hypothesis, there will be a tendency for the balance of payments between Britain and Greece to be drawn towards an equilibrium over a period of time. The Japanese buy Saudi Arabian oil. The Saudis buy Japanese technology. Trade tends to be reciprocal.

Another aspect of this mechanism is that if one nation's balance of payments is in deficit, another nation must have a surplus. Globally, there must be some approximate balance. If this were not so we could have nightmare visions of a world where all nations are in perpetual deficit and sliding further and further 'into the red'. The physicists tell us about those almost incomprehensible black holes in space. Perhaps we can add another frightening spectre – balance of payments red holes?

Yet, the accounting system in operation in all capitalist countries, and certainly in the world's banking fraternity, has surely convinced us that for every creditor there must be a debtor; and that is as true when we are talking about individuals as when we are talking about nations. Of course, it can be argued that our model is simplistic, but before we jettison the argument on that score, let us look at what happens when a country, because of its economic power, persistently exports more than it imports. On current account they amass enormous balances which they then proceed to lend (on capital account) to the so-called debtor nations. Current accounts and capital accounts when aggregated move back to a global balance.

Where you find nations with balance of payments surpluses, there you will find international bankers. The British became bankers as a result of the Industrial Revolution, the United States of America became the world's bankers through the destruction of its major competitors in the Second World War, and most recently we have witnessed the economic miracle in Japan. The world, hungry for Japanese technological equipment, has enabled Japan to build up an enormous trading surplus. In doing so Japan has become one of the world's great banking nations, with five of the six largest banks in the world being Japanese.

If the hypothesis is acceptable, two conclusions follow. First, adverse balance of payments are not as evil as they seem. It is governments interfering with the mechanisms which pose the real threats, for example with exchange rates and interest rates. Second, in looking for the next 'world bankers' we may have to look no further than our own back yards. If the USA benefits, as it surely does, from a free trade area of some 250 million comparatively rich people (including Canadians), what can we expect from a European Community with a population approaching 400 million people?

Your views

1. Can you see any flaws in these arguments? (Can you express your ideas in good English?)

2. How do you view the problem of international debts? What do you think should be done about it a) by the debtor nations and b) by the world's bankers?

3. Do you think the affluent states in the European Community should help the countries of Eastern Europe to develop? What form do you think such aid should take? Do you think the investment should come from governments or bankers, or both?

Part Three: Examination practice

21: ICM Certificate in Business English

In this part of the book students will be given the opportunity to test their skills and judge the level of examination they are capable of taking.

We look first at the ICM Certificate.

> **Aim:**
> To test the basic ability to understand and communicate in English as the language of business.

Written paper format

Question 1 Requires a suitable response to an incoming business letter or memorandum.

Question 2 Consists of a passage from which certain words have been omitted. The missing words will be listed and the passage has to be rewritten with the missing words included.

Question 3 Takes the form of a brief vocabulary test.

Question 4 Either calls for the completion of incomplete sentences, or takes the form of a multiple choice question.

Question 5 Involves summarising, reducing a passage of about 150 words to about 50 words.

All questions are to be answered.

If the written paper only is taken, the award will be a Certificate in Business English (Written). If the Oral Test is also taken, the award will be a Certificate in Business English (Written and Oral).

Oral test format

This will take the form of a short business case study which will be given to the candidate to study for 10 minutes before the test. The examiner will then ask the candidate a series of short questions relating to the case study.

The pass mark for these examinations is 61% and students scoring more than 85% will be awarded an ICM Certificate in Business English with Distinction.

A sample Written Paper is shown below, accompanied by suggested answers.

It is followed by an Oral Test with a list of questions such as might be asked by the Oral Examiner.

THE INSTITUTE OF COMMERCIAL MANAGEMENT
PO Box 125, Bournemouth, England BH2 6JH†
CERTIFICATE IN BUSINESS ENGLISH

Instructions to candidates

a) Time allowed: 2 hours.

b) Answer all questions.

c) All questions carry equal marks.

d) No dictionaries allowed.

Question 1

You are the Personnel Officer in Crampthorn and Barley Ltd and have been asked to deal with the following application for a reference. Draft a suitable reply in the light of the information contained in Joanna Sedgeley's staff report.

Barchester Bank plc
Midlands Area Staff Department
The Bull Ring, Birmingham BH6 8QY
Telephone: 031 222 4444

The Personnel Manager
Crampthorn and Barley Ltd
45/49 Hyde Road
Stedbury
Staffordshire ST11 5WX

3rd January 199-

Dear Sir or Madam,

Ms Joanna Sedgeley
Flat 65 Galway Mansions, Stedbury, Staffs ST8 9AD

The above named has applied to this office for a post as a temporary clerical officer, having left your firm we understand in December 1991.

We should like to know how long Ms Sedgeley worked for you; in what capacity; whether you were satisfied with her work; the reasons for termination of her employment with you; and above all, whether you deem her to be trustworthy.

Any background information you can give about Ms Sedgeley would be gratefully received.

Yours faithfully

George Webster

George Webster
Personnel Officer

Note: Your General Manager has reminded you that the company recently closed their account with Barchester and they now have a new banker.

---

† A selection of past examination papers can be obtained (free) from the Examinations Officer at this address.

21: ICM Certificate in Business English

Staff Record for: Joanna Sedgeley

Joined company: 15.7.1988   **Address:** Flat 65, Galway Mansions, Stedbury, ST8 9AD

Left company: 23.10.1991   **Telephone:** 010 000 1111   **Born:** 1.4.1967

Post: Telephone Receptionist/Filing Clerk

Reason for leaving:
Husband (employed in our Marketing Department) left her to live with another woman. Husband continues to be employed by us.

Annual Reports

1988   Joanna seems very shy and lacks confidence in dealing with customers.

1989   After giving birth to a baby daughter in October Joanna returned to work as a receptionist/cashier in our Marketing Department.

1990   A good year's work. Joanna given a 15% merit pay rise.

1991   Work has deteriorated since June and her departure has probably been for the best. She was making all sorts of mistakes in her work.

Suggested answer

Crampthorne & Barley Ltd
45–49 Hyde Road, Stedbury, Staffordshire ST11 5WX
Telephone: 040 445566

Mr George Webster
Barchester Bank PLC
Midlands Area Staff Department
The Bull Ring
Birmingham BH6 8QY

7th January 199-

Dear Mr Webster

Reference: Joanna Sedgeley

In reply to your letter of the 3rd January, Mrs Sedgeley joined this company as a telephonist/receptionist in July 1988, later becoming a receptionist cashier. She left us on the 6th December 1991 for for personal reasons which had nothing to do with her work.

According to her annual reports her work was generally satisfactory and she was considered honest and trustworthy.

Yours sincerely,

J Smith

John Smith
Personnel Manager

Question 2

Rewrite the following passage with appropriate words taken from the list below.

Communication is far more difficult than people imagine. Inadequate communication ...... to many divorces, not a few strikes, and even to international ...... on occasion. It is certainly a ...... problem in life generally, and in business particularly. The problem is that business units ...... to get larger and larger to achieve ...... of scale, and larger businesses have ...... communication problems than their smaller counterparts. So, while ...... costs may decrease as the scale of production increases, the ...... of managing a larger organisation multiply.

a) unit b) problems c) economies d) major
e) tend f) leads g) more h) conflicts

Answer

missing words in order:
leads – conflicts – major – tend – economies – more – unit – problems

But you are expected to rewrite the completed passage.

Question 3

Rewrite the following table adding the missing verbs and nouns.

verb	noun	verb	noun
believe	belief	refer	
threaten			pleasure
	enjoyment	lend	
clarify			receipt
	assistant	confirm	
suggest			expression
	requirement	elect	
agree			presentation
	franchisor	distribute	

Answer

Missing verbs in order:
enjoy – assist – require – franchise – please – receive – express – present.

Missing nouns in order:
threat – clarification – suggestion – agreement – reference – loan – confirmation – election – distributor/distribution.

Question 4

Complete the following sentences in your own words.

a) A bank manager ...
b) If a company is successful ...
c) Staff dealing with a telephone enquiry ...
d) The board of directors ...
e) An invoice is sent ...
f) When people are doing boring jobs ...

Suggested answer

a) A bank manager may have to refuse a customer's application for a loan.

b) If a company is successful its shareholders can expect to receive satisfactory dividends.
c) Staff dealing with a telephone enquiry should be polite and helpful.
d) The board of directors appoint the senior managers in a company.
e) An invoice is sent when goods are purchased on credit.
f) When people are doing boring jobs they need frequent breaks.

Question 5

Summarise the following passage in about 50 words.

Money is at the heart of business. Money is needed to pay wages, to acquire materials to make up into manufactured goods and to reward those who attempt to anticipate the needs of society and stand to lose if they fail to do so. Money is the lubricant which allows the diverse elements in the economic system to interact effectively. If a business runs short of money in the private sector it will be wound up (if a company) or closed down (if the proprietor is bankrupted). People will lose their jobs and the flow of goods and/or services it has been providing will dry up. Money is the life-blood of business and executives of all types will find much of their time and energy devoted to coping with problems of a financial nature. Finance becomes critical when a business is being first set up; when expansion is planned; or when a shortage of working capital is developed.

Suggested answer

Without money, business would be impossible. It is needed to pay wages, buy raw materials and to reward successful entrepreneurs. If there is a shortage of money the business will collapse. There will be no production, no jobs. This is why executives spend so much time dealing with financial problems

(50 words – but between 45 and 55 words would be acceptable.)

ICM CERTIFICATE IN BUSINESS ENGLISH
SAMPLE ORAL EXAMINATION

Time allowed :	10 minutes to read through the case study
	10 minutes to answer questions from the examiner

Case study

(You can take this into the examination room with you.)

Scene:

The Director's suite in the Head Office of Anglian Tobaccos. The Chairman, Matthew Ironside, is having a working lunch with the Managing Director, Tom Blanchard. Tom knows it is going to be a rather tough session because sales have been falling dramatically over the past eighteen months. Every effort has been made to reverse the trend – without great success. Tom hopes his team's latest ideas will please the Chairman.

IRONSIDE: I got your latest sales figures, Tom. Disappointing! I hate the thought of having to talk about redundancies again, but I don't see any alternative.

BLANCHARD: I share your disappointment, Matthew, but some of my people have been working on a new line.

IRONSIDE:	A new line? I didn't think there was anything new in this business. What is it?
BLANCHARD:	I think you'll like it. Our market research people have discovered that we're losing most of our share of the market in the under-twenty age group and so we've produced a new brand aimed at the younger smoker.
IRONSIDE:	What's new about it?
BLANCHARD:	Well, there are two new ideas. Firstly, the cigarettes are only 70% of the normal length. That would keep the price down. Secondly, in each packet of twenty we would include a very special cigarette-holder. It's short but attractive and allows all the tobacco to be smoked. It's not just a cigarette-holder because it also has a new filter we've developed. We think we can find a number of doctors and surgeons who will recommend it. Oh! And we're thinking of introducing coloured cigarette papers to make them more attractive to young people. Pink, blue (pale blue, that is), light brown and black.
IRONSIDE:	It sounds interesting, Tom. When can we see some samples?
BLANCHARD:	*(Obviously relieved at finding his boss interested in the scheme):* I hope to bring along some samples to the Board meeting tomorrow afternoon.

Questions which might be asked by the Oral Examiner:
1. Why do you think sales might have been falling at Anglian Tobaccos?
2. How is the Managing Director hoping to change the situation?
3. Do you think the new cigarettes are likely to be attractive?
4. How do you think the new cigarettes would be marketed?
5. Do you think cigarettes should be advertised on television?
6. What are your views on cigarette smoking? In restaurants? Cinemas? Discos?
7. Do you think government taxes on cigarettes are too high or too low?
8. Do you think businesses have a social responsibility to the public?
9. What should cigarette manufacturers do if their sales are falling?
10. If a company offered you a good salary would you care what they produced?

22: ICM Diploma in Business English

This qualification is designed for business executives and aspiring business executives and assumes an understanding of the major issues in business and management. However, if you have made a reasonable effort to complete the programme of study in this book, you should be able to take the Diploma with confidence. An Oral Test is obligatory for this qualification.

> **Aim:**
> To evaluate the candidate's ability to exhibit a composite knowledge of both the English language and basic business concepts, as is required by the modern business executive.

Written paper format

Question 1 Based on a short business case study of 400/500 words.

Requires the identification of the problem, a brief consideration of the options, and the offer of a solution or solutions.

Question 2 Takes the form of a vocabulary test.

Question 3 Involves summarising, reducing a passage of 250/300 words to about 100 words.

Question 4 Calls for an essay-type answer to a business/management question. One question can be chosen from four. The first question will cover a general business topic. The other three will relate to specific areas of business, specifically:

a) marketing and advertising;

b) business finance and administration;

c) banking and insurance.

Oral test format

This will take the form of a short business case study which will be given to the candidate to study 15 minutes before the test. For about 15 minutes the examiner will then ask the candidate a series of short questions relating to the case study.

The pass mark for the examination will be 61% and students scoring more than 85% will be awarded a distinction. The award will be the ICM Diploma in Business English (Written and Oral) with the words 'With Distinction' displayed on the Diploma, when appropriate. A sample Written Paper follows, together with Diploma level Oral Test.

THE INSTITUTE OF COMMERCIAL MANAGEMENT
PO Box 125, Bournemouth, England BH2 6JH†
DIPLOMA IN BUSINESS ENGLISH

Instructions to candidates

a) Time allowed: Two hours.

b) Answer all questions

c) All questions carry equal marks.

d) No dictionaries are allowed.

Question 1

Case Study: Gamma Furniture PLC

This company grew out of a one-man business established by Louis Steiner in 1951. From the start the business was operating on a small scale, with Louis, his two sons, and a handful of workers producing hand-made furniture of high quality.

Louis died in 1975 and his son Morris took over. His first step was to form a limited company. Next, he borrowed heavily from the bank to buy a new, large factory in East London, and the machinery and equipment to set up mass-production lines. There followed a period of poor results, but then Morris discovered a talented young designer on his staff who was able to change the fortunes of the company. Danny Schaffer produced a succession of very distinctive and highly successful designs for interlocking furniture which found a ready market. These were sold under the description of Unit Five Furniture.

Gamma became revitalised and was converted into a Public Limited Company with its shares quoted on the Stock Exchange. Morris Steiner and his family retained 40% of the voting shares. The demand for Unit Five Furniture has been so great that a new factory was opened up at Reading two years ago, and another is in course of construction on the outskirts of Bristol.

All that is history. This morning, Danny Schaffer sought an audience with Morris Steiner. 'I'm going into business on my own,' he tells his boss, 'I've been able to put my hands on a bit of capital and I want to try a few ideas out for myself.'

a) What problems might this create for Morris Steiner?

b) What options are available to Morris?

c) How do you think Morris should deal with the problem?

Suggested answer

You might include such points as:

a) Danny might set up in competition. If Gamma's profits fall, dividends will fall. 60% of voting shareholders at least may become dissatisfied. They may press for a new Board of Directors.

b) Offer Danny more pay or promotion. Company shares or a directorship? Try to delay departure until a replacement can be organised? Offer to finance his new venture assuming it looks OK? Form a subsidiary Danny Schaffer Productions Ltd, perhaps using the new Bristol factory? Flatter/entice him into staying with Gamma.

---

† A selection of past examination papers can be obtained (free) from the Examinations Officer at this address.

c) Interview him at length after Morris has had time to consider the full implications? Take him for a formal lunch/dinner? Find out more about Danny's project and his future plans. Apply whichever option is most appropriate to the situation which emerges.

Note: There are no right and wrong answers to these case study questions. Rather the examiners will be looking for a logical, analytic approach, and clarity of expression.

Question 2

Give opposites for the words highlighted in the following passage and synonyms for the words in italics:

The economist has a *vital* role to play in two **distinct** areas of the decision-making process. First he has a contribution to make in evaluating prospects in the economy generally and in *particular* industries. The data he **collects** and the forecasts he makes will determine to a large extent which *options* are **taken**, and which directions the investment flows take within the *overall* system. It is **logical** that the economist who is concerned with the allocation of scarce resources should have a role to play in *discussing* both the range of options and the pros and cons of such options.

The second area of interest for the economist is **related** to the economy's *growth*, which is tied up with savings and investment. Consider the machinations of the industrial company with regards to the distribution of profits to its shareholders. Profits *retained* by the company become **available** for investment and are thus used to *generate* higher profits and dividends in the future. This operation can be viewed as a microcosm of what is *happening* the economy at large. When individuals forgo immediate consumption their savings become available for investment, and the present scale of investment determines the **future** limits of consumption. Such factors are obviously related to economic growth and are therefore of concern to the economist. One of the facets of the problem is that the poorest people in society have the **least** opportunity to forgo immediate consumption. While this may be a truism it also represents a *dilemma* for a society which is **seeking** both a high level of investment and a fairer spread of wealth. The two goals are not **always** compatible.

Suggested answer

Synonyms		Opposites	
vital	important	distinct	indistinct
particular	specific	collects	distributes
overall	total	taken	given
discussing	debating	logical	illogical
options	alternatives	related	unrelated
growth	contraction	available	unavailable
retained	kept	future	past
generate	develop	least	most
happening	occurring	seeking	finding
dilemma	problem	always	never

Question 3

Give the following passage a title and summarise it in about 100 words.

An investor is concerned essentially with the degree of risk and the volume of returns likely to be associated with his investment. Risk has two particular dimensions. First, there is the danger that the whole or part of the capital sum might be lost. Second, there is the uncertainty about payment of interest and dividends. The objective of all investors is to minimise risk and maximise returns, but price can be seen to act as a regulator in that investments which are regarded as riskless and give high returns are comparatively expensive, while high-risk/low-return investments are comparatively cheap. In other words the price mechanism tends to compensate for the varying degrees of risk and the likely level of returns, introducing an equilibrium in much the same way as it does for the demand and supply of any commodity.

There are a number of ways of avoiding or eliminating risk, but it usually involves some expense. One way is to pool a large number of similar risks. For example, it would be very risky for an individual to meet any losses sustained during the course of a year by a motorist friend, in return for a single and comparatively small premium. Yet the insurance companies are able to eliminate risks both for themselves and their policy-holders by combining a large number of similar risks.

Another way of avoiding risk is to hedge against loss, and this necessitates choosing two eventualities which will cancel each other out. It is like betting that both teams in the football Cup Final will win.

Suggested answer

Risks and Returns

Investment inevitably involves risk. The investment may not provide the expected returns or, worse, the capital may be list. If the investor accepts risk, his rewards may be high. If he is looking for safety, the rewards are likely to be small. The demand for investments which are both safe and rewarding will be high, but so will the cost of such investments. Risk may be reduced by combining a large number of risks, which is what the insurance companies do, or hedging against an eventuality by choosing another happening which will produce exactly the opposite result of the first.

(99 words)

Question 4

*Answer **one only** of the following questions:*

a) What problems would you expect a manufacturing company to face when they move into the export trade for the first time?

or

b) How might a limited company raise funds for an expansion programme?

or

c) What factors would a bank manager consider when a customer applies for a loan or overdraft?

or

d) What special problems face the small business?

Suggested answer to (d)

What special problems face the small business?

Small firms (with, say, less than 500 workers) are often faced with the problem of limited capital. This has a number of side-effects. It means first that they are unable to benefit from economies of scale. Bank managers will be less inclined to lend them funds and will charge them higher rates of interest when they do. People will be prepared to buy shares in well-known companies. They will not want to buy securities of any sort from small unknown companies. Whereas large firms can threaten to withdraw their business, if debts owing to them are not settled in time, they tend to be regrettably slow in paying their own bills.

An engineer may set up a firm using his technical skills as the basis of the business. As the business grows, his defects as a marketing manager, accountant and personnel manager will begin to appear. He cannot be an expert in all sections of the business, nor can he afford to hire the quality experts to be found in the ranks of his larger competitors.

The small firm is also unlikely to be able to afford sophisticated technological equipment such as mainframe computers or visual display units, however useful they might be. Advertising cost spread out over a large number of units may be insignificant but given a smaller level of output they may prove an intolerable burden. Inevitably, television advertising tends to be a resource available only to the larger concerns.

Note: The key words are: capital; expertise; staff; unit costs.

ICM DIPLOMA IN BUSINESS ENGLISH
SAMPLE ORAL EXAMINATION

Time allowed: 15 minutes to read the case study.

15 minutes to answer questions from the examiner.

Case study

(You can take this into the examination room with you)

The New Jamaica Inn is one of the smaller hotels owned by the Pearmain Group. Situated in a well-known South Coast resort, the hotel has a two-star rating which has been given largely on the strength of the cuisine. The Chef is an Italian, Alberto Ciccetti, who would be able to choose a more highly paid job in almost any of the Group's hotels in Britain or the rest of Europe., but Alberto's daughter has married an Englishman and they are living within a few miles of the New Jamaica, and this accounts for his presence in this particular hotel.

Another distinctive member of the staff is Jane Garner. Jane is the Assistant Manager. Jane was appointed ten weeks ago and until now she has been understudying the Manager, but he has just started a fortnight's holiday. During the first week of the holiday Jane is faced with the following problems:

1. Alberto Ciccetti comes to her office. He is very upset. His daughter has decided to divorce her English husband and Alberto is going to take her and his two grandsons (aged six and ten) back to Milan.

2. A young couple on honeymoon have taken possession of Room 29, one of the best rooms in the hotel, with sea views, bath en suite and balcony. No other room in the hotel has all these features. Another guest has now arrived and claims he booked the room two months ago. It becomes obvious that a mistake was made when the receptionist recorded the booking. Although this guest is recorded as having booked Room 30, the amount of the deposit clearly relates to Room 29.

3. In the course of the last few days two different guests have complained about the loss of personal possessions. One of the guests, an elderly lady, has lost a small bottle of Chanel No 5. She is going around telling other guests what has happened. The second guest is a young solicitor who is staying at the hotel with a girlfriend. He has lost his nearly new electric shaver.

Questions from the Oral Examiner

These are likely to centre on the three immediate problems that Jane is facing. How would you (the candidate) deal with these problems? A framework of options follow to indicate the sort of approach which would be looked for.

Problem 1

A. Try to delay Alberto's departure, at least until the manager returns. Point out that it is unwise to make important decisions too hastily. Children's schooling? Possibility of a reconciliation? Can daughter and sons stay at the hotel for a few weeks? Need to protect daughter's interests in the event of a divorce.

B. Inform Group Head Office. They might offer him a hotel elsewhere, and organise a replacement for Alberto. They might want to see him.

C. Interview Alberto to obtain as many facts as possible, listening rather than talking.

Problem 2

A. Ask honeymooners to switch rooms with compensation in the form of a cash reduction or special meals, flowers, etc.

B. Ask the disappointed guest to accept the situation, with similar compensations. Introduce him to the couple? If they are likeable.

C. Offer a full refund and an apology, finding out if possible what went wrong.

Problem 3

A. Consult staff. Individually or collectively?

B. Inform police.

C. Put up warning notices.

Only a few of these ideas could be brought into a 15 minute discussion with the Oral Examiner, but it gives an indication of the types of questions which might be asked. The Examiner will be looking for a mature and professional approach to the problems, coupled with an ability to communicate ideas effectively in good English.

23: LCCI Level One

The LCCI syllabus for the First Level reads:

> **Aim:**
> To test basic knowledge of the written language and its use in brief office communication.
>
> **Criterion:**
> A successful candidate will have demonstrated the ability to write, briefly and intelligibly, the basic forms of office correspondence and the ability to understand and use them along with the most usual forms of information display.

Question paper format

Candidates will be required to attempt all 4 questions. Time allowed: 2 hours.

Question 1 The composition of a letter, or memo, communicating with or between organisations.

Question 2 A prose passage of about 300 words for comprehension. The brief answers required will oblige candidates to relate and use information across the passage, not merely to produce it in sequence.

Question 3 A 'look and think' comprehension task based on some graphic or numerical display stimulus and requiring only short answers.

Question 4 A 'look and write' production task, where candidates will have to label a diagram, a flow chart or an organisation tree, fill in a form or questionnaire, or re-order and supplement data.

Sample papers for the First Level now follow, together with suggested answers.

THE LONDON CHAMBER OF COMMERCE AND INDUSTRY
ENGLISH FOR BUSINESS: SAMPLE PAPER FOR FIRST LEVEL
(Formerly Elementary Level)
TIME ALLOWED: 2 HOURS

Instructions to candidates

a) *Answer all four questions.*

b) *Credit will be given for correct spelling punctuation and grammar.*

c) *Adequate and appropriate communication is required rather than a particular number of words.*

d) *When you finish check your work carefully.*

Question 1

In your company twenty employees receive, at the company's expense, a personal copy of a daily financial newspaper, which they collect from reception each day. There have been disputes with the newspaper delivery man about the correct number that should be delivered. Your manager has asked you to investigate and you have discovered:

- employees who are not entitled to newspapers take them from reception
- the newspapers are delivered, and taken, before the receptionist arrives for work
- there are spare copies when employees are absent or away on business trips.

Write a memo to your manager suggesting how to make sure that the correct number of newspapers is delivered each day and that the right people receive them.

(30 marks)

Suggested answer

```
To Mr Bryant*, Manager                    From J Smith+, Trainee
                                                       (date)
                    Daily Newspapers
I have looked into the problem of the staff's missing newspapers and it
seems there are two main explanations.
1.   Some staff who are not entitled to the newspapers are nevertheless
     taking them from the reception area, often before the receptionist
     arrives.
2.   When staff are absent or away on business trips their newspapers are
     surplus and tend to be picked up by people who are not entitled to
     them.
I think the answer is to ask the delivery man to place the newspapers in
a container for which only he and the receptionist will have keys. The
receptionist should then have a list of staff entitled to the newspapers
and tick the names off daily as and when the papers are collected. When
staff know they are going to be away for more than a few days they should
let the receptionist know so she can cancel their papers.
Inevitably there will be times when there are still surplus newspapers
and I would suggest these could be distributed at the discretion of the
receptionist. If you would like me to take any action please let me know.

J. Smith
```

* Although the Manager's name is not given it would be rude not to address him by name so a name has been fabricated.

+ This will be your name.

Question 2

You have heard the following dialogue at a meeting and wish to report the **main points** to your line manager.

Write an appropriately short memo to him containing the essential points.

MR WILSON:	I am the geologist who did the initial survey of this area. Perhaps I could help at this point.
CHAIRMAN	Ah, thank you. I am glad there is someone at this meeting who has actually been to the place. Most of the discussion so far has been very much based on second or third-hand reports. Well, do you think there is oil there in commercial quantities?
MR WILSON	It is difficult to say.
CHAIRMAN	Well, if you can't say it, who else can? I'm sure you can give some facts on which we can make a decision.

MR WILSON		The scientific evidence was not conclusive but I am working on a hunch. The geological samples indicate it is the sort of area where good grade oil might be found.
CHAIRMAN		But in commercial quantities?
MR WILSON		We are not even certain there is oil there yet. That will need further sampling. As for commercial quantities, we cannot possibly say that. And it's not a purely scientific question anyway. A lot depends on the price at the time we strike, and other factors like the political stability of the area. There is already talk of some trouble when the President dies. The security of delivery routes will then be a point to consider.
CHAIRMAN		How much more time will you need?
MR WILSON		About two months if the good weather holds. If we get an early winter, however, we won't be able to work for six months.

(30 marks)

Suggested answer

```
To Mr White, Line Manager                    From J. Smith, Trainee
                                                          (date)
           Report on meeting regarding oil drilling
Mr Wilson, the geologist who had done the initial survey, introduced him-
self to the Chairman and offered to help. The Chairman wanted to know
whether there was oil in commercial quantities. Mr Wilson was uncertain.
He said the scientific evidence was not conclusive but he was working on
a hunch. The geological samples indicate it is the sort of area where
good grade oil might be found, though it was too early to say whether it
would be in commercial quantities. That could depend on the price at the
time of the strike and other factors like the political stability of the
area.
The security of the delivery routes could be threatened by the death of
the President.
Mr Wilson reckoned a clearer picture should emerge within the next two
months though there could be a further six months hold up if winter comes
early.

J. Smith
```

Question 3

Look at the following charts showing the sources of energy in West Germany in 1957 and 1980.

Use the information in the charts to fill in the gaps in the sentences below. (Write your answers on your answer paper with reference back to the gaps e.g. 1a). Answer 5 b) Answer etc.)

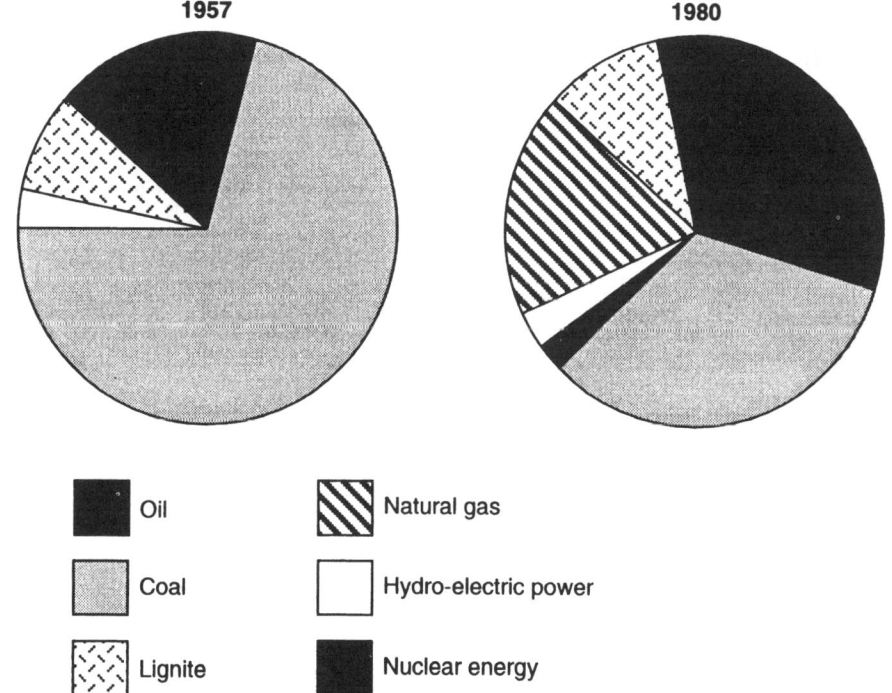

1. Between 1957 and 1980 the main trends in energy production were the sharp decrease in the use of a) ...... and the great increase in the use of b) ......

2. Coal accounted for almost a) ...... of West Germany's energy in 1957, but this figure had dropped to less than b) ...... in 1980.

3. Oil increased its share from considerably less than a) ...... in 1957 to just under b) ...... in 1980.

4. Two minor sources of energy – a) ...... and b) ...... – showed a slight c) ...... between 1957 and 1980.

5. The new sources of energy appeared for the first time in 1980: a) ...... and b) ......

6. Of these new sources, a) ...... made only a small contribution to the country's energy needs. b) ...... , on the other hand, was more important and produced approximately c) ...... of West Germany's energy.

7. West Germany produces most of its own lignite and coal, but imports most of its oil and natural gas. West Germany imported a) ...... of its energy sources in 1980 than it did in 1957.

(25 marks)

Answers

1. a) Coal   b) Oil
2. a) ¼   b) ¼
3. a) Fourteen   b) ½
4. a) Lignite   b) Hydro-electricity   c) Decrease
5. a) Natural gas b) Nuclear energy
6. a) Nuclear energy b) Natural gas   c) ¼
7. a) More

Question 4

Look at the organisation chart below, then answer the questions that follow.

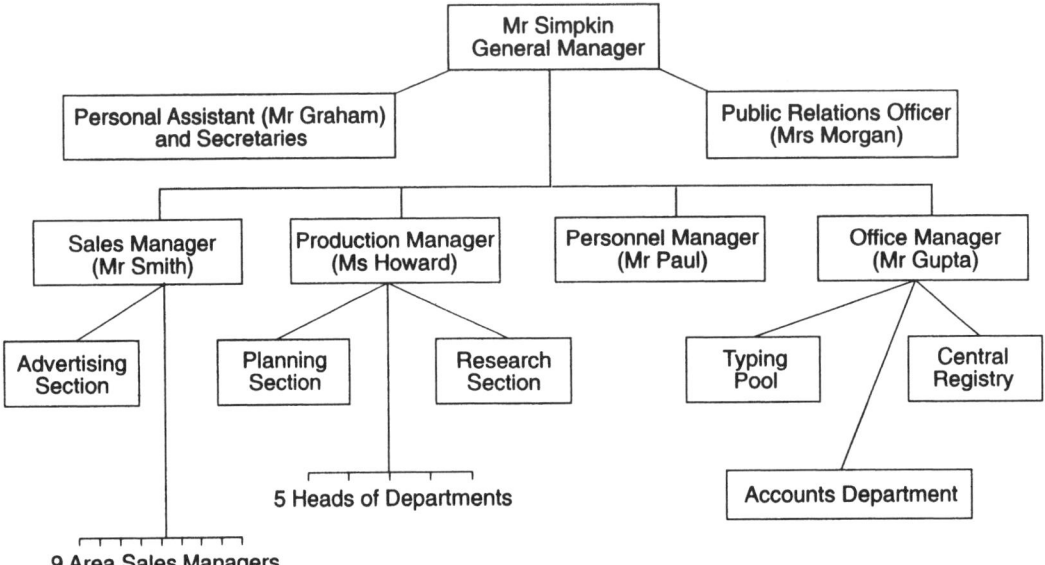

1. How many sections does Ms Howard control?
2. Who is responsible for Public Relations?
3. Who handles the General Manager's correspondence and telephone calls?
4. To whom do the members of Advertising Section report?
5. Why should Central Registry come under Mr Gupta?
6. Which of the four managers appears to have the least responsibility for other groups?
7. Is Mr Smith responsible to Mr Graham?
8. Through whom should the Heads of Process Departments approach Mr Simpkin?
9. To whom does Mr Smith give responsibility for selling the company's products?
10. Can Mr Smith give direct instructions to the members of Research Section?
11. From whom should Mr Paul seek clearance to interview a member of the Planning Section?
12. Which three rectangles contain the common support services which the whole company can use?

(15 marks)

Answers

1. Seven
2. Mrs Morgan
3. His Personal Assistant (Mr Graham)
4. Sales Manager (Mr Smith)
5. Because it mainly involves clerical activities
6. Personnel Manager (Mr Paul)
7. No
8. Production Manager (Ms Howard)
9. The nine Area Sales Managers
10. No
11. Production Manager (Ms Howard)
12. Secretaries, Public Relations and Personnel.

ANOTHER SAMPLE PAPER FOR FIRST LEVEL
TIME ALLOWED: 2 HOURS

Instructions to candidates

a) *Answer all four questions.*

b) *Credit will be given for correct spelling, punctuation and grammar.*

c) *Adequate and appropriate communication is required rather than a particular number of words.*

d) *When you finish, check your work carefully.*

Question 1

There are eleven typists in your company's typing pool and the Supervisor is greatly concerned at the bad timekeeping and absenteeism. Although they should be starting work by nine o'clock every morning, on Friday of last week the supervisor found that:

- five of the typists arrived more than ten minutes late
- two arrived more than twenty minutes late
- two were away sick, one with 'a cold', the other 'not feeling well'
- all of those present had both a morning and afternoon break in excess of the permitted fifteen minutes.

Write for the supervisor a memorandum which will have the effect of improving their behaviour. It will be circulated to all members of the pool.

(30 marks)

Suggested answer

To All Typing Pool Staff   From Adam Brown, Supervisor
                                                        (date)

Timekeeping and attendance

I have noticed recently a rather serious slackness developing. One day last week over half the staff were either seriously late for work or completely absent. I have no doubt there were some genuine reasons and explanations but this state of affairs cannot be allowed to continue. Firstly, because it makes the typing pool less efficient and all of our jobs are at stake, and secondly because when people are not here the workload of the more conscientious is inevitably increased.

In future we shall be using a signing-on book, in which you will be expected to show your time of arrival. At nine o'clock sharp I shall be drawing a red line across the page and anyone arriving late will be expected to come and see me, offering a good explanation.

I shall also be taking careful note of anyone who flouts the fifteen minute rule for morning and afternoon breaks. If anyone is absent from work I would ask them to give me a brief written explanation so this can be filed with their personnel records.

Please understand that my main concern is for the majority of the staff in the pool who work so hard and conscientiously. I do not think they should be burdened by a thoughtless minority.

Adam Brown

Question 2

You work in the office of a famous London department store and the following dialogue took place between yourself and a customer yesterday afternoon. *As this involved a complaint you are required by the company's rules to produce a brief memo to the Chief Buyer explaining what happened.*

MRS JOLIFFE:	I bought one of your Trolldolls for my daughter's birthday and when I got it home I noticed the head was a bit loose. I thought that might be the way it was supposed to be. Anyway, now it's come off completely and my daughter's in tears naturally.
YOU:	Could I have your name and address please?
MRS JOLIFFE:	Mrs Anthea Joliffe, Sunbeam Cottage, Trent Road, Ware.
YOU:	Ware that's in Hertfordshire isn't it? When did you buy the doll Mrs Joliffe?
MRS JOLIFFE:	I can't remember the exact day but it was 3rd of last month because it was Sarah's birthday the next day.
YOU:	Well, if you can bring it back with the till receipt we'll give you a replacement doll.
MRS JOLIFFE:	I'm not sure I want a replacement. As you know all the dolls are different and I don't know whether Sarah will find another one she likes. It's a long way to come to London on a wild goose chase.
YOU:	Why don't you bring Sarah along with you and see if there are any of them she likes? We've got a very big display of Trolldolls.
MRS JOLIFFE:	Alright. I'll probably be in on Thursday or Friday of next week. I take it I can get a cash refund if we don't find a suitable doll.
YOU:	We'll have to make a decision on that when we see the doll and the till receipt next week.

(30 marks)

Suggested solution

```
To Mr Ray Carter                                    From Julie White
Chief Buyer                                              Main Office
                                                              (date)
              Complaint by telephone - Trolldolls
   Mrs Anthea Joliffe, Sunbeam Cottage, Trent Road, Ware, Hertfordshire.
```
Mrs Joliffe bought her daughter a Trolldoll for her birthday at the beginning of last month. She noticed at the time that the dolls head was loose but now it has broken off completely. I told her she could have a replacement if she brought back the damaged doll together with the till receipt. She seemed to be looking for a refund but I suggested she brought her daughter to the store to let her see if there was another Trolldoll she liked. She will probably be coming in on Thursday or Friday of next week.

Julie White

Note: Although the heading is rather lengthy this allows you to concentrate on the message.

Question 3

The following bar charts show an analysis of overseas visitors to a famous South Coast seaside resort during the peak season (June to August) over the last two years.

Use the information in the charts to fill in the gaps in the sentences below.

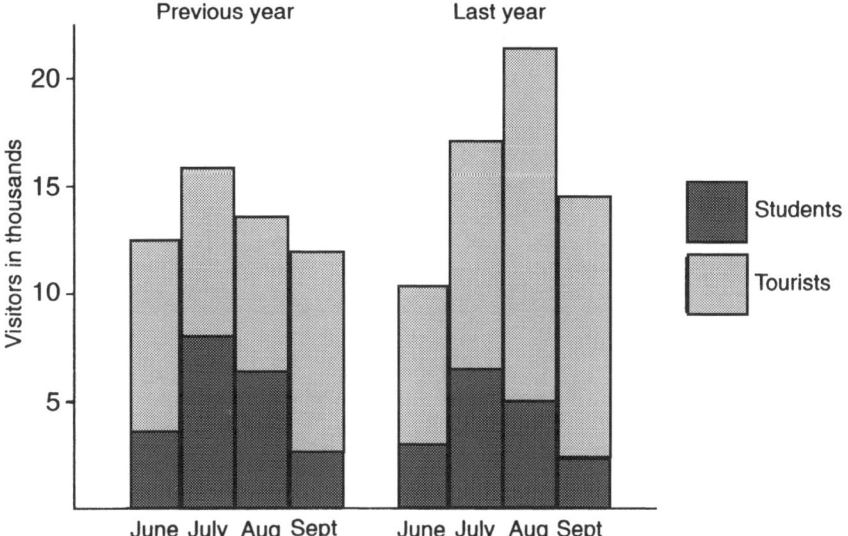

1. Last year a) ...... was the most popular month for tourists while b) ...... was the least popular month.
2. In both years a) ...... was the most popular month for students while b) ...... was the least popular month.
3. The number of students visiting the resort last year in July showed a slight a) ...... from the same month in the previous year.
4. Last year the number of visitors in August was a) ...... the number in June.
5. There were a) ...... students visiting the resort in the peak season last year, but there were significantly more b) ......
6. In August last year there was a total of a) ...... visitors to the resort of whom b) ...... were students.
7. On the evidence available here a) ...... and b) tend to be the most popular months for both tourists and students.

(25 marks)

Answers

1.	a)	August	b)	June	5.	a)	fewer	b) tourists
2.	a)	July	b)	September	6.	a)	21,000	b) 5,500
3.	decrease				7.	a)	July	b) August
4.	double							

Question 4

The organisation chart below relates to a company manufacturing fireworks.

Having studied the chart, answer the questions which follow.

23: LCCI Level One

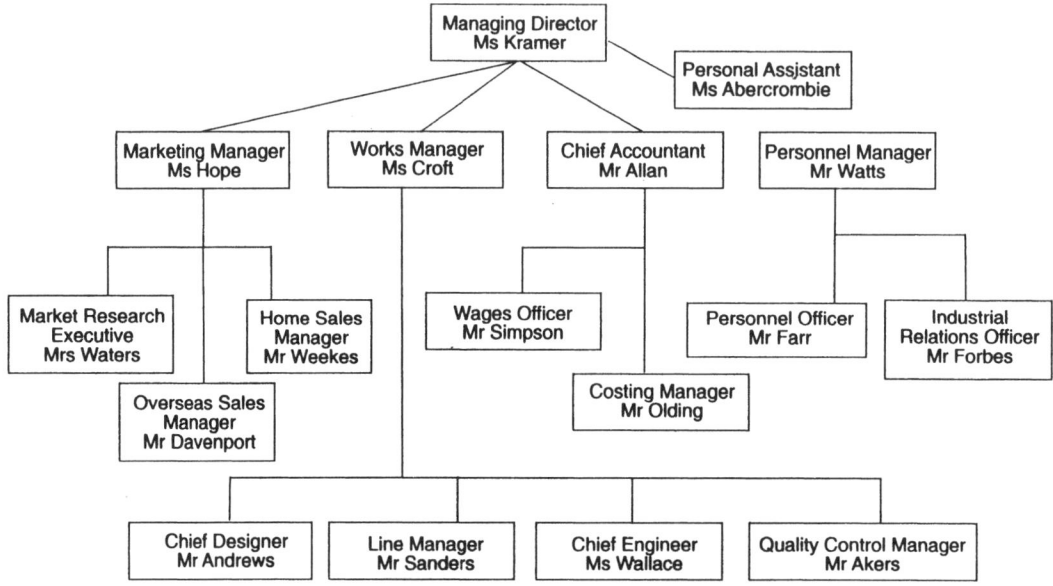

1. Which of Ms Croft's subordinates would he turn to for advice on new products?
2. If Mrs Waters was to send a report to Ms Kramer through whom should she submit the report?
3. Which of the executives would be dealing primarily with trade unions?
4. Which of the executives would be responsible for ensuring that the production standards were maintained?
5. Who would Mr Weekes receive instructions from?
6. If there was a conflict between Ms Hope and Mr Allan who would settle the dispute?
7. If stocks of fireworks were starting to pile up in the warehouses, with which of his subordinates would you expect Ms Kramer to confer?
8. How many people on this organisation chart are immediately responsible to Ms Kramer?
9. If Ms Hope called a meeting of her immediate subordinates who would be expected to attend?
10. If a Safety Committee were to be set up with three management representatives which of the executives shown here would you expect to be on the committee?

(15 marks)

Answers

1. Mr Andrews, Chief Designer.
2. Ms Hope, Marketing Manager.
3. Mr Forbes, Industrial Relations Officer.
4. Mr Akers, Quality Control Manager.
5. Ms Hope, Marketing Manager.
6. Ms Kramer, Manager Director.
7. Ms Hope, Marketing Manager, and Ms Croft, Works Manager.
8. Five.
9. Mrs Waters, Mr Weekes and Mr Davenport.
10. Mr Forbes (Industrial Relations Officer), Mr Sanders (Line Manager), and Ms Croft (Works Manager) as Chairwoman.

24: LCCI Level Two

If you have completed the full programme of exercises in this book you should be able to tackle this level quite comfortably; you now have the opportunity to test your progress.

Second Level English for Business

> **Aim:**
> To test a candidate's ability to understand and write connected English on business topics and in formats usual in business communication, and to confirm a parallel ability to speak English at an equivalent level.
>
> **Criterion:**
> A successful candidate will have demonstrated the ability to write creditable and accurate English on behalf of an employer, with minimal supervision, and choose the tone, form and content appropriate to the requirements of a particular situation.

Question paper format

Candidates will be required to attempt all 3 questions. Time allowed: 2½ hours.

Question 1   An extended writing task requiring candidates to **produce a report**, article, memorandum, essay, etc, on a **choice of role related topics drawn from business and economic life.** Candidates should display the virtues of good writing: order, clarity, balance, relevance, economy and logic.

(40 marks)

Question 2   A letter-writing task, the stimulus for which will be an incoming letter and the data needed to reply to it.

(30 marks)

Question 3   A reformulation task requiring candidates to **expand, reduce or selectively rewrite** a passage of English for some defined purpose within a **given role.** Candidates will be offered options that will draw on their ability to make notes, or reassemble elements of a text for a specific purpose, which will be stated.

(30 marks)

Oral test

Candidates whose mother tongue is not English will be required to pass an Oral Test before they can be awarded a certificate. The Oral Test will consist of a conversation (7 – 8 minutes) with the examiner.

THE LONDON CHAMBER OF COMMERCE AND INDUSTRY
ENGLISH FOR BUSINESS: SAMPLE PAPER FOR SECOND LEVEL
(Formerly Intermediate)
TIME ALLOWED: 2½ HOURS

Instructions to candidates

a) *Answer all three questions.*

b) *Credit will be given for correct spelling, punctuation and grammar.*

c) *Adequate and appropriate communication is required rather than a particular number of words.*

d) *When you finish, check your work carefully.*

Question 1

*Write on **one** of the following subjects.*

a) You work for a company that plans to spend a large sum of money on a new social and sports club for its staff. Employees have been asked to submit their ideas for such a club **in the form of a memorandum**, which should contain suggestions for social and sports activities, recreational facilities and any other relevant points. Write the memorandum you would submit.

b) Describe a thriving business enterprise that you know and say why, in your opinion, it is so successful.

c) You wish to open a shop and have applied to a bank to assist you financially. Write a report to the bank manager giving information about the shop and how you propose to use the money you hope the bank will lend you.

d) You have just had an accident in the office where you work. Your employer's insurance company who have been notified of the accident, have asked you to write a report about it, stating how it occurred, at what time, the injuries you suffered, the names of any witnesses of the accident, and any further information that you think may be useful to them when they deal with the case.

(40 marks)

Suggested answer

> To: Miss J. Peterson
> Personnel Manager
> Date:
> From: Andrew Smith
> Supervisor, Typing Pool
>
> **Ideas for a New Social & Sports Club**
>
> I was very pleased to hear about the plans for a new club and I am sure this will be welcomed by most of the staff. One of my concerns is that this should not just end up as a football and cricket club catering for the interests of a minority of the staff. I assume there will be some sort of building on offer and this gives us a wonderful opportunity to use this for a wide variety of social activities.
>
> Even if the building is comparatively small I think we could allocate one evening a week for the company's music society, another evening for the gardening club and so on. One evening should certainly be given over to a meeting for retired employees. My own father has recently retired from the company and I know he would support this idea. Maybe on a Saturday we could have a general social get together. I am not sure what form this should take, but I feel it should offer an alternative to the Saturday evening trip to the pub. Family entertainment should be 'the order of the day'. My own interest is badminton. I do not know whether the plans would include an indoor playing area, but I know another couple of people in the typing pool who are interested in this sport.
>
> Obviously there are lots of questions to be answered before we can make any detailed suggestions and I would have thought we might form a Social and Sports Committee as soon as possible. The committee could represent the employees and make sure their views are known to the company. Again I feel that the composition of the committee is important and I would like to see factory and office staff, workers and managers represented in about the same proportions as they are found in the company. As you will know, about half of our employees are women, and I would like to see their interests taken care of.
>
> *Andrew Smith*

Note: The ideas which are put forward are less important than the form and style of the memorandum.

Question 2

Your company, M Gilbert & Co Ltd, has received the following letter.

Using the company's Employee Report Form given after the letter, write a correctly laid-out and informative reply to it, ready for Mr L Eaton, your Office Manager, to sign.

Audio-Video Enterprises
Marconi House, Reith Road, Elmwood, Leashire AB3 4DP
Telephone 3269 014587

Your Ref
Our Ref: JAP/RS/VLJ

Mr L Eaton
Office Manager
M Gilbert & Co Ltd
100-110 Quiver Street
London UV1 5LS

30 November 1991

Dear Mr Eaton

Mrs Janet A Parsons
11 Rosewood Street, Elmwood, Leashire, AB6 5LX

The above has applied to us for the post of Assistant Office Manager and has given your name as a reference since she worked as a senior clerk in your office from 1 January 1984 until 31 December 1988.

The post for which Mrs Parsons has applied is an important one and involves much responsibility. We are looking for a mature person, well experienced in modern office procedures, able to fit in an office with a friendly atmosphere but who can be firm with staff under her control when the occasion demands it. She must also be able to take charge of the office in my absence and make decisions when required. We also require someone who is punctual and regular in attendance. I should be pleased if you would give me your opinion of Mrs Parsons from your knowledge of her and her work, and state whether or not you feel she is a suitable candidate to be shortlisted for the job for which she has applied.

Yours sincerely

Rachel Searle

Rachel Searle
Officer Manager

M Gilbert & Co Ltd						EMPLOYEE REPORT FORM
Name:	PARSONS, Janet Ann		Address:	11 Rosewood Street, Elmwood, Leashire, AB6 5LX		
Born:	12 March 195-		Status:	Married		
Appointed:	1 January 198-		Post:	Senior Clerk, Production Control Unit		

Yearly Report	Punctuality	Absence	Dress	Work Attitude	Staff Relations	Comments
198-	A	A	B	A	A	Excellent. Shows promise. Good example to others.
198-	B	A	B	C	A	Family problems affected attendance and punctuality.
198-	C	B	B	D	B	Warned about lateness. Rather disappointing after first year

LEFT: 31 December 1988

Note for senior staff completing this form:
Use the following abbreviations: A = excellent; B = very good; C = good; D = fair; E = poor.

Suggested answer

M. Gilbert & Co. Ltd
100-110 Quiver Street, London UV1 5IS Telephone: 081 100 1100

Ms Rachel Searle
Office Manager
Audio-Video Enterprises
Marconi House
Reith Road
Elmwood
Leashire AB3 4DP   (date)

Dear Ms Searle

Mrs Janet Parsons
11 Rosewood Street, Elmwood, Leashire AB6 5LX

I am writing in reply to your enquiry of 30th November and confirm that this lady was working for this company between 1st January 1984 and 31st December 1988. She was a Senior Clerk in our Production Control Unit. As you will appreciate it is some time since Mrs Parsons was with us so I am obliged to refer to our staff records in order to answer your queries.

The records show that she was well presented and got on well with other members of staff. Towards the end of her time with us she was having problems with her family and this was affecting her attendance and attitude to work, but otherwise she was apparently very satisfactory.

Yours sincerely,

L. Eaton

Mr L Eaton,
Office Manager

Note: Bearing in mind the lapse of time since she was employed by the company it would be wrong for you to say whether Mrs Parsons has (or does not have) the qualities Mr Searle is looking for. You can only report on the facts you have been given. In general it is unwise to give seriously critical references because these could give rise to a claim for libel. The manager receiving references will usually 'read between the lines' in any case.

Question 3

*Answer **either** a) **or** b) but not both.*

a) Your company, Metexport Limited, have received the following telex from America, where the Managing Director, Mr L S Stevenson, has been for the past month:

> ARRIVING HEATHROW MONDAY 3 DECEMBER 09.00. DON'T MEET. ARRANGE MEETING WITH ALL SENIOR ADMIN STAFF AND REPS TUESDAY 4 DECEMBER 0900 IN CARLTON ROOM TO DISCUSS U.S. EXPORTING POLICY AND TO ORGANISE NEW ADVERTISING AND SALES CAMPAIGN. STEPHEN SNAPE, HEAD OF SNAPE METALS INC, NEW YORK, WILL BE WITH US. WHOLE DAY MEETING. PROVIDE BUFFET LUNCH. NO ABSENTEES. URGENT.
>
>   STEVENSON

Your Office Manager, Andrew Bailey, asks you to write a memo about the meeting to be distributed to the staff concerned. Write the memo, covering all necessary points.

24: LCCI Level Two

b) Carefully read the following passage, which contains about 400 words.

Then *either*:

i) Using the information given in the passage, put yourself in the role of an office manager about to brief a new secretary on her first morning at work. List the points you would emphasise on professional etiquette, and on the attractions and limitations of the job.

or

ii) Write a summary of it in not more than 120 words, using your own words where appropriate, and supplying a suitable title.

Note: Indicate clearly which alternative you have chosen.

Most secretaries find that solicitors are generally very conservative in the presentation of their letters: they do not like (even resent) innovation and prefer to stick to the style which has been the accepted practice of the office all down the years. Some of the wariness on the part of lawyers stems from long experience of the need never to say too much nor to make admissions which may have repercussions later on to the detriment of their clients – hence the common usage of the expression 'without prejudice' at the top of their letters. A solicitor's office is therefore not the ideal place into which to try to bring ideas which may upset the decorum and established practices of the office. This is not to say that you should always refrain from offering ideas. To do so may be advantageous in that you may learn why they are not acceptable, thus improving your own knowledge of the practices of the law. Generally speaking, many solicitors are now 'spring cleaning' the office environment and the dust-laden shelves, while antiquated equipment is being replaced with modern machinery. Office routine and procedures are also slowly receiving improvements so one can now find many firms of solicitors whose decor and general working environment matches the most up-to-date commercial and industrial organisations. Work in a solicitor's office can be interesting and even absorbing if you have a logical and enquiring mind. It is certainly not dull, as some people seem to believe. Contrary to the general belief, many solicitors are bold and enterprising – subject to the limitations which must necessarily apply when dealing with the affairs of clients and you should act with caution for a very long time until you fully understand all the implications of the job and the problems you could create by even a little carelessness or indiscretion. You will learn, too, many Latin phrases and their meaning (and even how to spell them). Above all else, work in a solicitor's office is highly confidential because you are dealing with people and their private affairs: it must never be discussed or even mentioned outside the office. Even within the office it is wise not to comment on your work. The best thing is to do the work and not talk about it to anyone, but you would certainly find that the human aspect of other people's situations can become very interesting and absorbing.

(30 marks)

Suggested answer

Note: The candidate is only required to deal with one of the options but all three are dealt with here.

a)

Metexport Limited   *Memorandum*

URGENT

To   All Senior Administrative Staff and Representatives
From   Mr Andrew Bailey, Office Manager

Meeting with Managing Director 4th December

Telex just received from Mr Stevenson. He will be arriving at Heathrow on Monday morning in company with Stephen Snape, Head of Snape Metals Inc., New York. There will be an all-day meeting with all senior administrative staff and representatives on Tuesday 4th December in the Carlton Room, commencing at 0900. U.S. exporting policy and the organisation of new advertising and sales campaigns will be the main items on the agenda.

Mr Stevenson has emphasized that this matter is **urgent** and there should be no absentees. A buffet lunch will be provided.

Andrew Bailey

Note: The memorandum can be crisp and to the point because you are dealing with senior staff.

b)   i)

Briefing for new secretaries

In many ways the world of the lawyer is different from everyday life and the following notes are intended to help you make necessary adjustments. In undertaking your new duties always remember that:

1. The solicitor is acting to protect the interests of his clients.
2. Any information which comes into your hands is **strictly confidential**. It should not even be divulged to other members of staff.
3. Accuracy is vital, and a simple error in the wording of a letter can be extremely costly to either or both the firm and its client.

There are many good aspects of working in a legal environment. You will undoubtedly find being a member of a team which is helping people to cope with a great variety of problems both interesting and absorbing. If you have any ideas on how the services might be improved we are always glad to hear from you, but do not be surprised if we sometimes seem a little cautious in the way we approach problems. Lawyers are conservative both by their nature and their training and that is something you will need to accept and live with from now on.

A Student
Office Manager

---

ii)   **Secretaries in solicitors' offices**

Solicitors adopt conservative attitudes to letter writing partly to avoid saying things which might work against the interests of their clients. Although solicitors are geared to seeking accepted rather than radical solutions, many of their offices bear favourable comparison with the most up-to-date of their commercial and industrial counterparts. For those with an enquiring mind the work can be very interesting. The application of the law to a great variety of human predicaments often calls for boldness and enterprise but, since it is the welfare of their clients and their personal reputations which are at stake, the solicitors also need to be cautious. And their secretaries must understand that precision, discretion and confidentiality are the keynotes to their contribution.

25: LCCI Level Three

At this level your skill in the use of the English language, as well as your business knowledge and acumen, will be tested to the full but, if you have tackled the course conscientiously and feel confident, this could be your level. Bear in mind it is a slightly longer paper.

Third Level English for Business

> **Aim:**
> To test a high-level ability to understand, write and variously process the general and special varieties of English used in business, and the ability to use appropriate formats. The Oral Test will confirm a capacity to speak English at an equivalent level.
>
> **Criterion:**
> A successful candidate will have demonstrated the ability to write mature, fluent, accurate and idiomatic English on behalf of an employer, choosing technical terms, tone, form and content appropriate to the requirements of a particular situation.

Question paper format

Candidates will be required to attempt all 4 questions. Time allowed: 3 hours.

Question 1   The composition of a letter, the stimulus for which will be an incoming letter, or the employer's instructions, or both. The rubric will include data on which a reply might be based and an indication of the tone required. The candidate's letter must be 'mailable' and hence must be correctly laid out, linguistically accurate and appropriate in tone and content.

(25 marks)

Question 2   The draughting of an internal report based on raw data given in the form graphs, notes, press cuttings, charts, tables, etc Candidates will have to understand, select, collate and, if necessary, supplement this data in order to write the report in the light of the instructions given. The report must be clear, well-organised and logically paragraphed and – where appropriate – numbered. The language must be correct and stylistically appropriate, so that the report will be fit for internal distribution. The rubric will give guidance on the form and content required.

(25 marks)

Question 3   A comprehension task in which candidates will be asked to show understanding of a passage for a defined purpose. This might be a press article, an extract from a business journal, company report, circular, letter, tender, or some other form of business reading matter, with which candidates should be familiar at this stage. Questions will be asked to probe their understanding, not only of factual content but of argument, bias, persuasive devices and internal organisation. Their comprehension should be signalled by the most economic means available, e.g. incomplete sentences, figures, single words, diagrams, organisation trees, etc.

(25 marks)

Question 4   A conversion task involving the reformulation of a message for some defined purpose. Thus candidates may be required to produce a memo from a telex, cable, letter or computer printout; or an abstract from an article; or a summary of a phonecall for discussion; or a telex/telegram/cable from a company notice, employer's instructions, etc

The essential point is that a message received in one form is transmitted in another. This will involve reducing lengthy messages, expanding fragmentary messages, completing inadequate messages or selecting from redundant messages. In transferring the data from one form to the other, the candidates must adopt the appropriate format and tone.

(25 marks)

THE LONDON CHAMBER OF COMMERCE AND INDUSTRY
ENGLISH FOR BUSINESS: SAMPLE PAPER FOR THIRD LEVEL
(Formerly Higher)
TIME ALLOWED: 3 HOURS

Instructions to candidates

a) *Answer all four questions. Each question carries 25 marks.*

b) *While formal accuracy is expected, adequate and appropriate communication is essential and candidates must judge the length of their answers in this light.*

c) *When you finish, check your work carefully.*

Question 1

You work as Assistant Manager in the Sales Department of Rentax Ltd, a components manufacturer based in Birmingham (address: 398 Bristol Road, B2 5LH).

You have recently written to a major customer (RCF Systems Ltd) at New Estate Road, London SE1 1DD, to inform them of a price increase.

The following is an extract from their reply:

> And so, in conclusion, I must underline that we cannot accept this 10% increase in prices.
>
> Moreover, we would appreciate a full analysis of present and proposed costs which make up your prices. This information would be helpful if it were received in advance of a meeting at which we could discuss the prospects of cooperation between our companies. I would suggest a date towards the end of next month, if you agree.
>
> Yours sincerely
>
> *Donna Blackburn*
>
> Donna Blackburn
> Purchasing Manager

You made the following notes as your Sales Manager angrily read the letter:

1. Hard luck to them! It's the first increase in 3 years.
2. We can't tell them what our costs are!
3. We need to meet them *at once*. We'll both go.
4. They ought to remember the good service we give them!

Use these notes to write a reply to the customer's letter.

Suggested answer

> **Rentax Ltd**
> **Components Manufacturer** 398 Bristol Road, Birmingham B2 5LH Telephone 031 222 3333
>
> Ms Donna Blackburn
> Purchasing Manager
> RCF Systems Ltd
> New Estate Road
> London SE1 1DD   (date)
>
> Dear Ms Blackburn
>
> Thank you for your letter regarding our recent price increases. From my own experience I know how difficult it is to accept these additional burdens but, as a matter of interest, this is our first increase in three years so I feel we have been particularly kind to our customers. I wish our suppliers could have been as kind to us! We have only achieved this record by keeping our costs down to an absolute minimum - much to the disbelief of some of our competitors.
>
> Of course I understand and appreciate your concern. I would like to come and see you as soon as possible. I know my Sales Manager wants to join me. Would next Thursday be too soon? If you will telephone me as soon as you get this letter we can fix a time and date. I feel sure a discussion at this stage would be to our mutual advantage. I hope it also shows our intention to continue to provide a service to our customers which is second to none.
>
> Yours sincerely,
>
> *Jane Grimond*
>
> Jane Grimond
> Assistant Manager, Sales Department

Note: The problem here is to avoid giving ground without causing offence to an obviously valuable customer.

Question 2

Your company is considering a change to flexible working hours for office personnel. Your manager, the Head of Personnel, has asked you to write him a preliminary report on the initial reactions of the staff to this idea.

Write the report using the notes below to prepare it.

Office staff:	Good (lunchtime shopping).
Data Processing:	Difficult (they work as a team).
Accounts Department:	Good! (traffic, parking).
Sales Representatives:	'Doesn't affect us.'
Canteen:	Mixed - less rush at meals, but longer lunch period.
Security:	Oh no! (longer hours).
General Administration Office:	Most in favour (except Office Manager).
Points raised by Office Manager:	Open to cheating/abuse of system; lack of supervision; expensive.
Your recommendations:	Trial period (3 months?); information sessions; watch production closely.

Suggested answer

```
                     Preliminary Report
To Mr P Hardy, Personnel Manager     From Miss J Smith, Personnel Officer
                                                                  (date)
           Re: proposed introduction of flexible working hours
As requested I have been finding out informally how various members of
staff react to the idea of this change.
Findings - There was a lot of support for a flexible working hours
scheme. Some relished the thought of longer lunch breaks. Others thought
they would be able to avoid the worst of the traffic and that parking
would be easier. Resistance came from the Data Processing Department who
pointed out that they have to act as a team, and (understandably) the
Security people who appreciate the extra work it would involve for them.
The Office Manager felt that, apart from being expensive to administer,
such a scheme would need to be very carefully supervised.
Recommendations - I feel much of the resistance could be overcome by in-
troducing flexible working hours for a trial period, say, three months.
During this time people could generally find out for themselves whether
it was beneficial or otherwise. We could sort out some of the inevitable
snags as they appear. In the meantime I think we should arrange some in-
formation sessions so that people know exactly what we have in mind. I am
sure they would be able to offer some useful suggestions too. Finally, I
think we should accept that the purpose of the exercise is to improve ef-
ficiency. To that extent I think we would need to watch productivity
closely, but I believe we would find that the flexible working hours sig-
nificantly reduced absenteeism, lateness and even labour turnover. It
would not be difficult to monitor these figures.
```

Question 3

You have contact with Languedoc Marine, a French firm which is about to sign an agency contract with a UK manufacturer called Wizard Electronics. A copy of the contract is reproduced on the next page. As you are at present working in England, Languedoc Marine have asked you to visit Wizard on their behalf, to examine the agency contract, which they have not yet seen, and to find the answers to specific questions that concern them and which you have noted down below.

Make the notes which you will need before you can telephone them with your answers.

Record of questions from Languedoc Marine:

1. Will they pay all our expenses?
2. Do we handle customers' payments?
3. a) Do we get commission for sales in France in which we haven't been involved?
   b) If so how do we know what they are?
4. How do we renew the contract?
5. How can we cancel it?
6. If we cancel, can we change to representing similar products from another supplier?
7. a) Do we get paid at once?   b) How often do they pay us?
8. What are the dates for:
   a) the signing of the contract?   b) the start of the contract?
   c) arrival of demonstration samples?   d) the first payment of commission?
   e) earliest date by which the contract could be stopped?

9. If a customer doesn't pay for goods, will Wizard accept all the loss?
10. a) Are Wizard working with other agents for these products in France?
    b) Can we work with other manufacturers for different types of goods?

AGENCY CONTRACT

1. Wizard Electronics (Marine Department) Ltd UK, hereafter called the Principal, entrust Languedoc Nautique SARL, Le Phare d'En Haut, PORT GRUISSAN (11430) France, hereafter called the Agent, with their sole agency for France, for the sale of the following products:

   EASY-BEACON Radio Direction Finder   (Patent No ......)
   WIZARD 2000 Satellite Navigator   (Patent No ......)

2. The Agent will endeavour to serve the interests of the principal to the best of his ability and provide all information necessary to promote business. He will inform the Principal at once about every order received and follow the latter's instructions as to selling price, terms of payment and delivery.

3. The Agent pledges not to deal in products competing with those referred to in this contract throughout the period of validity of contract and within one full year after cancellation, if any.

4. The Principal will supply the Agent with all necessary advertising material free of charge, duties, and carriage. Two demonstration units shall be sent as soon as they are available but may not be sold and shall be returned by the Agent on request and at the expense of the Principal.

5. The Agent will be supplied with copies of correspondence with firms in his territory and of all invoices resulting from transactions within the said territory.

6. The Agent is not entitled to collect money from customers and may only do so by express authorization.

7. The commission will be $2^1/_2\%$ (two and a half percent) of the invoice for all transactions direct or indirect, carried out with customers within the defined territory.

8. A statement of commission shall be issued quarterly and forwarded to the Agent no later than the end of the following month, and payment falls due on the date the said statement is issued.

9. In the event of a customer defaulting, commission that has already been paid must be repaid and shall be debited to the following statement of commission.

10. Ancillary expenses may be claimed by the Agent only when supported by corresponding itemised receipts and shall not go beyond limits normally accepted in the trade between bona fide business partners.

11. The Agent will inform the Principal of any change in regulations that may influence the position of the products on the market.

12. The contract shall come into force on September 1st, 19 . . and is for a period of one year. This Agreement may be terminated by either party giving three months notice by registered letter, and shall be prolonged automatically for a further period of one year provided that notice of termination has not been given within the agreed time.

13. All disputes arising in connection with the present contract will be finally settled under the rules of conciliation of the International Chamber of Commerce by one or more arbitrators appointed according to the said rules.

14. This agreement cannot be transferred by either party and has been made out in two identical copies, one copy remaining with either party.

Place: CROYDON   Date: August 17th 199-

Signature of Principal   Signature of Agent

25: LCCI Level Three

Suggested answer

1. They will pay for advertising material including duties and carriage – and return of demonstration units (Clause 4). Other normal expenses require to be supported by receipts (Clause 10).
2. No. Only if expressly authorised by Wizard (Clause 6).
3. a) Yes. $2\frac{1}{2}\%$ on all sales whether direct or indirect (Clause 7).
   b) Quarterly statement will be sent (Clause 8).
4. Renewed annually automatically unless cancelled (Clause 12).
5. 3 months notice required – by registered letter (Clause 12).
6. No. Not for one year from termination of contract (Clause 12).
7. a) No. Payment due when quarterly statement issued (Clause 8).
   b) Quarterly (Clause 8).
8. a) 17th August (see foot of contract).
   b) 1st September (Clause 12).
   c) As soon as available (Clause 4).
   d) At end of first quarter – due 1st December (Clause 8).
   e) 1st December – 3 months from start – minimum 3 months notice required (Clause 12).
9. No. Languedoc must refund – will be deducted from next statement (Clause 9).
10. a) No. It is a sole agency (Clause 1).
    b) Yes. As long as they are not 'competing goods' (Clause 3).

Question 4

You are the European Distribution Manager of an international firm. You have found on your desk the following notes from James Inkster, your Sales and Marketing Director.

```
We need a meeting with Claude Dubosquet, Madame Schultz and the Paris
area sales force on 24 October. Say 10am, at the Paris office. Should
take a couple of hours.

I'll present the new advertising campaign (about 1/2 hour) and you can
deal with the distribution problems (1/2 hour?). I'll show them that video
on customer profitability (30 minute cassette), and then I want to know
if they can use those ideas in their sales areas.

We can take the flight that gets in at 8.45. Can you get a quick message
off to Dubosquet? Tell him to make sure everybody's there this time!
```

```
PS Better ask for a coffee break - 2 hours is a lot of English for them,
without a break!
```

Now draft both

a) *the text of a telex or telegram/cable to Mr Dubosquet and*

b) *an agenda for those attending the meeting.*

Use your own or an invented name if necessary.

Suggested answer

a)

> JAMES INKSTER TO MEET MME SCHULTZ AND PARIS SALES FORCE. 24TH SEPTEMBER. 10 AM TO NOON. PARIS. SUBJECT ADVERTISING AND DISTRIBUTION. OUR FLIGHT GETS IN AT 8.45. EXPECT EVERYONE TO BE ON TIME. PLEASE CONFIRM RECEIPT. JOHN DOE.

b)

> **Meeting at Paris office 10am**
> AGENDA
> 1. Roll call.
> 2. Presentation of new advertising campaign by Mr James Inkster, Sales and Marketing Director.
> 3. An explanation of distribution problems by Mr John Doe, European Distribution Manager.
> 4. Coffee break.
> 5. Video presentation on Customer Profitability.
> 6. General discussion on possible uses of video presentation.

Part Four: Dictionary and answers

Common business colloquialisms

May be used as a noun or a verb

Colloquialism	Meaning
A1	Without fault, good in every respect.
acid test	The ultimate test (originally a test on metal to see whether it was gold)
across board	Everywhere. Including everything.
airy fairy	Unrealistic. Not specific enough.
all at sea	Someone who is all at sea is confused. They do not know what is happening.
all in	Everything included in the price.
all right	Satisfactory. Acceptable.
at the drop of a hat	Immediately. Without hesitation.
back to the drawing board	Start again from the beginning.
beat about the bush	Talk without saying what is really in your mind.
big noise	A person who is a big noise is very important.
blind alley job	A job that has no future.
blowing your top	Losing your temper.
book of words	Instructions. The book of rules to be followed.
bounce	A cheque is said to bounce (like a rubber ball when thrown at a wall) when it is returned unpaid by the bank.
brass farthing	If you don't give a brass farthing it means you do not care at all.
bring home the bacon	Achieve the desired result.
brush off	When you are given the brush-off it means you are not wanted.
by and large	Generally.
by hook or by crook	By one means or another.
carry the can	Bear the responsibility. Take the blame.
chew over	To chew over means to discuss.
chip on one's shoulder	Someone with a chip on their shoulder is over-sensitive.
comfortably off	A person who is comfortably off has plenty of money.
cry off	To cry off is to cancel something which has been arranged.
do away with	To dispose of something.

drop a line	To send a letter.
fiddle*	To fiddle means to act dishonestly, either with cash or account.
for a song	When something is being offered at a very low price we say it is going for a song.
from A to Z	In great detail.
get away with it	When someone does something wrong but does not get caught, we say they are getting away with it.
get cracking	Work fast.
get into hot water	If you get into hot water you are getting into trouble.
get no change out of someone	This means they are not being helpful.
get wind of	Get to know about.
give up the ghost	When you give up the ghost you stop trying.
go by the book	When you go by the book you follow the rules strictly.
go it alone	Work on your own.
go shares	You each pay your own share of the bill.
good turn	A good turn is a kind act.
grit one's teeth	When you grit your teeth you are showing determination.
guinea pig	A guinea pig is a small rodent often used in medical research, hence humans who are being used to test something out are often also called guinea pigs.
hammer it out	Keep working at it until you solve the problem.
hang-up	Another name for an obsession or fear.
hassle*	If you hassle someone you are putting them under pressure.
have a bash	Make an attempt.
have your chips	You have had your chips if you are not going to get any more chances.
headache	A difficult problem is sometimes called a headache.
hell for leather	When a person goes hell for leather they are going extremely fast.
high and dry	If you are high and dry you are safe.
high-handed	A person who is being high-handed is being over-bearing.
hit the roof	To say someone hit the roof is to say they seriously lost their temper.
hog the floor	Someone who hogs the floor does not let anyone else speak.
hold down a job	If you can hold down a job you can keep a job and not lose it.

Common business colloquialisms

hold your horses	This is another way of saying 'Wait!'.
homework	You do your homework when you fully investigate a situation.
in a nutshell	Briefly and concisely.
in clover	In a very fortunate position.
in on something	Being involved in an activity.
in the kitty	Reserves of cash. Savings.
in the soup/in the cart/in a jam	In trouble. In difficulty.
jack of all trades	A person who is a jack of all trades can do a lot of different kinds of work.
jam on it	If someone has an easy job but still complains, we can ask whether he wants jam on it. In other words, he has got bread, does he want jam too?
jobs for the boys	Good positions in the organisation for one's friends.
jog my memory	I make a diary note of an appointment to remind me or jog my memory.
just as well	It is good that it happened.
keep your head	Stay calm.
keep your eyes skinned	Watch carefully.
keep on at	To nag, or insist.
leg-pull*	A leg-pull is a joke.
let the cat out of the bag	Disclose a secret.
let the side down	If you let the side down, you have failed to support your colleagues in the firm.
light-fingered	A thief is light-fingered.
loaded question	A question which has an ulterior or hidden motive.
long in the tooth	Elderly.
long-winded	Using more words than necessary to say something.
lose face	To lose prestige in the eyes of others.
lumbered with	Burdened with. Having to do something unpleasant.
make both ends meet	The ends are income and expenditure. Do not spend more than you earn.
moonlighter	A person who does two jobs, the second usually in the evening.
much of a muchness	similar.
mum's the word	Keep quiet about it. Say nothing.
narrow squeak	Escaped, but was nearly caught.
nest-egg	A sum of money put aside for retirement or for a rainy day (an unexpected financial commitment).

Common business colloquialisms

never-never	When you buy goods through hire-purchase, you are said to buy them on the never-never. The implication is that you will never finish paying for them.
nitty-gritty	Details.
off the cuff	Spontaneous. A remark which is made without reference to facts.
oil a palm/grease a palm	Bribe.
old hand	An old hand is someone with experience.
on appro'	An abbreviation of 'on approval'.
on-going	Something which is still happening, such as an advertising campaign.
on spec	If you do something on spec you are taking a chance, hoping it will be OK.
on the carpet	You are on the carpet when your manager is reprimanding you.
on the tip of my tongue	I cannot think of the word I want.
one-upmanship	Doing better than one's colleagues.
out of hand	If something is out of hand it is out of control.
out of your depth	In a situation over which you have no control (originating from swimming)
out of the frying pan into the fire	From a bad situation into a worse one.
pass the buck	Passing the blame on to someone else (originating from the USA, where buck is slang for dollar)
pat someone on the back	To give them praise.
pay lip service	Pretend to agree. Agree without enthusiasm.
pick someone's brains	To obtain information from someone.
pigeon holes	Places for letters and messages (originating from message-carrying pigeons).
plug something	To keep putting forward your ideas.
point taken	I accept your comment as valid.
powers-that-be	The authorities in control.
pull strings	Use your influence.
pull out all the stops	Make an all-out effort.
pull someone's leg	Play a joke on them.
put someone in the picture	To give them information.
put someone out	Cause them problems.
put the cart before the horse	See things in reverse. It is the horse that pulls the cart, not the other way round.
put-up job	A situation which was worked out previously, deceitfully.

Common business colloquialisms

put your foot down	As a manager you put your foot down when you insist on being obeyed.
quite a few/quite a number	An amount somewhere between few and many.
racket	A racket is an organised scheme for making money illegally.
rake-off	A commission with a hint of deceit.
rat-race	The competitive business world, pitting individual against individual.
recap*	To recap means to look again at what has happened, say in a management meeting.
rocks	A business is said to be on the rocks when it is collapsing (originally a nautical term).
roof, through the	When prices (or costs) go through the roof, they rise rapidly and excessively.
run-of-the mill	Ordinary.
rusty	Out of practice.
sack someone/give them the sack/ send someone packing/fire someone	dismiss them (for example, for unsatisfactory work, or misbehaviour).
safe as houses	Very safe.
sauce/cheek	It is a sauce (or a cheek) when someone treats you disrespectfully.
saved my bacon	Something which saved me from trouble is said to have saved my bacon.
save your breath	You are wasting your time trying to explain. Your explanation is falling on deaf ears.
say one's piece	Say what one wants to say.
scot-free	You get off scot-free when you do something wrong without getting punished.
scrape the barrel	To use our last (and probably worst) resources.
scrape through	You scrape through when you just manage to pass (for example, an examination).
second fiddle	If you are playing second fiddle you are playing a minor role.
sell like hot cakes	Sell quickly and without difficulty.
set off on the wrong foot	Start off in the wrong way.
set the ball rolling	Get things started.
shambles	When an organisation is a shambles it means it is in a mess.
shark	A businessman who is a shark is greedy and dishonest.
sharp	A businessman who is sharp is quick to take advantage of a situation. Perhaps to the point of dishonesty

Common business colloquialisms

shilly-shally	To shilly-shally is to be unable to make a decision.
shoestring	To manage on a shoestring is to manage when income barely meets expenses.
shoplifting	Customers stealing from shops and stores.
short-sighted	A manager is short-sighted when he fails to see what is ahead.
show-down	A confrontation.
show a leg	Wake up and do some work!
show your paces	Show what you are capable of achieving.
sick and tired	Irritated and fed up (with a situation or state of affairs).
sign on the dotted line	A light-hearted, friendly way of asking someone to sign a document.
sitting duck	Someone is a sitting duck when they are an easy target for criticism.
six of one and half a dozen of the other	Very little difference between the alternatives. Both parties were equally to blame.
sixes and sevens	You are at sixes and sevens when you are confused and do not know what to do next.
skate around a problem	You do this when you avoid facing a problem straightforwardly.
slippery customer	Someone who is unlikely to keep a promise.
small beer	Something or someone of little importance.
smart alec	A person who is too clever.
snarl-up*	A traffic jam (cars or computers).
so-so	What do you think of your new secretary? So-so. There are good points and bad points.
so what?	If someone tells you something, but you find it of no interest, you may say, 'So what?'.
soft option	The less complicated and/or troublesome alternative.
spade work	Preliminary hard work before a project can get started.
spiel	Glib talk. From the German *spielen*, to play. For example, we now use the term sales spiel.
split the difference	In bargaining it means coming to the centre of the difference between two figures.
spot cash	Immediate payment in cash.
squash an idea/plan	To reject it, firmly.
steep	If a price is too steep, or a bit steep, it means the price is far too high.
sticky business	A difficult and unpleasant problem.
sticky wicket/patch	A cricketing term meaning a difficult period.

Common business colloquialisms

storm in a teacup/making a mountain out of a molehill	A minor problem being treated as a serious one.
straight from the horse's mouth	A statement directly from someone in authority.
straw that broke the camel's back/the last straw	Too much! I cannot take any more!
stymied	A golfing expression meaning, in business, that you cannot reach your objective.
suss out	To investigate thoroughly. To find out the answers to the questions.
swallow it hook, line and sinker	An angling term. A fish takes the bait and so do you. You believe everything you have been told.
sweat/no sweat	If you say 'It's a sweat!' it means it is hard work. If you say 'It's no sweat' it means it is not a problem.
swings and roundabouts	A term related to the fairground. When you invest n a number of different projects some will be profitable, others will make losses. What you gain on the swings, you will lose on the roundabouts.
swing the lead	To avoid doing something by making things easy or by making excuses.
tail wagging the dog	When the subordinate makes the decision for the manager.
take a back seat	Let the subordinate decide the direction in which we are going.
take a knock	To take a knock is to suffer a setback.
take a leaf out of someone's book	To copy them.
take it in one's stride	To do something without difficulty.
take heart	Be encouraged!
take with a pinch of salt	Do not take too seriously.
take someone down a peg or two	Deflate someone's ego.
take the wind out of his sails/cutting the ground from under his feet	Making it difficult for someone to do what he or she intended to do.
talk the hind leg off a donkey	Talk too much.
talk out of one's hat	Talk rubbish.
tall order	Giving an order which is difficult to comply with.
tall story	A story which is hard to believe.
taped	When you have got someone taped it means you know what they are trying to do.
tea	When I say something is my cup of tea it means I like it.

teach your grandmother how to suck eggs	When you do this you are telling an expert how to do something.
tear someone off a strip	To reprimand them severely.
tell someone straight	To tell someone the truth whether or not it hurts them.
ten to one	A term used in betting, meaning there is a chance it will happen. A two to one chance means it is more likely to happen, and an odds on chance means that it is more likely to happen than not.
thank your lucky starts	You are very fortunate.
thin end of the wedge	There is much more (and worse) to come.
this, that and the other	All sorts of things.
three R's	The basic subjects taught at school – reading, writing and arithmetic.
throw a spanner in the works	To upset the existing arrangements.
throw out the baby with the bath water	To discard the important things with the trivia.
tied up	Not available at the present time.
tilt the scales	A factor which made it possible to reach a decision.
tit for tat	Retaliation.
tittle-tattle	Gossip. Idle chatter.
top dog	The person in charge.
topsy turvy	Things are not as they should be. They are upside down. Confused.
tot up	Add up (a bill for example)
touchy	Very sensitive.
trashy	Of very poor quality.
trendy	Fashionable.
trump/play your trump card	Put forward your best idea.
turn down	Reject.
turn over a new leaf	Make a fresh start.
turn the heat on	Put pressure on those who are being investigated.
twiddle one's thumbs	Do nothing.
two-faced	Someone who is two-faced is a hypocrite.
underhand	Devious.
up to your eyes in work	Overloaded with work.
use your loaf	Think! Use your head!
VIP	A very important person

Common business colloquialisms

waffle*	You are waffling when you are writing or saying something which has little or no meaning.
wangle*	A wangle is a trick. To wangle is to achieve something by manipulation.
wet blanket	A person who is a wet blanket reduces (or dampens) our enthusiasm.
whitewash*	A whitewash is a cover up of the truth.
windfall	An unexpected piece of luck, like an apple falling off a tree.
year dot	Something that happened in the year dot happened a long time ago.

Business dictionary

absenteeism – the practice of people staying away from work, often without good reason, but there is an assumption that the absentees probably do not enjoy their jobs.

actuary (plural –actuaries) –an official of an insurance company skilled in the calculation of risks and premiums.

adjournment – suspending the meeting for a later resumption, or transferring it to another place.

adjuster – an official who assesses losses and damages in connection with an insurance claim.

agency/agent – a firm/person who is acting on behalf of another person or party.

agenda – plan for discussions in a meeting.

Annual General Meeting (AGM) – once every year the company's board of directors is obliged by law to account for their stewardship to the shareholders. The agenda for the AGM usually includes: (i) declaration of dividends, (ii) consideration of the accounts and (iii) election of directors and auditors.

annuity – an investor pays a lump sum to a financial institution such as an insurance company and in return receives an annual payment for life.

apologies – regrets expressed for non–attendance at meetings – usually read out before the meeting proper commences.

appraisal – an attempt to rate an individual or team performance, possibly with a view to promotion or a pay increase.

archives – the place where records are stored, and from which they can be retrieved.

artwork – drawings and diagrams accompanying advertising material.

auditor – someone appointed to investigate a company's financial position on the evidence of the accounts.

bad debts – debts which are not likely to be recovered.

balance of payments – the difference between national income and national expenditure over a given period. The calculations are made monthly and annually.

balance of trade – the difference between the value of goods exported and the value of goods imported over a period of time.

balance sheet – a formal list of a business's assets and liabilities at a particular date.

Bank of England – a central bank which acts as both the government's and the commercial banks' banker. Private firms and the public generally do not have accounts at the Bank of England.

bankruptcy/bankrupt–the situation when someone is unable to meet their commitments and is sued by a creditor (or creditors). The individual concerned is called a bankrupt.

bill of exchange – it is similar to a cheque but payable at a future date (say three month's time). This gives the importer an opportunity to sell the goods before having to pay for them.

bill of lading – it is a list of the goods handed over to the captain of a freighter and signed by him. It becomes the document of title to the consignment while it is in transit.

bottleneck – something obstructing an even flow of production, for example where some essential machines are unable to cope with the supply of raw materials fed to them.

brokers – someone who deals as a middleman (or intermediary), such as a stockbroker on the stock exchange or an insurance broker who puts his clients in

Business dictionary

touch with insurance companies offering the most favourable terms.

budget – a set of projected accounts aiming to control expenditure. Each departmental manager will be given limits for both capital and revenue expenditure.

buffer stocks – the reserve needed to ensure you can always meet your customers' orders.

building societies – financial co-operatives some of whose members deposit their surplus funds in the society, while others borrow money mainly for the purpose of buying their houses. The societies hold the title deeds on mortgage until the loans are repaid.

bulk-buying – by purchasing goods in large quantities it is possible to obtain high discounts which have the effect of lowering your costs.

bureaucracy – a system of government by strict rather than flexible rules.

cash and carry – a form of trading usually associated with warehousing, whereby business customers buy their goods more cheaply because they pay cash for their goods rather than buy them on credit. They also provide their own transport.

cash discount – a reduction in the invoice charge available to the purchaser when cash is paid within a stipulated period (e.g. 21 days).

cash dispensers – by inserting a plastic cash card into the unit and keying in your account number you are able to collect money up to a certain limit. Your account will be debited automatically.

cash flow – a projection of cash inflows and outflows need to be made to ensure that the firm always has enough cash in its coffers to meet its commitments.

census – an official analysis of the composition of a population. Once every ten years an official survey of the population is made. There are also censuses of production.

chain of command – the lines on the organisation chart showing who is responsible to whom. These lines will normally be followed when one executive is communicating with another.

Chancellor of the Exchequer – the government minister in charge of the Treasury who deals with matters affecting business such as interest rates and taxation.

commuters – workers who live outside a big town like London but travel to work there daily.

comprehensive – covering a variety of matters. Usually related to an insurance policy in which case it means the policy covers a wide range of risks.

conciliation – peacemaking as between employers and trade unions. Called for when there are industrial disputes and threatened strikes.

consignee – the person to whom goods are being delivered. The person who is sending the goods is called the consignor.

consortium (plural – consortia) – a group (or groups) of companies working together on a single project. For example, consortia of international banks will provide funds for oil exploration and other very expensive operations.

consumer – the person who finally receives and uses the goods, such as the person who buys a television set or suite of furniture for his own use.

containers/containerisation – standardised pallets or containers are now used making it easier to switch cargoes from ship to shore, from train to road etc. The movement to this technique is called containerisation.

conveyancing – the legal process of transferring the title (i.e. ownership) of land and buildings from one person to another.

co-option – the act of nominating another person to join a committee.

co-ordination – the act of combining effectively a variety of activities or individuals.

copyright – the exclusive right given by law for a term of years to an author, com-

poser, designer etc. to make copies of his (or her) works.

corporate plan – the master plan for the organisation. The plan which determines where the organisation is going and how it is to get there.

corporation tax – a tax raised on the profits of companies.

counterfoil – a complementary part of a cheque or paying-in slip giving details of the transaction and retained by the customer.

cover-note – a document issued by an insurance company giving temporary cover against loss or damage until the formal contract is prepared.

crèche – a day nursery where parents can deposit their very young children while they go to work.

credit card – can be used to purchase goods or services without recourse to cheques or cash. Payment can be made to the issuing company at a later date without interest being incurred. After the specified date the amount outstanding becomes a loan and interest is charged. Examples: Barclaycard and Access.

creditor – someone to whom you owe money.

credit ratings – when a firm is allowing its customers to buy goods without paying for them immediately they need to place some limits on the amount of credit given. Those with good track records are given higher limits.

customs – government department collecting duties on imports from other countries.

data banks – retrievable information stored in a computer system.

days of grace – when an insurance contract has expired it is sometimes the convention to allow a short period to elapse before the cover is cancelled. The same convention is applied to bills of exchange to which three days of grace are added before payment is due.

debtor – someone who owes you money.

deficit – a shortfall. In connection with the national budget it implies that the government is going to spend more than it collects from taxes.

delegation – the act of passing down decision-making powers to a subordinate.

depreciation – assets gradually become less valuable through wear and tear or generally become out-dated and the writing down of the value is described as depreciation.

depression – the time when business activity is at its lowest and unemployment is at its highest.

devaluation – when a currency is made cheaper in comparison to other currencies, for example sterling is devalued when it moves from £1 = \$2.00 to £1 = \$1.50.

deviation – a movement away from the chosen path or objective, calling for a correction.

discount – a reduction in the price for prompt payment (cash discount) or large or regular purchases (trade discount).

discretion – power given to make decisions.

discrimination – treating employees unfairly on grounds of sex, race or religion.

distributor – an agent appointed by a manufacturer to deal with sales in a particular area.

diversification – the spreading of risks among a variety of projects or enterprises.

dividend – a distribution of profit to the shareholders of a company.

documentary credit – a document used to facilitate overseas trade whereby the importer's bank guarantees payment to the exporter.

draught – an indication of the size of a ship according to the depth of water required to float her and the weight of water it displaces.

drawer – the person who makes out a cheque or bill of exchange and whose account will be charged.

drawings – the withdrawals of cash or kind from the firm by the proprietor(s).

dumping – occurs when exporters sell goods overseas at a price below cost so as not to spoil prices in their domestic market.

economies of scale – as some costs remain fixed whatever the level of output the average costs tend to decrease as more units are produced.

EFTPOS – electronic funds at point of sale involving transfer of money directly from the customer's to the shopkeeper's bank account.

e.g. – an abbreviation of 'for example' (used at various points throughout the text).

ego – the part of the mind which relates to our individuality and gives us a feeling of self-importance.

employer's liability – if an employee suffers injury or death during the course of work the employer may be held responsible or partly responsible. Insurance cover is available to meet this contingency.

endorsement – see indorsement.

endowment – the type of insurance policy which is an investment and provides a sum for the insured after a fixed term of years.

equities – another name for the ordinary shares of companies. So-called because they have the right to what is left after others have received their entitlements.

etc – an abbreviation of etcetera, meaning 'and so on' (used at various points throughout the text).

European Community (EC) – the European free trade area in which all tariffs and trade barriers are being removed.

Eurotunnel – a tunnel between England and France making for easier access and trade between the UK and the continent.

excess clause – when the insured makes a claim against the insurance company he (or she) is required to bear the first, say, £100 of the cost. This sum is described as the excess.

exchange rates – how much one currency costs in terms of another.

Export Credits Guarantee Department (ECGD) – a government department which offers an especially valuable insurance facility to exporters, covering bad debts and political upheavals etc.

facsimile (fax) machine – equipment which allows copies of documents, plans and drawings etc. to be reproduced in distant offices.

factoring – the taking over of book debts at a discount by an agent who attempts to collect the full value of the debts. Often includes a full book-keeping service.

feasibility – a study to ascertain whether a proposed idea or concept is both possible and commercially viable.

fidelity bond – an insurance policy covering the risk that employees will defraud their employers or steal cash.

fixtures – assets which are fastened into position so they cannot easily be removed.

flexible working hours – a pattern of work which allows the employee to select which hours of the day he (or she) will attend.

forward exchange – a facility offered by the banks whereby a merchant trading overseas and obliged to deal in foreign currencies is able to buy and/or sell such currencies in advance. This eliminates the risk of loss when exchange rates change.

franchise – the authorisation to sell a firm's goods or services in a given area. The franchisers are increasingly offering finance and marketing expertise as backup.

Gantt chart – a diagram which makes it easy to compare expected performance (or standard) with actual performance.

generalist – a person who is competent in a number of different fields.

goodwill – customers who are satisfied with the treatment they receive will tend to return to do more business. This tendency is a business asset and is described as goodwill.

grapevine – refers to the informal network of communication which exists in all organisations.

grievances – matters of concern to the workers which will normally be taken up by the trade unions or shop stewards.

guarantor – the person who has agreed to repay a loan or overdraft if the borrower fails to do so.

hierarchy – an organisation with grades or classes ranked one above the other. Can also refer to a pyramid of needs as in Maslow's theory.

i.e. – an abbreviation for 'that is' (used at various points throughout the text).

indemnity – the principle of insurance which lays down that in the event of a loss the insured person is compensated to the extent that they are not worse off than they were before. They cannot profit from insurance but will be allowed to recover the financial loss known to have occurred.

indorsement – the signature on the back of a cheque or bill of exchange.

induction – the programme arranged for new employees so they can become familiar with their new working environment.

industrial tribunals – legal bodies set up to deal with complaints from employees on the subjects of discrimination and wrongful dismissal etc.

inflation – the situation in which prices are rising as too much money is chasing too few goods.

insolvency – when a company is unable to meet its commitments and is sued by its creditors.

inter alia – among other things (used at various points throughout the text).

interlocking directorates – a company benefits from having some of its non-executive directors serving on the boards of other companies.

invisibles – items in the balance of payments which refer to intangible services rather than tangible goods.

invoice – the document which gives the purchaser details of the amount which has been charged to his account.

job rotation – jobs are sometimes changed around to give workers wider experience or to reduce the monotony. The technique helps to cope with absences through sickness and holidays.

job satisfaction – there is more to a job than the pay packet. Some work is satisfying in itself.

Joint Consultation Committee (JCC) – a group of workers and managers meeting together to sort out problems which are of common concern.

laissez-faire – a government policy which deliberately avoids interfering with the normal market forces.

lapse – the termination of rights, for example under an insurance contract, because time has run out.

legislation – Acts of Parliament which change the law governing business.

limited company – a company in which the liability of the members or shareholders is limited to the money they originally subscribed for the shares.

line manager – a manager in charge of a production line.

liquidity – the degree to which a business can meet its immediate commitments.

litigation – a lawsuit, in other words, legal proceedings between contesting parties.

Lloyd's of London – the world's leading insurance market in which syndicates of underwriters provide cover for a great variety of business risks, but particularly marine insurance.

logo – a brand sign or symbol used by a firm for its products and publicity.

maintenance – keeping machinery running and in a good state of repair.

Business dictionary

manifest – cargo list for use by Customs officers. Also a list of passengers in aircraft, goods in trucks etc.

market research – the attempt to discover the nature and extent of the market for a given range of products. Interviews and questionnaires are among the techniques used.

market segmentation – the splitting up of a market into parts, such as old age pensioners, high income earners etc.

mark-up – the amount added by a retailer to the cost of goods to cover overheads and profit. Thus, if a product costs £1 and there is a mark-up of 50%, the price will be £1.50.

mass production – the production of large quantities of standardised units. Because of the large scale the units can be produced comparatively cheaply.

material facts – decisions should be based on facts, and material facts are those which are strictly relevant to the problem which is being tackled.

media – the institutions such as newspapers and magazines, radio and television which give us their version of what is happening in the world.

microchip revolution – the microchip is the tiny electric circuit which has miniaturised the computer and led to the further rapid advance of technology in the business sector. The robotisation of production lines and the advent of cash dispensing machines outside banks are just two of the applications.

minutes – a brief record of what was discussed in a meeting.

mortgage – a loan secured by the deposit of the title deeds with the lender (the mortgagee), who then has the right to retain the deeds until the loan is repaid by the borrower (the mortgagor).

motion – a proposal made in a meeting. It needs a seconder, and once it has been approved it becomes a resolution.

multinationals – companies which are operating in more than one country.

national income – the total earnings of all the firms and individuals in the country. Where there is economic growth the national income will become larger.

nationalisation – the taking over of private industry by the government. For example, in the late 1940s the railways, and the coal and gas industries, among others, were nationalised.

non-executive directors – company directors who do not have departmental responsibilities, so that they could and very often do, serve on the board of more than one company.

Official Receiver – an official appointed by the Court to deal with the affairs of bankrupts (individuals) and insolvent companies.

off-the-job – training of staff undertaken in places away from the workplace, such as colleges and polytechnics.

on-the-job – training of staff undertaken at the workplace, usually using trainers from the firm's own workforce.

ordinary shares – every limited company must have some ordinary shares and these normally carry the voting rights which elect the directors and therefore ultimately control the company.

organisation chart – this shows the levels of management, lines of communication, chains of command and spans of control for the hierarchy of managers.

overdraft – when the customer of a bank draws a cheque for more than there is in the account an overdraft is created, unless the bank manager returns the cheque adding the words 'insufficient funds' or 'refer to drawer', because no arrangements for an overdraft were made.

overheads – administration expenses over and above the cost of the raw materials and wages.

participation – when subordinates are allowed to become involved in the decision-making process.

patent – the official right to make, use or sell some new gadget or invention. The right is usually limited to a fixed period of years.

Pay As You Earn (PAYE) – the system of taxation by means of which the tax is deducted by the employer before the employee receives the wages or salary.

payee – the person to whom a cheque is payable.

paying-in slip – the document which is used to pay cheques and/or cash into a bank or building society account.

planning – the function of management which requires anticipating future events so that appropriate action can be taken.

PLC (public limited company) – a company which can sell shares to the public and may apply to have its shares quoted on the Stock Exchange.

ploughed back profits – that part of the profit which is not withdrawn or distributed by the proprietors. In a company the ploughed back profits are normally transferred to general reserve.

poverty trap – for people who are extremely poor it is difficult to do more than survive on a day-to-day basis. They will need help from outside if they are going to fight back against poverty. The problem applies to the underprivileged in our own society as well as people in the Third World.

premiums – the payments made to the insurers by the policy holders.

privatisation – the transfer of previously nationalised industries into the hands of private owners. Members of the public are normally invited to buy shares in the undertaking.

probate – the official granting of authority to the executor of a deceased person's estate.

product life cycle – after a new product is introduced it can be expected to increase sales until it reaches a peak. Then its sales will decline.

projection – statistics are analysed to show a trend and then the trend is projected so that (inter alia) future sales can be forecast.

proposal – an application for insurance cover giving personal data and details of the risks seeking to be covered.

proposer – the person who is putting forward a formal motion at a meeting.

prototype – the first or trial model for a new product. A preliminary version which will probably need to be modified.

questionnaire – a document containing a list of questions the answers to which will, inter alia, give market researchers information about the nature of the market.

quorum – the number of members who need to be present before a meeting is properly constituted.

quota – a stipulated quantity of goods, for example limiting the amount of imports.

quotation – when work is required which requires a mixture of raw material and labour inputs it is usual to obtain a quotation fixing the price for the basis of the contract.

quoted shares – shares of a public limited company which can be bought and sold on the Stock Exchange.

recession – the stage of the trade cycle when boom conditions are giving way to less activity. A time when unemployment is increasing and business confidence declining.

redundancy – this occurs when workers are dismissed because their jobs no longer need to be done. It has nothing to do with their efficiency or their personal qualities.

referee – a person to whom a potential employer refers when considering the merits of an applicant for a job.

rejects – finished goods, or goods purchased, which are not up to standard. If there is a Quality Control Department this is an aspect of their function.

Business dictionary

relocation – this is called for when it becomes necessary to move out of the existing factories or offices.

reserves – when a company decides not to distribute all its profits it will transfer the undistributed element to reserves.

resolution – a formal decision reached by a majority vote in a committee meeting, including a board of directors' meeting.

respondent – one who answers the questions contained in a market research questionnaire.

retrieval – recovery of data from a computer memory store.

rights issue – a company raises funds by issuing new shares to its existing shareholders on favourable terms.

robotisation – processes performed with human skills but impersonally and without human intervention.

salary scales – a salary structure which means that a member of staff will continue to get an annual salary increase so long as they perform satisfactorily and have not reached the top of the particular scale.

satellite – a communication network using space satellites to bounce off signals.

seconder – the person in a meeting who formally supports a motion which has been put forward.

security – another name for stocks and shares, but also means something which is held by a lender until a loan is repaid, for example property deeds or stock certificates.

share capital – the shareholders' original stake in the company. In the balance sheet the details of the different shares issued will be displayed. (163 ,206)

shop stewards – the trade union representatives who operate on the shop floor (another name for the factory). They are normally elected by a show of hands.

short-dated gilts – government securities which will soon be repaid/redeemed by the government.

signatory – the person who signs a letter or document.

social security – that part of the Welfare State which deals with unemployment and sickness benefits inter alia.

specialisation – the technique of breaking down jobs into narrow tasks so as to improve productivity. It can lead to boredom and frustration if taken to excess.

sponsorship – some firms are prepared to give financial support to sporting functions in return for substantial publicity.

standing order – an instruction to the bank to make regular payments for insurance premiums and club subscriptions etc.

status – a superior position in the organisation gives us ego food. It can also relate to a bank status enquiry as when a customer who wishes to buy goods on credit is asked to provide a bank reference.

sterling – the UK currency is described as the pound sterling to distinguish it from other currencies using the pound as a unit of currency.

stockbrokers – dealers in stocks and shares operating on the Stock Exchange. They charge a commission for their services in arranging purchases and sales.

stopped cheques – if the drawer of a cheque does not wish his bank to pay the cheque when it is presented he can give them written instructions to stop payment. This is a very useful device when, for example, a cheque has been lost in the post.

strategy – involves the choice of objectives for a business, and the determination of the resources which are going to be used to achieve those objectives.

subliminal advertising – audio-visual material which impresses itself on the subconscious. The audience are not consciously aware of the message they have received.

subordinate – the person to whom instructions are given.

subsidiary – a company which is controlled by another. The control is normally exercised by the parent or holding company through the ownership of a majority of the voting shares.

subsidy – payments or grants made by a government to support a particular industry.

suggestion scheme – an arrangement whereby workers can offer their ideas to improve productivity or the working environment. The workers who put forward the best ideas are usually rewarded.

surcharge – an extra charge incurred, perhaps when the rules have been broken.

syndicate – a group of individuals or firms joining together to profit from a joint venture. Lloyd's of London operate their insurance business through syndicates.

tabloid – a newspaper, popular in style, printed on sheets half the normal size.

tachograph – sometimes called the spy in the cab, it automatically logs a truck driver's journey to ensure he takes adequate breaks.

target audience – the people at whom the (media) material is aimed.

tariff – a government tax aimed at discouraging the imports of certain goods.

telex – a system of communication which allows written messages to be sent and received at the same time.

trade cycle – periodic fluctuations in economic activity – evidenced by booms, recessions, depressions and recoveries.

Trade Descriptions Acts – legislation aimed at protecting the consumer from grossly misleading advertisements.

Treasury – the government department dealing with the country's finances.

uncleared cheques – when cheques are paid into an account it takes some days for them to pass through the clearing system. Until they have been cleared the cash cannot normally be withdrawn.

unit trusts – an investment in blocks of shares which are then divided into sub units for individual purchasers. In this way the small investor is able to benefit from a diversification of risk.

upgrading – a promotion or pay increase based on an appraisal of performance by a senior manager.

utmost good faith – the principle of insurance that requires the insured to disclose all material (relevant) facts to the insurer.

Value Added Tax – a government tax paid on goods and services as they are purchased.

video conferencing – a system by which people in distant places can communicate with each other audio-visually using television screens or visual display units.

visual display units (VDUs) – desk – top computers used to retrieve statistical data etc.

word processor – a computerised machine used for producing texts and diagrams, having the advantage of both editing and reproduction facilities.

work station – a set place where a member of staff and his/her equipment are located.

Answers

In this section brief answers are given to the asterisked (*) exercises covered in Chapters 1 to 20 inclusive.

Chapter 1

Exercise 3

i) Crumble Cookie
ii) Crumble Cookie
iii) Chocolux
iv) rising
v) about to be overtaken
vi) about £50m

Chapter 3

Exercise 2

No date – error in address – capital H in hong Kong – error in salutation – Corrigan – in body of letter – is going – campaign – language – if the – then the – brochures – you) – of the – relieve – School's – ambiguity in sentence starting 'I will then have a stock ...' (rephrase) – complimentary close should be 'Yours sincerely'.

Exercise 9

1. Number of absences for each member of staff in the Sales Office between July and September inclusive.
2. No
3. August
4. Best Laura and Tharampal – worst – Edward
5. Year of joining.

Chapter 5

B. receive – reception – advertisement – hygienic – immaculate – various – mature – liquid – similar – gyrating – embedded plastic – attentive – imperfect – contemptuously – receptacles – moist – journey – piece – emerged – distinctive – recognise acquired – employees – policy – loose – lose – infinite – instrument – processed – supervisor – presence – relieved – disappeared – extracted – analysis – careful – faulty.

D. *Synonyms* – break/harm (alternatives) – loose/lax/lazy – join/ attach – tolerably/satisfactorily – fasten/lock – neat/orderly – tighten – slackly – busy/industrious – hide/cover/disguise – worker – stretch/expand – contamination – unlock/free – worsening – expand/lengthen – fault – repair.

Opposites – fix/mend – tight – part/detach – unacceptably – unlock – untidy – loosen/unfasten – tightly – lazy – show/reveal – employer – contract/shorten – cleanness/purity – hold/retain – improving – shorten – perfection – damage.

E. i/c ii/d iii/a iv/e v/b vi/h vii/k viii/i ix/j x/g xi/f

K. buffer – patent – prototype – availability – resources – overheads – batches – objective – maintenance – pollution – depot – rejects – budget – layout – schedules – sequence – workflow – flexibility – relocation – rationalisation.

Chapter 6

B. cyclical – fade – emerge – products – continues – tested – product – obliged – persuade – described – trend – setters – attitude – recoup – during – economies – develop – customers – reaction – queue – bound – reach – stabilize – sales – attracted – provided – perfected – careful – flow.

Answers

D. *Opposites* – sell – employer – unattractive – mismanage – unstable – hide/disappear – insecure – careless – dissuade – subordinate – ineffective – secrecy – powerful – simple – appoint/employ – praise – inability – dismiss – inadequate – purposeless.

Synonyms – purchase – worker – pleasant/pleasing – control/organise – unfluctuating/unchangeable – escape/appear – safe – cautious – influence – executive/leader – influential/useful – propaganda – helpless/ineffective – difficult – sack – rebuke – capacity – employ – sufficient – intentional.

E. i/l ii/c iii/i iv/b v/a vi/g vii/k viii/j ix/f x/h xi/d xii/e

K. persuade – modification – diversification – discount – copyright – turnover – salesperson – publicity – segmentation – enquiry image – consumer – motivation – survey – exhibition – distributor – sample – franchise – contract – gimmick – order – invoice – mark-up – market – quotation.

L. 1B – 2C – 3B – 4C – 5B – 6C – 7B – 8C

Chapter 7

B. establish – principal – agencies – behalf – create – artists – prepare – normally – field – design – build – brand – economies – artwork – advertising – implement – programme – detailed – charges – media – customers – magazines – obtain – specialist – economical – executive – involving – maximum.

D. *Synonyms* – gain – contract – lavishly – collect – representative – depressingly – roughly – earnings – focus – urge – important – criticise/assault – illogically – stop – likeable/liked – requirement/need (economic) – hide/disguise – influential – wholly – notable/superior – responsive.

Opposites – loss – expand – cheaply/inexpensively – distribute – principal – happily/confidently – precisely/exactly – expense/ expenditure – diffuse/spread – discourage – inconsequential – defend – rationally – allow/permit – unpopular – request/supply (economics) – reveal – unconvincing – partially – undistinguished – insensitive. – insensitive.

E. i/f ii/h iii/i iv/a v/j vi/b vii/c viii/l ix/d x/e xi/g xii/k.

K. showcase – persuasion – audio-visual – gimmick – ego – brand – exhibition – exclusive – audience – logo – slogan – hoarding – leaflet sponsor – profile – bulletin – tabloid – teaser – publicity – feature – stimulus – artwork – presentation – media – dry – run.

L. prepared – specimens/examples – drawings – recommend/propose – idea/concept – readership/sales – factors/points – regions – advantageous – charges – aspect – responses.

Chapter 8

B. urgently – spare – expensive – combat – contagious – spread – perishable – favourable – elsewhere – caring – present – peak – training – emotionally – unsettle – experience – foreign – reinforced – panic – burden – bulk – precious – gold – consignment – security – greatly – airports – finish.

D. Adjectives: fastest – major – regular – longer – heavy – few
   Adverbs: regularly – quickly – often – frequently – commercially – urgently.

E. 1C – 2C – 3A – 4B – 5C – 6B – 7A – 8C – 9B – 10B.

K. ferry – carrier – freighter – congestion – consignor – peak – freight – tachograph – tanker – draught – merchant – consignee – wreckage – commuter – diesel – log – manifest – terminus – exporter – airship – tourist – hovercraft – haulier – conveyance – capacity.

Answers

L. vii   iv   ii   viii   ix   i   iii   v   vi.

M. f   h   j   k   l   a   d   c   e   g   i   b.

Chapter 9

B. parties – transmitted – frequency – similar – political – conversing – overcome – considers – different – concentrate – language – signals – research – feedback – attitudes – barrier – problems – crackle – astray – aborted – messages – sensitive – impart – compliment – rude – embarrassed – tone – handled.

D. *Prepositions* – on – in – into – among – in – in – at – which – in – who – to – at

Verbs – compare – recover – refer – dealt – checked – leave – display – inspected – discover.

K. emphasis – document – acknowledgement – receptionist – feedback – tidiness – recipient – impolite – query – archives – retrieval – catalogue – colleague – telecommunication – complaint – signatory – stereotype – summary – agenda – minute – diary – docket supervisor – excess – reminder.

L. 1) T F T F T F T F   2) F F T T T T T F   3) T T T T T

Chapter 10

B. proceeds – benefits – identification – invitation – food – valuable – particular – quality – between – predict – enthusiasm – sound – routine – reactions – accept – fewer – participation – pleasant – reflected – labour – involved – poach – contribute – irrelevant.

D. There – their – They're – their – there – their – their – they're – There – They're – their – There – their.

E. 1B – 2C – 3A – 4A – 5B – 6C – 7A – 8C – 9B – 10A.

K. report – adjournment – agenda – adequate – interview – audience – referees – grievances – minutes – motion – proposer – neutral – resolution – quorum – command – relevant – amendment – auditors – seconder – convene – liaison – apologies – co-option – casting – procedures.

L. 1B – 2C – 3A – 4A – 5A.

Chapter 11

B. individually – improved – achieved – shortfall – prelude – scale – deserve – upgrading – merit – purpose – candidates – thorny – hopefuls – quality – measure – significantly – colleague – judgement – receptionist – attendance – question – akin – indisposed – flimsy – discouraged – unreasonable – professional – teamwork.

D. *Synonyms* – encourage – upgrading – normally – fulfilling/ rewarding – conformity/submission – pertinent/appropriate – enlist/employ – talent/capacity – temporary – choose – possible – surplus – consent – intellect – often – cleverly – private – skill – trainee – lively – personable – place.

Opposites – demotivate/discourage – demotion – unusually – unsatisfying – nonconformity – irrelevant – dismiss – disability – permanent – reject – impossible – insufficiency – disagree – dullness – infrequently – inexpertly – impersonal – inefficiency – craftsman – static/lethargic/lazy – introvert – move/shift/displace.

K. foreman – bonus – overtime – frustration – moderate – militant – dismissal – personal – personnel – applicant – morale – counsellor – induction – interviewee – personality – participation – discretion – courtesy – redundant – remuneration – environment – referee – aptitude – questionnaire – representative.

Answers

Chapter 12

B. primary – adequate – expenditure – wages – purchases – storybook – computer – assets – examining – creditors – debtors – insolvency – vital – problems – solutions – statistical – deduction – cheaper – answered – mechanisms – corrective – continuous – possible – accuracy.

D. often – co-operative – probably – new – always – obsolete – invariably – essential – between – credit – some – immediately – quickly – high – increasingly – given.

E. 1A – 2C – 3B – 4A – 5C – 6A – 7C – 8B – 9A – 10B.

K. expenditure – fixtures – dividend – bankrupt – equities – auditor – assets – discount – liabilities – invoice – balance – ledgers – returns – drawings – capital – debtors – depreciation – creditor – goodwill – bankruptcy – revenue – budget – overheads – security – investor.

Chapter 13

B. complex – capital – buy – provided – run – directors – appointed – General – management – spent – advertising – company's – post – combines – link – appointed – actively – company's – certain – course – sell – overseas – Marketing – increase – coming – Financial – coming – delay – mixture – benefit – faced – brand.

D. directors – ensure – send – accounts – make – board – resolution – proposed – passed – votes – undertake – responsibilities – elected – shareholders – answers – team.

E. 1C – 2A – 3B – 4A – 5A – 6B – 7C – 8B – 9C – 10A.

K. diversify – executive – enterprise – integrity – curtness – dividends – co-ordinate – strategic – administration – conflicting – compliance – generalist – eminent – arbitrary – obligations – objectives – initiate – majority – shareholders – expertise – remuneration – delegation – take-over – frequently – tactical.

Chapter 14

B. mixed – tackled – objective – relates – mechanics – problem – complex – assembled – range – involves – appears – short-term – context – monetary – minimum – point – required – actions – complying – opportunity – early – provide – choice – remains.

D. involved – greater – day's – deal – astute – avoid – typing – reach – achieve – same – consider – likely – maintain – public – development – evaluated.

E. i/e   ii/f   iii/b   iv/g   v/c   vi/j   vii/l   viii/k   ix/a   x/d   xi/i   xii/h.

G. *Synonyms* – post-mortem/investigation – control/organise unintentional – teamwork – suggest – aim/intention – direct/manage – lively – objectively – minor – complain – convince – divulge/indicate – orderly/inflexible – gratefully – caring/friendly – plan/forecast/predict – thin – skinned – record – discuss – data/details.

Opposites – whitewash – mismanage – intentional/deliberate – conflict/disharmony – accept – vagueness/uncertainty – free/disobey – stationary – irrationally/illogically – superior/manager – agree/ accept – dissuade – enquire – easy-going – ungratefully – uncaring/unfriendly – recollect/reflect – insensitive – ignore – dictate/instruct – misinformation.

K. flexible – autocratic – analytic – evaluation – redundancy – supportive – hazardous – complex – anticipation – implement subordinate – options – discretions – emphasis – remedial – permissible – frivolous – criteria – feasibility – projection – cooperative – bureaucracy – deviation – ineffective – competitive.

Answers

Chapter 15

C. 1A – 2A – 3C – 4C – 5A – 6B – 7B – 8A – 9B – 10C – 11B – 12A.

E. optics – satellites – orbits – microwave – graphics – lightpen – terminals – binary – programs – retrieval – manipulation – backing – library – integrated – operating – software – utility – translators – code – computers.

F. *synonyms* – speech – disregard – danger – influence/effect – revolutionary/fundamental – crucial – distinction – try – recovered – policy – data – add – target – discerning/discriminating – enterprise – handled/applied.

opposites – unrecognisable – least – unprepared – liability – answer – questioned.

G.
| i/e | ii/h | iii/b | iv/j | v/a |
| vi/c | vii/f | viii/d | ix/i | x/g |

H. matrix – floppy – track – bugs – algorithm – uses – off-line – core – byte – digital – screen – punched – access – chip – decoder – cursor – flowchart – robot – on-line – spreadsheet.

Chapter 16

A. equities – profits – dividend – takeover – shareholders – directors – hedge – control.

B. major – elected – substantial – bidder – unprofitable – nature – acquired – surprise – worthless – wound – described – attractive – prepared – mortgage – devoted.

C. interesting – technique – cost – factor – increase – unreal – supporters – before – wrongdoers – period – misinformed – undiscovered – discussed – control.

H. T T T T F F F T F T.

I. 1C – 2B – 3A – 4A – 5B – 6A – 7C – 8B.

K. dividend – equities – risk – broker – asset-stripping – premium – voting – majority – supplies – inflation – replaced – auditor – Guinness – capital report – taxation – annually – satisfactory – securities – quotation.

Chapter 17

B. withdrawal – surplus – interest – amount – addition – grant – excess – credit – then – approach – conducted – income.

D. *Verbs* – authorise – overdraw – require – imply – abbreviate – indorse – confide – cancel – prescribe – benefit – remedy – legalize – complete – negotiate – fabricate – neglect – define – enforce.

Adjectives – applicable/applied – overdrawn – altered – implicit/ implied – specific/specified – indorsed – secure/secured – cancelled – modified – beneficial/beneficent – economic – legal – accumulated – negotiable/negotiated – confirmed/confirmatory – neglectful/ neglected – agreeable/agreed – enforceable/enforced.

Nouns – applicant – authority – alteration – requirement/requisition – specification – abbreviation – security – confidence/confidentiality – modification – prescription – economy/economics – remedy – accumulation – completion – confirmation – fabrication – agreement – definition.

I. 1C – 2B – 3A – 4C – 5A – 6B – 7C – 8C – 9A – 10B.

K. indorsement – counterfoil – security – excess – principal – confidentiality – building – liquidity – payee – guarantor – authorisation – mortgagor – credit – negligent – drawer – application – bankrupt – bankruptcy – overdraft – central.

M.
| 1. fall | 2. rise | 3. rise | 4. fall | 5. fall |
| 6. fall | 7. fall | 8. fall | 9. fall | 10. rise |

Answers

Chapter 18

B. principle – actuaries – expectation – expect – premiums – younger – remove – burdens – bear – exceed – injuries – pilferage.

D. *Verbs* – calculate – expect – propose – adjust – comprehend – mature – differ – depend – succeed – convert – specify – protect – specialise – consider – expire – investigate – consolidate.

Adjectives – indemnified – expected – diversified – adjustable/ adjusted – invested – mature/matured – renewable – dependable retiring/retired – converted – satisfying/satisfied – protective – concentrated – considerable/considerate – speculative – continuous – consolidated – classified.

Noun – indemnity – calculation – diversification – proposal/ proposition – investment – comprehension – renewal – difference – retirement – success – satisfaction – specification – concentration – specialisation – speculator/speculation – expiration – continuation – investigator/investigation – classification.

G. i/d ii/a iii/j iv/f v/l vi/g vii/e viii/i ix/h x/k xi/b xii/c.

I. IB – 2C – 3A – 4C – 5A – 6C – 7A – 8B – 9C – 10B.

K. catastrophe – lapse – renewal – confirmation – annuity – fidelity – broker – syndicate – excess – comprehensive – cover-note – insured – insurer – actuary – indemnity – cancellation – claim – premium – adjuster – underwriter.

M. *Synonyms* – damage – personal – obligations – authorised – visits – part – willing.

Opposites – infamous – uncovered – reject – worse – rejection.

Missing words – signature – broker – cargoes – risk – proportion – cover – majority – commitment.

Chapter 19

B. currency – element – contract – completion – rate – result – transaction – fluctuate – agreement – problem – rose – benefit.

D. historically – manufactured – transportation normally – export – delivered – fierce – encounter – import – political – largely – selecting – enter – vary – general – formulated – vitally – invoicing – shipped – satisfy – inevitably – vital – increasingly – systematically .

J. i/d   ii/e   iii/a   iv/f   v/b   vi/h   vii/i   viii/j   ix/g   x/c.

K. bond – convert – licence – accepted – multinationals – invisibles – tariffs – peseta – documentary – surcharge – lira – shipper – devaluation – agent – quota – guilder – intermediary – consignment – subsidiary – procedures – irrevocable – customs – maturity – franc – dumping.

Chapter 20

B. prosperity – poverty – democracy – system – presents – collected – benefits – assessed – encourage – includes – purchased – earners.

D. *Synonyms* – shortfall – fair – moving/unstable – state/communal – sufficiently – changeable/changing – affirm/corroborate – disclose – deterioration/wear/diminution – jointly – collect – unarranged/ unorganised – likeable/approved/admired – differentiate/contrast decreasing – planned – purposefully – helpful – foolishly/stupidly – authoritatively.

Opposites – surplus – unfair – immobile – private/personal – inadequately – stable – deny – conceal/hide – appreciation – individually – distribute – ordered/contrived –

Answers

unpopular liken/relate – increasing/expanding – purposeless – indecisively – unco-operative – wisely/thoughtfully – democratically.

K. depression – recession – legislation – bullion – redistribution – corporation – inflation – minister – boom – nationalisation – census – privatisation – stability – subsidy – conciliation – recovery – sterling – deficit – Treasury – budget.